Praise for Cross-Cultural Dia

Jay Levy and colleagues' *Cross-Cult..*
From Pretreatment Strategies to Psychol..   ..*ments*
provides wonderful insight into the profou   ..up-building that is
the core of street outreach to the unshelter.. nomeless. Jay distills many
decades of his own street experience, and by cross comparing his brilliant
schema of Pretreatment with the British model of Psychologically Informed
Environments (PIE), he reveals the underlying common processes of effective street engagement. Essentially, Jay shows us how to compassionately
embrace the reality of those who fall within the underwater portion of the
"pre-contemplative" iceberg of behavioral change. As a long-time practitioner of street medicine, I recommend this book to anyone who seeks that
sacred place on the streets where healing begins.

Jim Withers, MD, Founder and Medical Director
Operation Safety Net and the Street Medicine Institute (Pittsburgh, PA)

In *Cross-Cultural Dialogues on Homelessness*, Jay Levy and co-authors
provide the conceptual tools, the hitherto "missing language", needed by
practitioners and policy makers working with excluded individuals. This
well-written and insightful book outlines the psychologically informed
approach that has been successfully used in the US, UK and other countries
to re-integrate people who have experienced homelessness, severe mental
illness and, frequently, other traumatic life events. It offers a common language, and, more importantly, a common vision of working across professional boundaries to redress social exclusion. This book has been informed
by the authors' practice and should come with a warning: it will revolu-
tionise how you work - irreversibly and, undoubtedly, for the better.

Clíona Ní Cheallaigh, MB, MRCP, PhD
Senior Lecturer in Medical Gerontology, Trinity College
(Dublin, Ireland)

I cheer the approach, which sees homeless people as survivors of
complex, ongoing trauma rather than any of the many stigmatizing descriptions thrown at them. The philosophy and approach described here can, and
indeed should, be applied to all client populations, not only to homeless
people with long histories of trauma and its effects. As well as the theory,
and descriptions of practice, the book is full of case studies that illuminate
and inspire.

Bob Rich, PhD,
(Wombat Hollow, Australia)

At Anna Maria College, we have always felt fortunate to have had Jay Levy teach principles of outreach counseling to our student body. Now, through *Cross-Cultural Dialogues on Homelessness*, readers will get the opportunity to learn from Jay's experiences—as well as his collaborators experiences—in working with people on the homelessness spectrum. For those of us who are new to the topic of homelessness, the text offers a valuable overview of theory, postmodernism, systems, application, and practice. For those of us who are deeply entrenched in the topic of homelessness, this book simultaneously offers refreshing, new insights. The text presents an ongoing conversation on homelessness that expands beyond the "silos" of professionals working (hard) in isolation of each other. It provides an international discourse and techniques to professionals; it provides resources to the people who need them and the hope for a better future.

John M. Pratico, MA, CAGS, PsyD
Director of Psychology Programs
Anna Maria College (Paxton, Massachusetts)

Cross Cultural Dialogues on Homelessness is a timely and important collection of the latest thinking on how we should respond to the traumatic life experiences of so many homeless people. Fascinatingly, the contributors show that therapists, counsellors and key workers on both sides of the Atlantic are reaching similar conclusions on the best way for services to think about their work with traumatised, excluded clients. Maybe it turns out we are all human? An implicit and passionate call for constructive dialogue at every level, the book shows how progress always depends on the development of shared languages, trust and communication. Levy and company suggest a commitment to reflective dialogue will improve both the quality of frontline services and the way policy makers, managers and commissioners think about responding to the needs of people pushed to the margins of our societies.

Alex Bax, Chief Executive, Pathway (London, UK)
BA, MA, MFPH, & Visiting Fellow, IHHD, University of East London

The title of this book caught my eye and Loving Healing Press, in small print, struck a chord. I read it carefully through a variety of lenses, mindful of the fact that a lot of time has passed since I started working with people labelled homeless." The dialogue taking place then had elements of what this book promotes. I lived and worked in a shelter with very damaged people interspersed with people from various backgrounds and experiences. We were inspired, challenged and supported by a psychologist and psychiatric nurse. Later, my "research" involved working with recently qualified doctors, including one who later trained as a psychiatrist and psychotherapist.

The questioning of the medical model was at the top of our agenda; lively discussions took place. Later, when TRUST, now the Alice Leahy Trust, was set up (1975), we always involved people who were in their own care. We met people where they were - mentally and physically. We were the first doctor and nurse team in Ireland visiting people sleeping rough. Our work was greatly supported, up to the time of his death, by Professor James McCormick, a GP and first head of the Department of Community Health at Trinity College, Dublin.

This book is different because it is based on theory and practises, dialogue and the sharing of ideas - from both sides of the Atlantic. The human interest stories add great value to the book, which should be required reading for anyone interested in creating a better world for his/her fellow human beings. It should be read and debated by all with a vision for a better future for those who need services and those attempting to provide them. People with the responsibility of planning services with no "on the ground" experience would benefit greatly from this book.

Alice Leahy, Director of Services,
Alice Leahy Trust (Dublin, Ireland)

Cross-Cultural Dialogues on Homelessness:

From Pretreatment Strategies to Psychologically Informed Environments

Edited by Jay S. Levy, MSW with Robin Johnson

Loving Healing Press

Ann Arbor * Milton-Keynes

Cross-Cultural Dialogues on Homelessness: From Pretreatment Strategies to Psychologically Informed Environments.

Edited by Jay S. Levy with Robin Johnson

ISBN 978-1-61599-366-6 Paperback
ISBN 978-1-61599-367-3 Hardcover
ISBN 978-1-61599-368-0 eBook

Loving Healing Press   info@LHPress.com
5145 Pontiac Trail   www.LHPress.com
Ann Arbor, MI 48105
Toll free: 888-761-6268 (USA/CAN)   FAX: 734-663-6861
Distributed by Ingram Book Group (USA/CAN/AU), Bertrams Books (UK/EU).

Library of Congress Cataloging-in-Publication Data

Names: Levy, Jay S., 1961- editor. | Johnson, Robin Giles Hillary, 1948- editor.
Title: Cross-cultural dialogues on homelessness: from pretreatment strategies to psychologically informed environments/edited by Jay S. Levy with Robin Johnson.
Description: 1st Edition. | Ann Arbor, MI: Loving Healing Press, [2018] | Includes index.
Identifiers: LCCN 2017043564 (print) | LCCN 2017052186 (ebook) | ISBN 9781615993680 (ePub, PDF, Kindle) | ISBN 9781615993666 (pbk.: alk. paper)
| ISBN 9781615993673 (hardcover: alk. paper)
Subjects: LCSH: Homeless persons--Mental health services.
Classification: LCC RC451.4.H64 (ebook) | LCC RC451.4.H64 C76 2018 (print) |
  DDC 616.890086/942--dc23
LC record available at https://lccn.loc.gov/2017043564

Confidentiality

The case illustrations depicted in this book are based on actual persons and events from our field experiences. However, names, places and events have been altered as warranted to protect client confidentiality.

Dedication

We dedicate this project to people without homes, and to all those who have survived homelessness, and to the homelessness service workers who help the most vulnerable among us. Their courage, strength and dedication serve as an inspiration to all.

Contents

Table of Figures

Words of Appreciation

I am indebted to the generosity of others whose input made this project possible. I am especially thankful to my British colleagues who provide a UK perspective based on both their personal experiences and field research. They are Robin Johnson, Ray Middleton, John Conolly and Suzanne Quinney. Robin in particular has gone above and beyond in his writing, editing and encouragement for all of us to produce something of value.

I am honored that my US colleague, Joe Finn, also contributed to this book. His tireless efforts to end homelessness have resulted in many innovative Housing First programs across Massachusetts, and have served as a national model for remediating homelessness. Much credit goes to our publisher, LH Press, and its CEO, Victor R. Volkman, for encouraging our writing and always showing interest in the next project.

I have endless appreciation and love for my wife, Louise Levy (high school teacher and environmental educator), for her tireless reviews of the manuscript, astute observations and suggestions, as well as being a willing soundboard on our exceedingly long walks.

Last, but not least, thanks to my two daughters, Talia and Sara, for their emotional support, playfulness, and thoughtful discussions culminating in Talia's design of the bar graph shown in Fig. 12-3.

Most importantly, all of us believe in one another and share the ideals of inclusion, diversity and social justice.

Jay S. Levy, MSW, LICSW
Editor

US Foreword — Creating a Common Language

The "Housing First" movement, like most social movements, grew out of a sense on the part of many that something in society was fundamentally wrong. In Massachusetts, I witnessed the late 1980s and early 1990s from the views of those in the trenches responding to unaccompanied adult homelessness. One had to be particularly insensitive, or wholly blinded by the conviction that they were involved in some noble mission to shelter the poor, to not understand that something had gone fundamentally wrong. Homelessness represents the failure of multiple systems of care, especially those systems meant to serve people whose lives had been impacted by serious behavioral illnesses and disorders.

For me, working those days at Boston Intake, the Newton Overflow Shelter, and eventually Father Bill's Place in Quincy, Massachusetts, it was a shocking revelation to see the number of people with serious mental illness simply cut adrift. How does one explain the frustration of trying to have a person in the midst of a psychotic episode evaluated, only to be told from the clinician at emergency services that you would have to transport the client to a hospital or a police station because the clinician did not feel safe coming to your shelter?

During those times, people with serious mental illness were being directly discharged to homeless shelters. There were few opportunities for residential programs, and often the subtle or sometimes explicit message was that the person was not "housing ready" or even program ready. They were seen as noncompliant clients. It was painfully apparent that such "clients" would never improve their wellbeing if the system was built around clinicians sitting in clinics waiting for these people to show up and say they needed help.

Over time, this realization grew among many of us serving homeless individuals. We asked: "What if we tried using our various housing resources to house them?" This idea was not grasped by all; there was hardly universal acceptance for such a concept. Those who opposed it felt that these individuals were not capable of sustaining housing. Some argued that an urban shelter was the best you could ever expect for this population. Some even promoted the idea that shelters should be considered an acceptable urban housing niche. Fortunately, a critical mass of homeless providers did not share this view.

Yet, once committed to the cause, then what? How should we reach out, approach homeless individuals and serve them in such settings? What expectations should we place on such tenants? Out of this questioning, our own particular form of "low-threshold" housing grew into place. The Massachusetts Housing & Shelter Alliance (MHSA) advocated for and began an effort to shape a statewide movement to make Housing First a reality in the Commonwealth. MHSA's founding Executive Director Philip Mangano's early advocacy for the conversion of resources toward housing and services emerged as the national vision of Housing First. Not only would housing result in a reduction of costly emergency and acute resources across systems of care, it would actually improve peoples' chances for recovery. Over the past ten years, MHSA, with the vital work of agencies across the Commonwealth, is proud to have been a part of housing nearly 2000 people who were chronically homeless. The claims of cost savings have been substantiated by a number of different studies (Byrne and Smart, 2017; Wright et al., 2016; Buchanan et al., 2009; Larimer et al., 2009).

But, this is not the whole story of how such an approach came to be. The emergence of any great innovation has a complex causal structure. From my perspective, the low-threshold approach to housing would never have emerged in Massachusetts without the long practice of clinicians committed to providing outreach to the very population described above. The core wisdom of accepting people where they are, without judging or pigeonholing them, grew from the work of clinicians engaged with the Department of Mental Health (DMH) Homeless Outreach Team in Boston, or the work of Projects for Assistance in Transition from Homelessness (PATH) Counselors across the Commonwealth, which proved that one could connect, communicate and inspire people to seek the resources they needed.

My own perspective on the possibilities of low-threshold housing was often reinforced by outreach counselors sharing their personal experiences with me. They, too, seemed to know that the conventional and institutional approaches had failed. I think it was their approach, honed in the urban streets and alleys, under bridges, and in the forests of our rural areas, that shaped housing providers' views on new possibilities beyond the compliance-based, abstinence-based programs that had existed for years, and yet failed to put a dent in homelessness.

As office-based clinicians worked with this population, it occurred to me that many of the existing clinical modalities or treatment models failed to capture the reality of what these dedicated outreach workers were practicing on the streets. Even some of the most progressive social work models that emphasized the experiences and articulated needs of the person did not encapsulate for me, an advocate and not a clinician, the essence of my encounters with homeless individuals experiencing serious mental illness.

It was Jay Levy who finally provided the missing language. The story of the progression from outreach to shelter to housing approaches is, in many ways, his story as well. However, he was one of the first to begin to shape a language to an effective practice or approach.

"Pretreatment" was a concept that anyone working direct care with homeless individuals could immediately identify with. Jay's development around a "Pretreatment" approach to homeless individuals experiencing serious mental illness opened ways to communicate with them in the midst of crisis. Not only did he practice this approach for many years — his distillation of his learned wisdom and experience in writing resulted in a useful tool for all of those in the trenches trying to move people out of crisis and into housing, or, for that matter, sustaining people in crisis in their housing. His concept of establishing a "common language," where practiced, was useful to direct care worker and clinician alike.

Now, in partnership with Robin Johnson and others throughout the UK, Jay has begun the first steps toward a cross-cultural discussion on homelessness. This is most appropriate, given the lessons already learned in the United States and the United Kingdom in addressing and prioritizing the needs of chronic homelessness. We learned much from the "rough sleepers" focus of providers in England. What makes this dialogue important is that the discussion of Pre-treatment strategies and the concept of Psychologically Informed Environments (PIE) are shaped out of real-time practice and are most applicable and meaningful to those actually working with this population.

These efforts at such a dialogue constitute an attempt to mainstream practices that could actually end homelessness for people with significant mental health issues and complex needs. Jay displays the fruits of such dialogue by highlighting the importance of the language of systems, and how that shapes various responses to the problem of homelessness. We should not deceive ourselves for a moment here in our country: if the various systems of care accepted such practices, we would see far less homelessness. The inability of mainstream care systems to adjust to this population is one of the primary causes of homelessness.

Make no mistake about it: Jay is not a theorist. His writing comes from his actual work. The philosophers of knowledge might suggest that Jay's writing is grounded in *praxis*[1]. The book is full of his personal experiences, as well as the experiences of his British colleagues; everywhere from the streets of Boston and the woods of Western Massachusetts to London's urban landscape. If you have actually been in the situation of engaging with homeless individuals such as the ones captured throughout these pages, you will immediately get the sense that you, too, have been there. That is what makes this work so compelling. It is so much more grounded in the realities of homelessness and of serious mental illness than our office and clinic-bound colleagues will ever comprehend. It should be required reading for all in the fields of counseling and social work, or, at a minimum, for anyone who aspires to work with homeless individuals with serious mental illness.

My more direct work with homeless individuals, with a few remarkable exceptions, ended when I assumed the leadership of MHSA in 2003. Most of my work today is dedicated to the development of and advocacy for the resources necessary to house homeless individuals, with a strong emphasis on promoting the dedication of resources toward the low-threshold model of permanent supportive housing. The introduction of Housing First in Massachusetts; the first flexible funding for low-threshold housing; the first model of Medicaid reimbursement for tenant-based services; and most recently, the introduction of Rapid Re-housing and the first Pay for Success (Social Innovation Financing) initiative in the nation for homeless individuals are all great successes that ultimately strive for the same end Jay has dedicated his life to: ending homelessness.

However, it should be noted that despite the success of the past decade or so, I have known Jay for the past three decades, during which I have been professionally engaged in the fight to end homelessness. It has been an honor to work with Jay, and I know no one as dedicated to this cause as he has been. His work and this transatlantic project are important contribu-

---

[1] Greek, German and French philosophers debated the meaning of *praxis*. Greek philosophers, Plato and Aristotle understood praxis as action in and of itself and an end in itself, not guided by moral or rational motivations. German Philosophers Hegel and later Marx understood it as conscious action that brings about social transformation — an explanation that fits in well with dialectics and dialectical materialism. French philosopher Jean-Paul Sartre understood it in terms of intentional individual action directed toward a specific project that ultimately leads to self and social transformation. I use the term praxis using this latter interpretation.

tions toward ending the scandal and social failure that causes people to live outside.

Throughout these chapters, authors from both the US and UK describe practices to better serve vulnerable people without homes. A real and vital dialogue has begun with our colleagues across the sea. Hopefully, the reader of this work will, too, become part of such an important conversation.

Joe Finn, MA, Sociology, MA, Theology, JD
President/Executive Director of MHSA
MHSA, March 20, 2017

References

Buchanan, D., Kee, R., Sadowski, L. S. & Garcia, D. (2009) The Health Impact of Supportive Housing for HIV-Positive Homeless Patients: A Randomized Controlled Trial. *American Journal of Public Health.* 99(S3): S675–S680

Byrne, T. & Smart, G. (2017) *Estimating Cost Reductions Associated with The Community Support Program For People Experiencing Chronic Homelessness* (CSPECH). Boston: BCBSMA Foundation, Pine Street Inn & Massachusetts Medicaid Policy Institute. Retrieved from: http://bluecrossmafoundation.org/sites/default/files/download/publicatio n/CSPECH_Report_Mar17_FINAL.pdf.

Larimer, M. E., Malone, D. K., Garner, M. D., Atkins, D. C., Burlingham, B., Lonczak, H. S., Tanzer, K., Ginzler, J., Clifasefi, S. L., Hobson, W. G. & Marlatt, G.A. (2009) Health Care and Public Service Use and Costs Before and After Provision of Housing for Chronically Homeless Persons with Severe Alcohol Problems. *JAMA.* 301(13): 1349-1357

Wright, B. J., Vartanian, K. B., Hsin-Fang Li, Royal, N., & Matson, J. K. (2016) Formerly Homeless People Had Lower Overall Health Care Expenditures After Moving Into Supportive Housing. *Health Affairs*, 35(1): 20-27

UK Foreword — Transatlantic Dialogue: Different Journeys with Common Goals

Currently, several innovative pathways are being constructed for people with complex needs who experience homelessness. Despite their differences, all these innovations have a common purpose — to create better journeys into social inclusion for those without a home. Anyone interested in better serving the people society excludes could benefit from reading this book. Within these chapters are some of the most innovative practice ideas on homelessness from both the US and UK. Collecting these differing ideas into one place allows a creative dialogue to open up between best practices on either side of the Atlantic.

The variety of authors contained here illuminate innovations that can help us all on our collective quest to create better journeys for people without homes. Each chapter contains succinct summaries of very useful concepts with direct practical application for services, such as Pretreatment, Trauma Informed Care (TIC) and Psychologically Informed Environments (PIE). Several contributions are from the originators of the concepts such as Robin Johnson (PIE) and Jay Levy (Pretreatment). Reflecting on how these ideas resonate with, and differ from, our own practices within our local cultural contexts can help us all get better at reducing homelessness and increasing social inclusion.

Although contributors to this project differ in their valuable insights, common themes also emerge. All of the chapters are to some extent a description of creative responses to systemic failure of traditionally offered services to effectively engage people with complex needs (combination of housing, legal, medical, mental health, and/or substance misuse needs). In chapter 9, Jay Levy explains how part of the problem is the way traditional services have developed in "silos" with their own "silo-thinking," professional languages and bureaucracies of eligibility criteria, which often serve the smooth running of the service at the expense of excluding people without homes with complex trauma histories.

This resonates with our experience in the UK. Service delivery often has little effect, with a revolving door of entry into and discharge from services, leading back to homelessness. It is not just that repeated ineffective costly contact with services reduces trust, but systemic failures and neglect from services re-traumatises people with insecure attachments through repeated rejections, early discharges, evictions, etc. At worst, ineffective services can mirror the abuse and neglect people experienced in their early life, an experience that has become entrenched for decades. The ineffective engagement from traditionally "siloed" services necessitates the needs for new approaches to help services get better, several of which are outlined in these chapters. *New work requires new genres.*

Currently, I am a System Broker at Fulfilling Lives in the North East of England, where we work with people with complex combinations of needs around homelessness, substance misuse, reoffending and mental health, who have difficulty engaging in services. Because of my own lived experience of complex needs, I have always been a champion of involving and employing "experts by experience" (aka: Peers). We emphasise the value of genuinely co-producing, with the people who have "lived experience" of these needs, the offer from services reaching out to people with multiple needs.

The Peer movement has an important role to play in the UK and US in improving how services are designed and delivered, in homelessness, substance misuse and mental health domains. Although it is evolving in both countries, and is more prominent in addiction services, the level and quality of involvement of "experts by experience" does vary considerably in mental health and homelessness services. Despite some good examples on both sides of the Atlantic, it is fair to say there is still further distance to travel on the valuable journey of "service user involvement." Employing and/or genuinely involving Peers who have experienced the needs that a service is trying to meet is often an underdeveloped potential source of service improvement.

Whilst creating online PIE training resource films with experts by experience, I discovered a new technology of live-streaming, which allowed me to run a public talk show live online. I started experimenting with this new technology as I saw the possibility of interviewing both experts by experience and experts by training and/or professional practice in the field of complex needs and homelessness. I brought people together to open up a dialogue, share ideas internationally and record these films to spread innovation and develop staff knowledge and skills.

It is through these live-streaming "talk-show" genre films that I first met Jay Levy. This introduced me to the great work he has been developing in the USA for over three decades, and I was inspired to read his book on Pretreatment. I could see the potential of new technologies to spread good practice ideas in Homelessness. On one of these transatlantic discussion films https://youtu.be/nHw1XK7exEI (Middleton, et al., 2016), we had Robin Johnson, who originated PIE, Claire Ritchie, who wrote the Westminster Council PIE guidance, and Jay Levy, who originated Pretreatment — all opening up a dialogue and exchange of ideas about better meeting the needs of people experiencing the effects of complex trauma and homelessness.

New technology allowed me to meet Jay and learn about the great work he has accomplished in a variety of roles, from homeless outreach counsellor to overseeing and directing several homelessness programs. I believe that the ideas Jay develops around common language construction outlined in chapter 3 have great value for engaging with people. As he illustrates with the example of Miguel who interprets/ reads the word "Therapist" as "The Rapist" from within his "*house of language;*" listening to and appreciating Miguel's linguistic world is key to engaging him with help around his mental health, which involves sensitively negotiating and using the word *counselor* instead of *therapist*. For me, reading Jay's chapters resonated with my own work in the UK applying some principles from "open dialogue" (Siekkula and Arnkil, 2006) to the habitual patterns occurring within the narratives of people with complex needs who are without a home.

Open Dialogue is an approach originally developed in Western Lapland forming a social network response for people experiencing a psychotic crisis which draws on Bakhtin's Dialogical epistemology (Bakhtin, 1984). I have found that taking an open dialogue approach does help staff reduce their anxiety through accepting they *only ever partly know* what is going on with clients. It also helps staff appreciate that we understand the client's world dialogically from the *relatively remote context* of our own narrative world. Drawing on Bakhtin's concepts, I encourage staff to see both themselves and their clients temporarily journeying together, meeting dialogically in overlapping worlds as *unfinalised personalities,* who can listen to and learn from each other at crossroads on our life-journeys.

Another common theme emerging from these chapters is the increasing appreciation of the role of trauma in resolving entrenched homelessness. In chapter 2, Robin Johnson reflects on his transatlantic journey by skillfully comparing and contrasting Psychologically Informed Environments (PIE) and Trauma Informed Care (TIC). This draws out several valuable resonating points, such as the need for trauma training, increasing peer support, collaborative strength based work with clients, promoting a sense of control through choice, emphasising safety, and developing staff skills for building relationships of trust.

As Robin rightly concludes, those of us trying to improve services in different ways on both sides of the Atlantic are indeed on "much the same journey." By journeying through dialogue together, we can travel faster and further than travelling alone. This book is a significant contribution to extending collaboration and connecting fellow travellers who are on a shared quest to improve the journeys of people with complex needs who experience homelessness.

Ray Middleton, B.Sc.
Systemic Practitioner and Doctoral Researcher in Social Psychology
Fulfilling Lives
http://www.laddder4life.com/

References

Bakhtin, M. M. (1981) *The Dialogical Imagination*. Austin, TX: University of Texas Press

Levy, J. S. (2010) *Homeless narratives & pretreatment pathways: From words to housing*. Ann Arbor, MI: Loving Healing Press

Middleton R. Johnson, R., Ritchie, C. & Levy J. S, (2016) [video discussion] Transatlantic exchange of ideas (PIE & Pretreatment https://youtu.be/nHw1XK7exEI

Siekkula, J. & Arnkil, T. E. (2006) *Dialogical Meetings in Social Networks*. London, UK: Karnac (Books) Ltd.

Introduction — Cross-Cultural Dialogues on Homelessness
Jay S. Levy

I first met Robin Johnson, who has edited the UK chapters of this book, almost by chance. Only a few short years ago, a passing comment I had made in a LinkedIn discussion on homelessness in 2014 first aroused Robin's curiosity. He posted a question; I replied; we messaged; and so began a conversation, a discussion — we should perhaps now call it a dialogue.

Later, one of Robin's colleagues — Ray Middleton, who is also writing here — introduced us to the possibilities of live streaming for discussions, not just between two people, but also in a small group. Before long, we had had several such live online discussions with me in the US, and Robin and some of his circle of colleagues from across the UK; sharing ideas, and seeing each other's nods and smiles.

Many such discussions followed. It was a meeting of minds; a shared commitment and vision; and an attempt to understand not just the points in common, but also the apparent differences between our worlds, our language, and our ideas about where the promise of the future lay. Shot through it all, though, was the sheer excitement of finding novel ways to communicate, especially in the new world that the internet has suddenly made available to us.

From the very start, this developing dialogue made full use of all the possibilities that these new technologies have to offer, and some of this is captured on video. During this same time period, Robin was gathering material for the website (Pielink.net) he had created, to share ideas and practice on mental health and homelessness. Eventually, Robin was able to make a trip to the US, meeting me and several of my colleagues, including Joe Finn, who writes here.

And so we began to see through the veils of mutual miscomprehension between what Winston Churchill once famously called "two countries divided by a common language." It was then my idea to put some of this into book form, and Robin and his colleagues in the UK gladly agreed to contribute chapters. Just as in our initial live conversations, theory and practice are interwoven continuously throughout this book, as they are in all the work we do. Deeply involved though we are with gaining a wider understanding, informed by psychology, by social theory, linguistics and the pragmatics of social policy, we are all equally committed to action learning, and above all, to learning from sharing experiences — from each other, and from the next encounter with the client.

So this is our story, and the importance of such narrative as an approach will emerge as we write, and the reasons why we have so often chosen to make some key points in the form of stories. Everywhere, and at all levels, we want to stress the importance, the crucial validity, of dialogue. So, the title — *Cross-Cultural Dialogues on Homelessness* — then has multiple meanings.

First, it presents a basic question for all "homeless service workers" to consider. How do we cross the cultural divide between ourselves, in our stable homes and lives, and those people without homes? This question takes us right to the heart of the issue of engagement. We are confronted with the essential challenges of initiating a trusting relationship, and attempting to really consider a person's words, ideas, values, aspirations, as well as their immediate needs. In other words, "Getting where the person is at," which is the hallmark of Pretreatment philosophy.

Second, there is the challenge of building bridges between the world of the person experiencing homelessness and the available resources/ services. In essence, homelessness workers are both bridge builders and interpreters. Our task is to understand these two often disparate worlds and develop pathways for communication and consideration. For example, we operate in a treatment-based culture that is often more focused on diagnostic categories, labels, compliance and "readiness for change" than on a person's own narrative, their unique strengths and vulnerabilities.

This is yet another cultural divide we must somehow cross and negotiate, by developing a common language that facilitates engagement between those who are homeless and the various providers of resources and services. We thereby attempt to bring together the complex challenges, abilities and the strident need for autonomy that many of our clients express with an entrenched office culture that determines eligibility for resources and services based on very general rules and quite specific regulations that often make no sense at all in the world of the client.

Third, and central to the task of this book, there is another cross-cultural dialogue now opening up, in the fostering of a transatlantic communication on homelessness with service providers throughout the US and the UK. In these chapters, we want to tell many new stories, yet the bigger tale we want to tell here is precisely one of how two countries can perhaps understand themselves better, by seeing what is done elsewhere.

The rapid change in telecommunications has brought us the opportunity to share our stories from the field. We are no longer bound by geographical limits — though it is perhaps particularly ironic that those of us who work with people who are disconnected in space now find ourselves, too, in a world without our familiar spatial boundaries. These conversations began only in 2014; and yet by 2018, we are able to bring them together, for the first time, in the form of a book.

So, here we will find some significant contributions from both sides of the Atlantic; the coming together of our collective wisdom on homelessness. This may even bring about a shift to new and improved perspectives that can guide our future efforts of reaching out and helping people without homes.

1 Homelessness on Both Sides of the Atlantic
Jay S. Levy

> Injustice anywhere is a threat to justice everywhere. We are
> caught in an inescapable network of mutuality, tied in a
> single garment of destiny.
>
> > –Martin Luther King, Jr. (1963)

Introduction

I can still hear echoes from a distant place. It was a time when people did not believe in the possibility of directly housing long-term homeless individuals without first requiring treatment. There was a din of naysayers and doubters who thought it could not or must not be done. Yet here we are in the midst of a movement. Over the past several years, we have unveiled the promise of finding homes for the most vulnerable among us who live on our streets and at the edges of our communities. Through the hard work of outreach, Housing First and the transatlantic truth of trauma-informed care, we have begun to make that promise a reality.

This project is another important step on our journey... an invitation to share our thoughts and challenges across borders and beyond the limits of cultural boundaries.

International Perspectives

Back in October of 2013, I had the privilege of presenting at the 9th annual International Street Medicine Symposium. It was inspiring to meet doctors, nurses, social workers, and other human service professionals from around the globe. Without exception, they were dedicated to providing quality healthcare to people without homes who experienced significant medical, mental health, and addiction issues. Upon my arrival at the conference, I was weighed down by the systemic barriers to care that most of us encounter on a daily basis. Locally, this translated to separate silos of mental health, addiction, and medical services with varying eligibility requirements that limited access to needed treatment and resources.

I listened intently to people's stories of outreach and the difficulties inherent in providing healthcare for excluded homeless populations throughout the world. One of the prevailing problems encountered by me and many others is the ongoing treatment bias. It demands that a person shows a level of readiness to directly partake in medical and/or mental health services, rather than addressing the immediate concerns of people without homes who experience complex trauma, addiction, and an array of physical ailments.

We were unified in our efforts to help, though some of us experienced barriers far worse than I could have ever imagined. I was astonished to hear that the governments of certain countries considered homeless outreach across cultural-tribal boundaries to be subversive. It therefore became a secretive practice with the accompanying risks of detection by authorities. In contrast, this provided a new and more optimistic view of our efforts in both the United States and England.

In many respects, we are fortunate to live in open societies whose governments support Homeless Outreach services to varying degrees. That being said, systemic barriers in both countries remain, including the criminalization of homelessness, the high cost of housing, lack of social supports, widespread poverty, and far too many vulnerable people suffering dire consequences due to their inability to access affordable housing and healthcare.

My first book, *Homeless Narratives & Pretreatment Pathways*, was completed during the summer of 2010. As this was both cause for celebration and during the pinnacle of Harry Potter mania, my family and I decided to travel to London. Off we went to visit the British Museum and an array of city parks and English gardens. At the Royal Academy of the Sciences, we were humbled by the great history of observation, experimentation and discovery. Throughout the many sights and sounds of London, which of course included Kings Cross Station's platform 9¾ and numerous city cafes, there were also the sights and sounds of poverty, homelessness and the day-in and day-out struggle for survival.

Suddenly and without intention, I had entered the familiar territory of urban homelessness. Once I took notice, it was hard not to be reminded of my numerous experiences of homeless outreach throughout the streets and shelters of New York City and Boston. This led to some initial curiosity that fueled my search for further information. I spent several days inquiring about the network of homeless services in London by browsing bookstores, online websites of various helping agencies, and occasionally directly approaching someone in need. I soon discovered that people without homes either stayed in hostels (as opposed to large US shelters) or for an array of reasons may have ended up on London's streets as "rough sleepers." Little did I know that my initial curiosity would eventually result in this project — *Cross-Cultural Dialogues on Homelessness.*

My Writing and Practice

I began my professional journey as a Homeless Outreach counselor during the winter of 1987. Since my initial meeting with my first client (who called himself Old Man Ray) at NYC's Port Authority, I have never turned back. My outreach experiences with Old Man Ray and others made me realize that people are experts on their own worlds (Epston & White, 1992), and that my role is primarily to foster client-centered relationships and shared objectives. The rest of my work flowed from there.

During the past thirty years, I provided outreach counseling, advocacy, clinical supervision, and directed housing programs that served formerly homeless individuals. I loved meeting people literally and figuratively where they were at, and this brought together my interests in grassroots social work and activism. Homeless Outreach afforded me the privilege of being welcomed into people's lives, as well as witnessing both the richness and debilitating effects of their day-to-day experiences and challenges.

During my time in NYC, I learned the art of engagement and respect for those who struggled to survive, while searching for their own sense of meaning and dignity among the city streets, shelters, and soup kitchens. This window into the realities of homelessness helped me to realize the importance of relationships, while also valuing our need for autonomy, finding purpose, and having a safe place to reside.

Over time, I realized that Homeless Outreach seemed to be more of a personal art among the most dedicated in the field, rather than a cohesive philosophy with guiding principles of care that outreach professionals could follow. My desire to write was fueled by the long and winding road of field experience, feedback from my work peers, as well as those without homes, which directly led to my formulation of the Pretreatment approach. I tried to right a wrong by putting pen to paper. I witnessed too many people being left out in the cold... too many people without homes deemed "not ready" for help, and the human service community saddled with too many rules and too little compassion.

Of course there were those who knew better. Outreach workers across America and leaders in the field such as Dr. Sam Tsemberis, founder of Pathways to Housing, and Dr. James O'Connell of Boston's Health Care for the Homeless, as well as Dr. Jim Withers of the Street Medicine Institute, among others, demanded help for the most vulnerable people living on the streets. Momentum for positive change was further supported by renowned author Malcolm Gladwell's (2006) *New Yorker* magazine article, "Million Dollar Murray," which espoused the merits (cost savings) of a Housing First approach for ending chronic homelessness. Many things have changed for the better. Outreach, Housing First, and other Harm Reduction approaches are now not only accepted, but favored by many of us who provide homeless services.

Throughout the years, I published several journal articles and books on the subject of Pretreatment. These works share people's stories, while also providing the theory behind the practice in an effort to elucidate effective ways of helping people to overcome trauma and homelessness. The end result was my second book, a *Pretreatment Guide* for homeless outreach counselors, case managers, and social workers, as well as a resource for others who serve people without homes in a variety of settings, which includes supporting transitions to Housing First apartments.

Outreach begins with getting "where the person is at" to form a trusting relationship in an effort to jointly work on goals to alleviate homelessness and improve one's quality of life. These goals need to resonate well with the client and are communicated via a "Common Language" (Blankertz, et al., 1990.; Levy, 2000; Levy, 2004) that serves as a bridge between the person experiencing homelessness and available resources, supports, and services. The foundation of Homeless Outreach (Levy, 2010) is a client-centered relationship, while common language construction is the main tool for facilitating positive change.

This is at the heart of a Pretreatment Model that also values supporting the process of transition and adaptation to new environments, as well as promoting safety through crisis intervention and harm reduction strategies. An important goal of my writing is to open up the conversation about Pretreatment and other trauma-informed perspectives in an effort to develop more effective strategies for helping people who have experienced multiple or extended episodes of homelessness, trauma, and loss.

Two Approaches to Helping: Pretreatment and Psychologically Informed Environments (PIE)

My most recent book, *Pretreatment Guide for Homeless Outreach & Housing First (2013),* was reviewed in the UK's *Housing Care & Support* journal. Its editor, and founder of PIE, Robin Johnson. contacted me on LinkedIn to initially inquire about a posting I made on effectively targeting Housing First programs to a chronically homeless sub-population, as opposed to generally applying it to all people experiencing homelessness.

It was during these initial conversations with Robin that I first learned about Psychologically Informed Environments (PIE) and its applications to trauma and homelessness. Robin seemed excited about the connections that he saw between PIE and Pretreatment. In fact, our initial discussion about Pretreatment was as a Psychological Model that neatly fit into a PIE approach for helping persons without homes who experienced complex trauma. This piqued my curiosity, and Robin was kind enough to introduce me to an online community that focused on sharing best practices and information about PIE via video, online chats, access to Library reference materials and more at www.Pielink.net.

So, what is PIE?

Robin Johnson (2015) among others identify a Psychologically Informed Environment at its most basic level as "one that takes into account the psychological make-up — the thinking, emotions, personalities and past experience — of its participants, in the way it operates." Robin further specifies, "But as all human social environments tend to do that to some degree, we tend now to reserve the term for those environments — places, services — that do so consciously, and with some particular purpose or goals in mind. This site is primarily about how we develop psychologically informed services to meet the challenge of homelessness." His description fits nicely with the objectives of homeless outreach, drop-in centers, and safe haven programs.

In fact, Robin now suggests, having recently been to visit services in the States, as he describes in a chapter later in this book that many of our long-term and permanent supported housing programs could be described as PIEs. There would be considerable benefits to further modifying many existing shelters and residential programs by applying the basic elements of PIE. Writings and research (see Pielink.net library) on the development and impact of Psychologically Informed Environments on homeless services throughout the UK lends valuable insight to our cause.

Over the past couple of years, I've been inspired by multiple video conference conversations with homeless service workers in England. This has led to an ongoing dialogue about the similarities, differences, and benefits of varied approaches to helping the homeless, as well as sharing specific strategies of outreach and engagement. Our aim is to facilitate a cross-cultural fertilization of ideas and practices that are rooted in a common language. This sharing of perspectives can help guide outreach counselors, social workers, and homeless service employees with the formidable task of reaching folks without homes who are most at risk and in desperate need of assistance.

In turn, this book explores the phenomenon of homelessness on both sides of the Atlantic. In particular, it focuses on people without homes who have been marginalized due to traumatic experiences and/or disability through the lens of Pretreatment and PIE. This brings a cross-cultural sharing of ideas and approaches to the vexing and complicated issues that homelessness inevitably presents. It is a societal ill that is in need of many voices from different places to spur compassion, discovery, and action.

I invite the reader to join us in an open dialogue that spans both time and space in an effort to create solutions to an age-old problem. Together we can provide both the inspiration and hope necessary to energize a movement, and thereby provide the optimism that successful change demands. I believe that both Pretreatment Strategies and Psychologically Informed Environments are among the seeds from which new ideas and innovative approaches to "hands on" practice can and will grow.

References

Blankertz, L. E., Cnaan, R. A., White, K., Fox, J., & Messinger, K. (1990). Outreach efforts with dually diagnosed homeless persons. *Families in Society: The Journal of Contemporary Human Services,71(7): 387-396.*

Epston, D. & White, M. (1992) Experience, contradiction, narrative, and imagination: *Selected papers of David Epston and Michael White, 1989-1991.* Adelaide, Australia: Dulwich Centre Publications

Gladwell, M. (2006) Million Dollar Murray: Why problems like homelessness may be easier to solve than to manage. *The New Yorker*, February 13 & 20.

Johnson, R. (2015) Published on PIElink website: http://pielink.net/

King, M. L. Jr. (n.d.) BrainyQuote.com. excerpt from April 16, 1963 Martin letter from Birmingham jail. Retrieved March 19, 2017, from BrainyQuote.com Web site: https://www.brainyquote.com/quotes/quotes/m/martinluth122559.html

Levy, J. S. (2000) Homeless outreach: On the road to pretreatment alternatives. *Families in Society: The Journal of Contemporary Human Services*, 81(4): 360-368

Levy, J. S. (2004) Pathway to a common language: A homeless outreach perspective. *Families in Society: The Journal of Contemporary Human Services*, 85(3): 371-378

Levy, J. S. (2010) *Homeless narratives & pretreatment pathways: From words to housing.* Ann Arbor, MI: Loving Healing Press

Levy, J. S. (2013) *Pretreatment guide for homeless outreach & housing first: Helping couples, youth, and unaccompanied adults.* Ann Arbor, MI: Loving Healing Press

2 Principles and Practice in Psychology and Homelessness: Core skills in Pretreatment, Trauma Informed Care & Psychologically Informed Environments
Robin Johnson

You Wait Years

You wait ages, it seems, for a humane and enlightened, emotionally intelligent approach to homelessness to come along; and then, like buses, three come at once. For some years it had seemed that the only really new and radical thinking on addressing all the psychological and emotional problems that so often are found in homelessness was something which had begun in the US, and was more recently coming to the UK and Europe, under the name of "Housing First", or "HF" (Tsemberis, n.d.; Busch-Geertsma, 2012; Evans, 2012: Pleace & Brotheton, 2012).

Originally seen as calling for fully individualized housing for those with the most complex needs, it is now becoming apparent in the US both that congregated or single site housing may be more affordable, and in some ways, for some people, actually more suitable. (Malone et al., 2015; Nichols & Doberstein, 2016; Kwong, 2016; Pereira 2016; True, 2016)

Meanwhile, there is still a valuable role for short term, transitional housing, in the form of "shelter"—or what we in the UK would call "hostels", "foyers" and "refuges" (Eastlund, 2017; Miller, 2016; Gaetz, 2013). In an earlier paper (Johnson, 2017a) we argued that there is a place even for the programme- or compliance-based housing that had been so out of favour, in the HF philosophy; and it's interesting to see that, in the last couple of years, the US government seems to be trying to find a way (HUD, 2015; Levy, 2017) to reconcile HF principles with a recognition of the valuable role of what they call "Recovery Housing", in which belonging in a community is an important, integral part of the support service.

But this quite recent development in the US seems so far to have only a fairly minimal vocabulary to describe what matters here, and what works. So, we suggest, when we look for models of shared living innovation in practice, it becomes useful to look further afield, and explore what lessons might be learned from other countries. Here, therefore, we will compare and contrast some new approaches to identifying the nature of care service environments that have more recently entered the field, on both sides of the Atlantic, each with their own vocabulary of key themes or principles.

We start with an analysis of the interpersonal skills needed for engagement with marginalized and excluded individuals with complex and entrenched difficulties that may have contributed to their radical alienation from the help that mainstream services hope to offer. Fortunately, much of the work has been already done for us here, in Jay Levy's writings on Pretreatment; so here we can focus on the connective tissue between this work with individuals, and the contexts and settings in which other services operate.

The next sections of this extended essay therefore go on to explore two new ideas that look not just at the immediate, interpersonal skills of engagement, as Pretreatment does, but at the networks of relationships, and the kinds of cultures and social environments that we create, or can aim to create, in services. In the US and Canada, such approaches have gone by the name of Trauma Informed Care, or TIC, in recognition of the central role of trauma in people's troubled lives.

Meanwhile, across the pond in the UK, we have also seen a parallel development in homelessness services, which are now being described as "psychologically informed environments"—PIEs. Here, in this chapter, we will aim to explore in some depth that last term, which will still be new to many US readers. Through that, we aim to get a glimpse of what is going on currently in new thinking on homelessness work.

Core Skills: Pretreatment

One of the most valuable new approaches to emerge in recent years adds to our understanding of the issues we address, in homelessness work; and also helps identify and foster the skills and the professionalism—in the best sense of the word—that we find in the work of homelessness workers. This is the concept of Pretreatment—or "pre-treatment"—in homelessness, as spelled out recently in a very useful couple of books by Jay Levy (2010, 2013), a social worker by profession.

This approach had its origins in substance abuse work, where workers often have to negotiate a complex harm minimization stage, long before the actual treatment programme can start (Joe et al. 1998; Miller and Rollnick, 2002; Salloum et al., 1998). Levy himself has described the essence of Pretreatment as follows:

> "One: to get where the client is at. Two: to always ask ourselves, how do our words and actions resonate in the client's world? And three: to really understand that the engagement relationship process, the foundation of our working well, are skills and interventions that are required for common language development, as the main tools..." (WAMC, 2011)

Levy here defines Pretreatment more formally as "an approach that enhances safety while promoting transition to housing and/or treatment alternatives through client-centred supported interventions that develop goals and motivation to create positive change".

He then characterises that in practice as consisting of five key elements or principles—relationship building (in the stages of engagement); common language construction; supporting transitions, as well as facilitating positive change; and promoting safety. To then unpack that a little, pre-treatment in outreach work focusses first on forming a relationship with the (potential) client, through finding, negotiating or constructing what Levy calls a common language, by which he means, a way to describe the situation and the possibilities that both worker and client are at home with.

Only then can the worker look to facilitating and supporting any possible change; always promoting safety, especially as a central issue for the homeless client; and always bearing in mind a range of other, cultural or "ecological" considerations, by which Levy means an acute awareness of how the client is situated and lodged in their world, with their own concerns. However, if from that it might appear that the 5 key elements of pretreatment follow in sequence, a staged engagement, this is not so. These are all simultaneous processes to take into account continuously in our work, and, for example, in ongoing assessment.

Levy himself has worked in a wide range of homelessness services, in New York, in Boston, and in the more dispersed townships of Western Massachusetts. He now manages a range of outreach services, and provides consultation for the REACH – Regional Engagement and Assessment of the Chronically Homeless – which follows their clients through all the stages of their own journey, from the streets or the woods, through temporary and settled accommodation, and even finally, where appropriate, into treatment services. In this way, they can provide what is, for many, a single stable relationship in a world of fragmented experiences and equally fragmented services.

Olivet and colleagues at the Centre for Social Innovation had similarly stressed the centrality of relationships, in their early work on identifiers of the Trauma Informed Care (TIC) approach (Olivet et al., 2010). This focus on relationship building as a core task, perhaps *the* core task, is also central to the PIE concept, which we will explore later in this chapter; and is also reflected in some of the writings of other UK writers, such as Laban (2009/2016), who writes on the need to work with clients—"service refusers" as much as service users—who are in what the cycle of change would call the "pre-contemplative" stage (Prokaska & DiClemente, 1982: Johnsen & Teixeria, 2010, Seal, 2005).

True to the theme of the need to search for those shared terms and concerns—what he calls entering their "universe of language"—Levy's writing and teaching approach avoids a reliance on the abstractions of data, and instead is based in narratives. Each of his key themes is shown in working practice in his accounts—verbatim at times—of encounters with individuals (and some couples). More than just case studies as illustration, Levy uses these narratives to exemplify and model a framework that can be used across the board, in social work/housing support training, in supervision, evaluation and reflective practice (Vickery, 2014).

Pretreatment (PT) explores and articulates all the essential skills in engagement, without which no treatment or support offer can ever be effective. These are the fundamental skills that underlie all services, not just across the homelessness spectrum (Van Doorn, 2015) from street outreach to Psychologically Informed Environments (Keats et al., 2012; Johnson R, 2013b, 2017a) and Trauma Informed Care (Fallott &Harris, 2009; Olivet et al., 2010: Prestidge, 2014) through to HF. Such skills are central in any of the "people-centred" professions including teaching, ambulance work etc. (Johnson & Haigh, 2012).

If these relationship building skills have been under-recognised, under-described and under-valued hitherto, it may be because with other groups and in other contexts they may be taken for granted. But these skills are particularly important, when working with those marginalised and excluded, distrustful and despairing, with whom we cannot expect the willing and easy compliance that other more mainstream treatment approaches may presuppose. The issues are simply starker, stripped down, in outreach work, where there are so few other props and prompts to help, and the issues and skills of relationship building must stand alone, to survive.

Note also that in articulating clearly and vividly the *pre*-treatment (sic) approach, Levy is careful not to take issue with the fundamental tenet of Housing First, that is, the idea that formal treatment should follow housing, and not be a requirement. Instead PT argues for a better recognition of the skills of engagement that must precede any form of treatment, even if the formal treatment stages are left until after the individual is housed. But they lie, by implication, on the same spectrum of skills.

With such a stress on finding and development of a common language that both worker and client can share between themselves, and construct a working relationship within, there is an irony here. In our own "universe of language", it seems to be the different ways that as professionals we have described HF, PIEs and TIC that now lead us to expect significant differences in the way our services approach the client. But Levy's writings, by putting the client at the absolute centre of the task of approaching, may also help us find the commonalities in all the real life challenges of engagement (Middleton & Levy, 2016).

The Past Casts a Long Shadow: The recognition of trauma

A UK government practice guidance document was published in 2010 by the homelessness directorate at the Department of Communities and Local Government, jointly with the National Mental Health Development Unit (NMHDU/DCLG, 2010). Entitled "on meeting the psychological and emotional needs of people who are homeless", this document had marshalled, besides many case study accounts of creative practice in homelessness services, a wealth of more formal research evidence on the prevalence of expressions of major psychological distress in this population. In behavioral problems such as self harm or suicide, substance abuse, etc. (Maguire et al., 2009: Rees et al., 2009) they noted that such presentations often amounted to levels of long-standing difficulty that fell well over the threshold for a diagnosis of personality disorder.

At that time this kind of poor mental health was a relatively new area for health services' attention. It was only a few years earlier that the UK Dept. of Health had argued (in 2003) that many people with such a diagnosis—or rather, with the problems that would justify giving them that diagnosis—were in effect excluded from mental health service care, even accusing these services of "therapeutic nihilism". A number of pilot projects had been set up, funded by the Department of Health, in an attempt to explore and learn lessons from new, more "optimistic" approaches to the needs of this group; and the written reports were only just beginning to surface (Dept. of Health 2009).

The authors of the NMHDU/DCLG guidance—which includes the author of this paper—were aware of this change of direction, in the UK mental health policy world, though it was then still little known outside of it, and had been largely un-noticed in homelessness circles. But they had argued nevertheless that a better term than "personality disorder" for these difficulties was "complex trauma". This, they suggested, was a less diagnostic and clinical way to describe the accumulated adverse life events so many had experienced, and lived with. This term also seemed to place the stress on what people had been through, rather than what they were; and so it opened some hope that, with new experiences, people could still change (Johnson & Haigh, 2012, Eastlund, 2016).

Despite its very much longer official title, that first NMHDU/DCLG "guidance on meeting the psychological and emotional needs of people who are homeless" was quite commonly simply referred to as "the complex trauma guidance". It had argued that this alternative term was the most useful way to describe and understand the problems of many who become stranded in long-term homelessness. It also helped to recognize and appreciate the work of those services working constructively with them. In the absence of mental health service in-put for these needs in the past, they argued, it was the homelessness services that seemed to have been developing the services and the skills.

Embedded Understanding: Psychologically Informed Environments

The next contribution that we consider here only entered the vocabulary of services in 2010, in the UK, and here it goes by the name of "psychologically informed environments", or PIEs. First suggested in an article on homelessness in a mental health journal (Johnson & Haigh, 2010), the term PIE was originally simply an attempt to describe, in very broad terms, the creative work being found in homelessness services with many that mainstream mental health services had been struggling to reach.

Many of the actual services we were describing in this way were perhaps still too new, and often too variable, to have any fully developed evidence base comparable to that of Housing First, for example. These new approaches are also usually so flexible, so customised to circumstances, that they do not lend themselves easily to the kind of "one size fits all" consistency of practice that quantitative outcomes evidence demands. It simply takes time to develop a research programme, let alone produce and publish any studies and findings. Studies of whole environments, what's more, need to be multi-faceted and often multi-disciplinary; and this is generally a challenge for more routine research methodologies (Johnson, 2017d).

This article however was one of a series, three linked papers on social psychiatry and social policy, outlining the way that more progressive thinking on mental health was now to be found outside, as much or more than within, formal mental health services, and this more enlightened thinking on community mental health was now expressed in many areas of social policy. Homelessness work was the chosen example here; but it was not unique.

Nevertheless, the idea of a psychologically informed environment in homelessness clearly struck a chord, and the term itself was quickly adopted in the formal guidance mentioned above, issued in 2010 by the homelessness directorate at the Department of Communities and Local Government, jointly with the National Mental Health Development Unit (NMHDU/ DCLG, 2010). As stated earlier, this document made much of the issue of complex trauma found among the homeless population in the UK. But this official document is also significant in being the first to endorse and adopt the concept of a PIE, as a suitable approach within resettlement services.

The response that followed within the UK homelessness services community was very positive. Some services were simply pleased to have the real nature of their work finally recognized, and given a name. Others – and especially those who plan and commission services – wanted to ask what more they might do, to develop services on these lines. This original guidance was therefore followed two years later by "operational guidance", written by the same team, which attempted to tease out what seemed to be the key features, the "active ingredients", perhaps, of a PIE (Keats et al., 2010).

A PIE Framework Emerges

Many or most, for example, seemed to be adopting some form of psychological approach—at least in the broadest sense of the word—to guide an understanding of people's behaviour. Note that this did not necessarily mean adopting any particular recognized clinical psychology treatment philosophy or model, such as CBT or psychodynamic thinking— though there are some that did. But more commonly the "psychology" would be quite intuitive—informed empathy, or emotional intelligence.

There were many examples of use of what mental health services would have called a "strengths model"—that is, one that emphasizes and works with whatever abilities and positive characteristics people may have, or may be helped to find, rather than focusing primarily on their difficulties. For some, a faith-based philosophy might add a core of respect for human dignity, and (perhaps ironically) some broadly humanistic thinking that echoed positive psychology's insights. But most could probably be best described as eclectic, drawing insights from anywhere.

Yet overall, one common feature was that creating and managing supportive relationships and aspirations was seen as central to the task. This took precedence even over the limited range of quantifiable "outcomes" that services were ostensibly expected to meet, and this was at times the cause of some creative tension and dialogue with funders.

There would then be some thoughtfulness and "psychological awareness" evident in the design of day to day routines, creating opportunities to participate positively. This might be via social and educational activities, or an attached employment scheme, or by creating roles within the organisation to try out and develop new strengths, such as resident's advisory councils, or peer mentoring. The management of conflicts and infractions of the rules, similarly, would aim to recognize and work with the fragile and fractured emotional state of many users, and allow cooling off time, or create opportunities to make reparations (the Crypt, n.d.; Gardiner, 2012). Later this aspect came to be dubbed "the Three R's" – meaning the rules, the roles and the responsiveness that these services offered.

Where services had an accommodation base—typically what in the US is called "transitional housing", and in the UK is known as hostels, refuges or foyers (i.e.: a service for young people) —they were giving careful thought to the use and design of any buildings. This would include not just their physical condition but the subtler "messages" they convey, in posters, lighting and furnishings; and also in their layout of spaces, the opportunities and barriers—the "social spaces" they create (Boex & Boex, 2012).

Taken together the conscious design of both the services and the building to suit the challenge of meeting complex and chaotic needs meant that these homelessness services could be seen as going far beyond offering basic food and shelter, and even beyond highly personalized "individual packages of care". They were creating an integrated and quite holistic, "wraparound" recovery environment (and hence the E in the term "PIE").

With better recognition of the challenging nature of their work, in serving some of the most vulnerable and chronically excluded, comes also more attention to the training and other support needs of staff and volunteers. Finally, there was a commitment to learning from experience, and even of adding, in some way, to the growing body of evidence of "what works", or "evidence-generating practice". Some had participated in pilot studies of new ways of working (Cockersell, 2011).

Though there was generally no culture of individual supervision in the homelessness sector, many services were becoming adept at learning lessons from incidents, and developing new ways to respond, sometimes in the form of action learning, but more commonly via a general philosophy of being "needs-led", and so becoming a "learning organization" (Quinney & Richardson, 2014: Woodcock & Gill, 2013).

In the years immediately after the Second World War, progressive psychiatrists, attempting to transform mental hospital care, had developed what was then called "therapeutic communities", using group therapy, and everyday social activities as material for therapy; and promoting what they called a "culture of enquiry" amongst staff as well as patients, to learn how to respond better. Something rather similar, a learning and enquiry culture in and for the organisation itself, now seemed to be emerging in homelessness circles.

Flexibility and Fidelity

Note that there is no easy "tick box" list of things to do here, to become or be seen or to qualify as a PIE. Rather, everything needs to be customised to circumstances, and hence the greatest stress is on action learning throughout, and what the authors termed as reflective practice, or what others have called a "culture of enquiry" (Jones, 1968; Main, 1983). This constant action learning means that being or becoming a PIE is more a journey than a destination; and arguably everybody is somewhere on this path, even if some are further advanced than others.

The remarkable flexibility that these services enjoyed, and which were able to put to good use, was a happy accident. It was a by-product, on one hand, of the peculiarity in the way these services had been funded, through a UK government-run programme called "Supporting People" (JRF, 2000, Johnson, 2006, 2007). On the other hand, there was the fact that almost all these services were run by the not-for-profit sector, and often in relatively small organisations with a strong local connection. A values base that stressed being "needs led" was nevertheless endorsed and positively encouraged by the Supporting People programme, and spread through such services.

But it also meant that this upsurge of creativity was largely confined to this sphere - what the UK calls hostels (including refuges and foyers) and short-term, transitional resettlement recovery work; and all the exciting new learning on working with the most excluded was originally largely confined to this sector, too. Nevertheless, these were the key themes and common elements that the authors of the 2012 operational guidance—largely the same writing team that had produced the 2010 guidance—had felt they could identify clearly enough to recommend as constructive practice.

Quite quickly after this, in a series of discussions, presentations and workshops, a version began to emerge that we might now see perhaps as the original or "classic" formulation of the PIE framework (this is the version adopted, for example, by Ray Middleton and his colleagues in the North East). This version identified as key elements the adoption of a psychological model or approach, training and support for all staff (and volunteers) to manage the complex emotional demands of the work; a stress on relationship building and the whole environment created in a service; and a constant concern to learn and adjust practice, evaluate and respect evidence for what works – reflective practice at both frontline and whole system levels.

But gradually, as the idea caught on, more services—not just in home-lessness work - found themselves "at home" in this account of their work, explicitly using it to see how they might develop further. We found the ideas being taken up with enthusiasm in outreach work, and in after-care. One thing - most usefully, for current purposes - the framework seems to apply both to short term services, recovery-oriented medium term services, AND equally to longer-term supported accommodation; it seems to work, to identify the core elements across ALL these services.

There are also attempts currently now to spell out what psychologically informed policy and commissioning needs to look like—to see the whole system, and its multiplicity of needs and pathways—the whole Continuum of Care, as they would call it in the US—as an environment of services As the scope and the number of variants expanded, some of the earliest attempts to pin down what a PIE was all about began to need some re-visiting. There continues to be considerable further development and evolution of the thinking and practice since 2012, and we have argued that the original PIE framework may even need constant up-dating to reflect such changes (Johnson 2016a, 2017c).

Nevertheless, the original formulation of the term PIE, in the first article published (Johnson & Haigh, 2010), had suggested a still simpler test:

> ".... for the moment, at least, the definitive marker of a PIE is simply that, if asked why the unit is run in such and such a way, the staff would give an answer couched in terms of the emotional and psychological needs of the service users, rather than giving some more logistical or practical rationale, such as convenience, costs, or Health and Safety regulations."

A similar concern to keep the concept and the actual development of services rooted in ordinary, non-technical language, in order to reflect and appreciate ordinary workers' experience, runs through these two authors' subsequent presentations—including this chapter.

Thus, for an illustration of "psychological model", the same authors suggested that adherence to any particular "model" was an option, but it really was not the central issue. Rather, the key question to ask was:

> "Granted their background and past life experience, what is the person in front of me likely to be making of what I am saying?"

It's not having the right answer that makes for a "psychological approach". It's the fact that the question is asked at all (Johnson, 2013; also Haigh, 2012).

Trauma-Informed Care

Meanwhile, across the Atlantic, another new term was being used to describe what would appear in fact to be a remarkably similar approach. In the US, we also find a range of resettlement services that take psychological trauma as the central issue — that is, as the "psychology" that "informs" the way these services operate. Their approach, which extends to many areas of social practice and not just in homelessness, goes by the name of Trauma Informed Care, or TIC (Fallot & Harris, 2009; Hopper et al., 2010; Olivet et al., 2010).

In a review of US homelessness organisations using TIC, Hopper and her colleagues (2010) identified the four key themes of TIC as: an awareness of the nature and later expression of past trauma; an emphasis on safety; creating, within or through the service, opportunities to rebuild control; and adopting a strengths-based approach. This foursome is at first sight a different list from the five or six key principles identifying a PIE. But— with the possible exception of safety, which is explicit in TIC, but only implicit in the PIE framework— it is entirely consistent with the broader view of a PIE.

In a paper published subsequently by the US's SAMHSA (2014), there is another account of the operational principles of TIC, which suggest six principles. These it lists as safety, trustworthiness and transparency, peer support, collaboration and mutuality, empowerment, "voice and choice," and an awareness of cultural, historical, and gender Issues. This account suggests a focus not just on the input of trauma awareness in services, but on the outcome in the way the services then operate.

What's in a Name?

This account of TIC, as it is embedded in the way a service works, brings the whole approach closer still to the PIE framework, which was primarily a description of the ways of working of these services in the UK context. When we then look "under the bonnet" (or "under the hood", in US parlance) the similarities and overlap become still more pronounced.

In an account of a programme of transatlantic exchange visits arranged in 2014 between the UK's HomelessLink and the US National Alliance to End Homelessness, an outreach worker in London describes (Prestidge, 2014) visiting services that we would have no hesitation in describing as PIEs; likewise the author of this paper, in visiting a range of services in the US, found services developing with what appeared to be a very similar underlying philosophy (See chapter 10; Conolly & Yazwinski, 2016).

But are there nevertheless some differences in emphasis that come with those terms?

Firstly, TIC is found in a wider range of environments than homelessness services. It has been developed, for example, in school teaching, where trauma awareness may help teachers to understand a pupil's disruptive behavior. We would certainly want to argue that the impact of trauma can be seen in a wide range of different environments; and an understanding of trauma can help enlighten our response to problematic behavior in a range of contexts.

But yet the roots of the PIE concept also lay in a wider set of observations on social policy and social psychiatry (Johnson & Haigh, 2010; Haigh et al., 2012); and there is actually nothing specific to homelessness in the PIE framework. It was, perhaps, particularly timely to have a term to describe innovative practice in the homelessness field as it was emerging, as it had not been described before; and that was well overdue (Johnson 2016c). But much the same could be said of TIC, which is closely linked to the spread of Housing First—in some areas, it seems, funds for training in TIC came "bundled in" with funds as incentives to develop a HF style of service (Grand & Thomas, 2016).

Secondly, the PIEs concept was first described in the context of what in the US would have been called "transitional housing"; but that difference simply reflects the different way that homelessness service improvements were pursued, in the UK, where a good deal of state funding went into decanting the huge hostels of the inter-war and post-war years, and replacement with smaller units with constructive activities. This does not seem to have happened, or not to the same degree, in many US states; and the antipathy in HF to transitional housing may reflect the comparatively poor quality of such provision in the US, which did not see the investment in improvement that we saw in the UK.

Yet with the development of "single site" or congregated care in Permanent Supported Housing (Malone et al., 2015; Nichols & Doberstein, 2016; Conolly & Yazwinski, 2016), in the absence of any other language or conceptual framework to describe or analyse what works there, it may be that the PIEs framework, alongside TIC, may help fill the gap and prove useful in identifying and promoting good practice.

Thirdly, it might perhaps be argued that, since both "trauma" and "complex trauma" are terms that derive from psychology, then psychology is the broader concept. It includes trauma-awareness, but it goes further. In fact, the original PIE paper authors have stressed repeatedly (Johnson & Haigh, 2012) that we would have included sociology, anthropology and any other keys to human understanding, if that weren't simply making the term too long to be useful. The services they had been describing were actually more often driven by values, and by emotional intelligence, than any particular psychological theory.

Certainly there are many other issues that come into play—such as the role of stigma and the dynamics of exclusion, the power (for good or ill) of group processes, the impact of demeaning institutional thinking and the wider social policy or cultural frameworks – that are independent of trauma psychology. We might say that PIE is perhaps a broader concept; or perhaps it is simply just a looser concept. If so, TIC can perhaps be seen as a specific psychological model—a range of insights on trauma that inform the development of a suitable environment, the training of staff etc., etc.

Nevertheless, both the PIEs guidance papers (2010, 2012) had proposed complex trauma as one of the most significant developments in psychological understanding. What's more, it would seem that in practice TIC does draw upon any wider issues or concepts or practice (Fallot & Harris, 2009; Hopper et al., 2010; Olivet et al., 2010). Finally TIC makes quite a good case for arguing that it is our growing understanding of the nature of trauma shows why these practice responses are appropriate. So that apparent distinction in the chosen terminology for TIC and PIEs does not seem such a rift in practice.

Nor is there real, definitive significance in the use of the terms "care" and "environment", which may at first sight seem different, but they are similarly interwoven. Over and above the most basic need for shelter, in Maslow's terms, the essential environment of human beings is social; it is other human beings. Care services create such an environment, both a building and a social environment, just as PIEs do; and the environments that PIE thinking promotes are providing care in the broadest, non-technical sense.

The Language of Policy Context

In fact, the real reason why homelessness services in the UK didn't and still usually don't use the word "care" is more pragmatic, to do with funding and regulation issues. Until recently, "care" services were funded differently and separately from "support" services, organised by different departments; and the distinction was maintained by government, which held the purse strings.

So it was important to both funders and service managers in the UK to talk as if there was a real difference. Even now, in the UK, "care" services are regulated and inspected by a different body. Still now, in the UK, we tend to avoid the term "care", to avoid confusion. But it seems that all we have done thereby is to create a new confusion, when we try to compare these services, by name, with those in other countries.

That said, there genuinely are considerable differences between the way that homelessness services in the UK and the US have developed, over a 20 year period. The UK had seen, over that time, substantial investment in modernizing the buildings, and in training of the staff, in what we call "hostels", which in the US would be called "transitional housing". We have seen far less investment in the kind of "permanent supported housing" that the Housing First programme calls for. But to fully understand all those differences, we would have to go far deeper into the comparative history of housing and health policy between our two countries.

Yet the PIE framework, like TIC, would apply to improving practice in both kinds of services; and there seems really very little substantive that separates the two concepts, beyond the differing contexts in which they arose, and a dialogue between the learning in context might be especially fruitful. If anything, then, we might perhaps say that the PIE concept lays greater stress on the creation of an environment as a whole, over and above the awareness and actions of staff; and that there is a somewhat greater explicit emphasis on reflective practice, on encouraging the culture of a learning organisation.

But the overlap between the TIC approach and a PIE is therefore clearly not just a coincidence in their middle names; the services they describe, offer or promote seem to be very much comparable, both in spirit and in practice. It does appear that it is only the fact that we use different terms to describe our housing "offer" that has stood in the way of such dialogue in the past. If so, and if we can say that a PIE is a journey, then just as England has pavements where the US has sidewalks, and the English have lifts where the US has elevators, and our cars have "bonnets" not "hoods", we may be in fact on much the same journey (Various, n.d.).

But this is what we might expect. It's certainly what we would hope for: that services that are really engaging effectively with much the same underlying issues would evolve until they start to look like each other, whatever the starting point or language they began with (Johnson 1981). Both Trauma Informed Care and Psychologically Informed Environments began life simply as attempts to describe what was actually happening in homelessness services, to identify, endorse and promote the best in such practice.

If both concepts seem to have developed a life of their own, and are now seeking to leverage in the research to confirm such practice, it is a tribute to all those in frontline services who developed such practice in the first place. Working primarily with empathy, imagination and a commitment to finding what works, it was they that replaced a culture of control, blame and exclusion with a culture of inquiry, in which more formal research now finds a natural home.

References

Boex, S. & Boex, W. (2012) "Well-being through design: transferability of design concepts for healthcare environments to ordinary community settings" in *Housing Care and Support,* 15(2):120-128

Busch-Geertsema, V. (2012) *The Housing First approach in Europe* Keynote address to AHURi/RMIT Homelessness Research Conference

Cockersell, P. (2011) "More for Less? Using PIEs and Recovery to Improve Efficiency in Supported Housing" in *Housing Care and Support,* 14(2): 45-50

Conolly, A. & Yazwinski, J. (2016) Interview conducted at Father Bill's & Mainspring, available at www.pielink.net

Dept. of Health (2003) *Personality disorder; no longer a diagnosis of exclusion* London: HMSO

Dept. of Health (2009) *Recognising complexity: Commissioning guidance for personality disorder services*, (London: HMSO), available at http://www.dh.gov.uk/en/Publicationsandstatistics/Publications/Publicat ionsPolicyAndGuidance/DH_101788

Eastlund, E. (2017) *Rainbow services, Trauma Informed Care and PIEs*; a presentation at the National Alliance to End Homelessness conference, Los Angeles, 2017, available at http://pielink.net/videos/rainbow-services-tic-and-pies/

Evans, W. (2012) *Housing First: an interview with Sam Tsemberis.* Substance Abuse and Mental Health Services Administration (SAMSHA), available at http://homeless.samhsa.gov/resource/housing-first-an-interview-with-sam-tsemberis-54965.aspx

Fallot, R. & Harris, M. (2009) Creating Cultures of Trauma-Informed Care (CCTIC): A Self-Assessment and Planning Protocol, *Community Connections* Version 2.2/ 7-09

Gardiner, G. (2012) Banking on Time: Potter Street TimeBank, in R. Johnson & R. Haigh (2012) *Complex Trauma and its effects; perspectives on creating an environment for recovery* (Brighton: Pavilion)

Grand, B. & Thomas, D. (2016) Interview conducted with Boston Public Health commissioner, available at www.pielink.net

Haigh, R. (2012) Everybody's problem, in R. Johnson & R. Haigh, (2012) *Complex Trauma and its effects; perspectives on creating an environment for recovery* (Brighton: Pavilion)

Haigh, R., Harrison, T., Johnson, R., Paget, S. & Williams, S. (2012) Psychologically Informed Environments and the "Enabling Environments" initiative, in *Housing Care and Support*, 15(4): 34-42

Hopper, E., Bassuk, E., & Olivet, J., (2010) Shelter from the Storm: Trauma-Informed Care in Homelessness Services Settings. *The Open Health Services and Policy Journal*, 3, 80-100.

HUD (Housing and Urban Development) (2015*) Recovery Housing Policy Brief*, available at the HUD Exchange website: https://www.hudexchange.info/resource/4852/recovery-housing-policy-brief/ (NB: also available, with commentaries, at the PIElink: http://pielink.net/download/a-european-commentary-on-recovery-housing/)

Joe, G. W., Simpson, D. D. & Broome, K. M. (1998) Effects of readiness for drug abuse treatment on client retention and assessment of process. *Addiction*, 93(8): 1177-1190

Johnsen, S. & Teixeira, L. (2010) *Staircases, Elevators and Cycles of Change: Housing First and other Housing Models for People with Complex Needs* Crisis and the University of York, available at: http://www.homelesspages.org.uk/node/24176

Johnson, R. (n.d.) *Editorials* (passim) for the Housing Care and Support journal, 2010-2015

Johnson, R. (2006) Health and Social Care and the Supporting People Programme *Housing Learning and Improvement Network Viewpoint no 8,* online published, Care Services Improvement Partnership, available at www.poelink.net

Johnson, R. (2007) This is not a pipe. *SITRA bulletin*, Nov. 2007, available at www.pielink.net

Johnson, R. (2013a) *Evidence-generating practice for Psychologically Informed Environments*, presentations at the Institute for Mental Health, Managed Innovation Networks inter-agency workshop series, various venues.

Johnson, R. (2013b) Editorial: The concept of a "Psychologically Informed Environment" in *Housing Care and Support,* 15(2): Retrieved from: http://www.emeraldinsight.com/products/journals/journals.htm?id=hcs

Johnson, R. (2016a) Memes; a cautionary tale in three parts: Part One — the Psychologically Informed Environment, August essay on the PIElink: www.pielink.net

Johnson, R. (2016c) *Is a PIE just about homelessness?* — SITRA bulletin online, now available at the PIElink: www.pielink.net

Johnson, R. (2017a) Principles and Practice in Psychology and Homelessness, Part One: Housing First — Addressing the Community Dimension, available at the PIElink: http://pielink.net/download/housing-first-addressing-the-community-dimension/

Johnson, R. (2017b) A European commentary on "Recovery Housing," available at: http://pielink.net/download/a-european-commentary-on-recovery-housing/

Johnson, R. (2017c) *Pizazz? Results from the working party survey on the range of PIEs, and a proposal on the next steps* (YouTube video for the working party on expanding the 'classic' PIE framework; available at: https://www.youtube.com/watch?v=Q7qQiAF2cmc&feature=em-upload_owner

Johnson, R. (2017d) *Attachment, stress, and the social environment; biology, psychology and neuroscience in homelessness resettlement work*, available at pielink.net

Johnson, R. & Haigh, R. (2010) Social psychiatry and social policy for the 21st Century, Part One: the psychologically informed environment. in *J Mental Health and Social Inclusion*, 15(1) 17-23

Johnson, R. & Haigh, R. Editors (2012) *Complex Trauma and its effects; perspectives on creating an environment for recovery* (Brighton: Pavilion)

Jones, M. (1968) *Beyond the therapeutic community; Social learning and social psychiatry.* (New York: Yale University Press)

JRF (2000) *An overview of the Supporting People Programme*, JRF website https://www.jrf.org.uk/report/overview-supporting-people-programme

Keats, H., Cockersell, P., Johnson, R. & Maguire, N. (2012) *Psychologically informed services; good practice guidance*; London, Dept. Communities and Local Government

Kwong, J. (2016) Blighted Santa Ana motel to be 71 apartments for homeless. *The Orange County Register*. 10/28/2016. Retrieved from http://www.ocregister.com/2016/10/28/blighted-santa-ana-motel-to-be-71-apartments-for-homeless/

Laban, R. (2009) *Take a chance on me* Winter 2009/10 edition of Homeless Link's "Connect," available at the PIElink, www.pielink.net

Levy, J. S. (2010) *Homeless narratives & pretreatment pathways: From words to housing.* Ann Arbor, MI: Loving Healing Press

Levy, J. S. (2013). *Pretreatment guide for homeless outreach & housing first: Helping couples, youth, and unaccompanied adults.* Ann Arbor, MI: Loving Healing Press

Levy, J. S. (2017) *A US commentary on HUD's Recovery Housing Policy Brief*; available at the PIElink, at: http://pielink.net/download/recovery-housing-policy-brief-2/.

Maguire, N. J., Johnson, R., Vostanis, P., Keats, H. & Remington, R.E. (2009). *Homelessness and complex trauma: a review of the literature.* Southampton, UK. University of Southampton

Main, T. (1983) The concept of the Therapeutic Community; Variations and Vicissitudes in M. Pines (ed.) *The Evolution of Group Analysis* (London: Routledge & Kegan Paul)

Malone, D., Collins, S., & Clifasefi, S. (2015). Single-Site Housing First for Chronically homeless people. *Housing, Care and Support, 18*(2): 62-66.

Middleton, R. & Levy, J. S. (2015) *Homeless Engagement: 5 Principles of Pre-treatment: Jay Levy in discussion with Ray Middleton*, broadcast and recorded, available at the PIElink, at: http://pielink.net/videos/the-5-principles-of-pre-treatment/

Miller, K. (2016) *Using Shelter Strategically to End Homelessness* Retrieved November 12, 2017, from https://www.usich.gov/news/using-shelter-strategically-to-end-homelessness

Miller, W. R. & Rollnick, S. (1991). *Motivational interviewing: Preparing people to change addictive behavior.* New York: Guilford

Nichols, N. & Doberstein, C., Eds. (2016) *Exploring Effective Systems Responses to Homelessness,* Toronto: Homeless Hub Press, available at: http://www.homelesshub.ca/systemsresponses.

NMHDU/CLG. (2010) *Non-Statutory Guidance On Meeting The Psychological And Emotional Needs Of People Who Are Homeless.* Retrieved November 12, 2017, from http://www.homeless.org.uk/sites/default/files/site-attachments/Mental_Health_Guide.pdf

Olivet, J., Bassuk, E., Elstad, E., Kenney, R. & Jassil, L. (2010) Outreach and Engagement in Homeless Services: A Review of the Literature, *The Open Health Services and Policy Journal, 3,* 53-70.

Pereira, A. (2016) *LA is Converting "Nuisance" Motels into 500 Apartments for Homeless Vets.* Retrieved November 12, 2017, from http://www.sfgate.com/news/article/L-A-is-converting-a-nuisance-motel-into-500-7953278.php

Pleace, N. & Brotherton, J. (2012) *Will Paradigm Drift Stop Housing First from Ending Homelessness? Categorising and Critically Assessing the Housing First Movement from a Social Policy Perspective.* Presentation at the Social Policy in an Unequal World - Joint Annual Conference of the East Asian Social Policy Research Network (EASP) and the United Kingdom Social Policy Association (SPA) University of York, July 16th-

18th 2012, retrieved from
http://www.york.ac.uk/media/chp/documents/2006/NPJB-EASP-SPA-
2012.pdf

Prestidge, J. (2014) Using Trauma-Informed Care to provide therapeutic
support to homeless people with complex needs: a transatlantic search
for an approach to engage the "non-engaging," *Housing Care and
Support,* 17(4) 208-214

Prochaska, J. O. & DiClemente, C. C. (1982) Trans theoretical therapy:
Toward a more integrative model of change, *Psychotherapy: Theory,
Research, and Practice, 19*(7): 276-288

Quinney, S. & Richardson, L. (2014) Organisational development, appreciative
inquiry and the development of Psychologically Informed Environments
(PIEs). Part I: a positive psychology approach, *Housing Care and
Support,* 17(2): 95-102.

Rees, S. (2009). *Mental Health in the Adult Single Homeless Population*
PHRU/Crisis, retrieved from:
http://www.crisis.org.uk/publications_djhsearch.php?submitted=S&fulli
tem=235

Salloum, I. M., Moss, H. B., Daley, D. C. & Cornelius, J. R. (1998) Drug use
problem awareness and treatment readiness in dual diagnosis patients,
American Journal on Addictions, 7(1): 35-42

SAMHSA (2014) Six Principles of a Trauma-Informed Approach, Extracted
from: Substance Abuse and Mental Health Services Administration.
*SAMHSA's Concept of Trauma and Guidance for a Trauma-Informed
Approach.* HHS Publication No. (SMA) 14-4884. Rockville, MD:
Substance Abuse and Mental Health Services Administration, 2014

Seal, M. (2005) *Resettling Homeless People: Theory and Practice* Lyme Regis:
Russell House Publishing

The Crypt (n.d.), interview with (un-named) manager' at the PIElink, at:
http://pielink.net/audio/st-georges-crypt-leeds/

True, M. (2016) *Former motel becomes permanent housing for homeless,* VT
digger, available at: https://vtdigger.org/2016/01/24/former-motel-
vermonts-first-permanent-housing-for-homeless/

Tsemberis, S. (n.d.) *Selected works of Sam Tsemberis* (collection): available at:
http://works.bepress.com/sam_tsemberis/

Various (n.d.): podcasts and videos appearing on the PIElink under
'Transatlantic dialogues: a two way trade', at
http://pielink.net/partnership/transatlantic-dialogues-a-two-way-
conversation

Vickery, L. (2014) Book review, in *Housing Care and support* 17(4) 224-226

WAMC (2011) radio interview with Jay Levy. Retrieved from
http://wamc.org/post/alan-chartockin-conversation-jay-levy

Woodcock, J. & Gill, J. (2014) Implementing a Psychologically Informed
Environment in a service for homeless young people in *Housing Care
and Support* 17(1) 48-57

3 Miguel's Narrative: Challenges of Common Language Construction
Jay S. Levy

I don't want to end up in a mental straightjacket, while they experiment with mind control pills... They'll extract all of your most personal thoughts against your will.

— Miguel

The main objective of Pretreatment is the formation of a person-centered relationship that is goal-focused. The key to success is rooted in our striving to develop a common language between outreach counselors and vulnerable, hard to reach people. Whether it is engaging with an individual client, or referring people to potential resources and services via social agencies, or advocating for change in governing policies, our mission is to find an effective means to cross these many cultural divides. Our task is to become interpreters and bridge builders across systems of care. The main tool for achieving this is through the development of effective communication, which is based on the art of common language construction.

We are engulfed by language, yet challenged on how to develop a common language with others. Freedman and Combs (1996, p. 29) state, "Speaking isn't neutral or passive. Every time we speak, we bring forth a reality. Each time we share words, we give legitimacy to the distinctions that those words bring forth." Berger and Luckman (1966) describe language as our pathway toward knowing what is real in everyday life, influencing our social interactions, and the formation of our inner worlds. There is a power in words to transform our reality. In this sense, language creates the world in which we communicate and live. The question of outreach and engagement is how to become welcomed into a person's world.

Entering Miguel's House of Language

Observing, listening, and attempting to understand a person's words, ideas, and values is a good place to start. Our ultimate success in reaching out to disaffiliated persons with complex needs is dependent upon how responsive we are to their immediate needs, daily concerns, and future aspirations. I am reminded of my work with a sixty-four-year-old Latino male named Miguel. We met on the Boston Common during the early spring of 1996. I approached Miguel because he was shoeless and carrying a blanket. I responded to what appeared to be his immediate needs by offering socks and asking if he'd like us to go shopping for footwear.

At first, Miguel proudly declared the toughness of his feet. He then informed me of his childhood history of walking barefoot along the roads, rocks and sands of Puerto Rico. I quickly agreed with his assessment, but then gently pointed out that getting something for his feet would simply provide the choice of when to go barefoot. In the end, he was very appreciative and agreeable to my offer, so together we purchased sandals.

The process of engagement was off to a good start and Miguel shared with me details of his impoverished childhood, yet strong community bonds, followed by the slow unraveling of family ties after his move to the mainland. He connected his current difficulties as related to ageism, cursed his isolation from others, and in many ways felt driven to drink. Our strong connection was further confirmed when he later showed me his bottle of rum and offered me a "hit," which I politely declined. This was the beginning of our journey. Many outreach meetings soon followed.

Understanding Language

Miguel wanted very much to be housed and part of a community, but often felt disrespected and left out. In contrast, our relationship helped to bring him a sense of connection. Together, we agreed to search for an affordable place to live. Miguel had a steady income through Social Security benefits, and he was eligible for elder housing. This was a great opportunity, because the wait for subsidized housing in Boston was several years unless you were able to document priority status as an elder or Veteran. This reduced the waiting time from years to just a few months.

However, this was tricky because Miguel did not consider himself to be an elder and really despised the term. He believed that being an "elder" meant that you were feeble, weak, and cast aside by others. I quickly learned that any mention of the term brought about an angry response. In this manner, the words we use and their perceived, not necessarily intended, meanings can have major ramifications. This is why the first and most critical step of Common Language Construction (see Fig. 3-1, p. 47) begins with *understanding* a person's words, ideas, and values.

Utilizing and Bridging Language

The question was whether or not there was a way to develop a common language with Miguel that would empower him to accept housing for elders. In response to Miguel's negative reaction, I joined with him by sharing my dislike for the term "elder," stating, "People often believe that I am older than my actual age, but I let them know that what's important is my state of mind. I am young at heart and I believe that you are too!" Miguel smiled and nodded in agreement. I continued, "Besides, with age comes wisdom, so perhaps we should consider folks who are over sixty to be wise men. People who have been here the longest often know the most." In this manner, I reframed the notion of being an elder to a more positive reference that Miguel could more actively consider and hopefully accept.

He then went on to share with me the wisdom of his grandmother and the hard lessons his father taught him, while growing up in Puerto Rico. By the end of our session, we were able to laugh together about the need to rename elder housing as "Homes for the Wise" or simply "60 and Over Housing." We entered the next phase of Common Language development by agreeing to some useful and acceptable terminology. In a manner of speaking, we were creating a playground of language from which we could further explore current linguistic connections and future possibilities to guide our work.

The next time Miguel and I met, we discussed his hard road to home-lessness and how he deserved a better life, which included having a home. I then drew from our playground of language and brought up the prospects of applying for "60 and Over Housing," so he could have an affordable place to live. In this manner, I was speaking or *utilizing* common words and phrases that we both agreed was a better descriptor of elder housing. Miguel seemed interested, but still a bit hesitant around being labeled as an "elder." I assured him that we could show up at the housing authority together and inform them of our preference for the term "60 and Over Housing." While they may not be willing to change the words on the housing application, we could both voice and write our opinion down for them and others to see.

This plan resonated well with Miguel, and so we contracted for services. Our next task was to fill out the subsidized housing application for seniors. Miguel signed a release of information and I further bridged him over to the worker (aka Housing Specialist) at the Housing Authority by calling her in advance in preparation for our arrival. This consisted of some advocacy, while also giving the housing authority worker some advance warning of the particularities of Miguel's situation, and his sensitivity to the term "elder."

My engagement process with the Housing Specialist went well. She understood Miguel's situation and promised to be sensitive. She allowed us to write suggestions for terms that would be synonymous with elder housing, but also made it clear that she would not and could not change the actual terminology on the application. This was enough of an accommodation to empower Miguel to effectively take part in the application process for subsidized housing. Ultimately, I was able to form a common language with Miguel that bridged him to the language of the system, while remaining true to our agreed-upon ideas, words and values.

In this manner, Miguel was successfully transitioned over to a new house of language of the Housing authority and eventually received acceptance into subsidized housing for people of 60 years and over. We had successfully completed the last phase of Common Language Construction (see Fig. 3-1, p. 47) by bridging together two different interpretations of housing for seniors. Approximately three months after completing the application, he moved into his new place, and welcomed me into his home for weekly outreach counseling visits.

Houses of Language

Heidegger declares (1971, pp. 63 & 135), "Language is the house of being." It is through language that we define our relationships with ourselves, others, and the world around us. Each person we meet, as well as the services, resources and programs we attempt to access, resides in its own house of language. It is a house built upon the words, ideas, and values that are critical to one's sense of self, purpose, or the mission that a particular program or service sets out to achieve.

The goal of outreach is to be welcomed into our prospective client's house of language and to develop pathways to the houses of language that define essential resources/services such as Social Security Benefits, AA/NA Groups, and Mental Health Clinics, as well as Subsidized Housing resources, and many others. This requires the willingness of the worker to tune in to what is actually being said, as well as experimenting with language utilization, or perhaps a bit of playfulness with words as we attempt to establish meaningful connections between others and needed resources. This is consistent with Derrida's post-modern philosophy of language

(1976) that views our communication as a relational, creative and playful process in which the meanings of words are subject to change, yet contextually defined.

Once Miguel was successfully housed, our work continued to help assure housing stabilization. Major aims of outreach counseling consist of helping people transition to housing and cultivating pathways to treatment. A primary concern that Miguel had was feeling isolated from others, so, much of our post housing work focused on building community connections. This included the challenge of referring him to a local Senior Center, which brought up similar concerns as our initial work in regard to subsidized housing. The term "senior" was a bit less charged than "elder," and so it was easier to reframe as a term that denotes respect for people who have more life experience. Together, we would laugh and say "No juniors allowed at the Senior Center!" My use of humor and Miguel's willingness to join in showed evidence of us being on the same wavelength, or working from the same playground of language. Fortunately, Miguel agreed to a tour of the center and immediately felt a sense of belonging when he met a staff member who was also from Puerto Rico, and fluent in Spanish.

The experience of facilitating a successful transition to the Senior Center provided me with an important realization. I witnessed how readily Miguel connected with someone who was from Puerto Rico. This led to multiple discussions about different Spanish-speaking groups Miguel could check out in order to increase natural community supports.

The longer I got to know Miguel, the more evident it became that he had repeated experiences of trauma and loss, from childhood to his most recent homeless episode. The effects of this were most evident in regard to his sensitivity to others. He very easily felt criticized and belittled. Unfortunately, this became a major challenge for him at the Senior Center. In spite of my efforts to mediate things, which included meetings with Miguel and the staff member with ties to Puerto Rico, Miguel attended the center less consistently as he became more critical of other members.

The dilemma at hand was twofold. First, my attempts at building community supports may continually run into the formidable obstacle of Miguel's trauma-induced feelings of mistreatment by others. Second, once someone is housed, my outreach services are time-sensitive, due to our service contract explicitly targeting literal homelessness. While I would make the case for extended outreach services to help assure housing stability, I still needed to work on a plan for Miguel to receive some ongoing counseling in the community to better address his feelings of abuse and isolation from others. I therefore offered Miguel the opportunity to connect with a culturally sensitive therapist.

My offer reflected values and concepts from my house of language. Heidegger (1971, p. 131) explains that our understanding of language is further impacted by the speaker's use of words and silence, which provides evident and not so evident "unsaid" connotations for the listener to interpret. In particular, my "unsaid" context and meaning for the word "therapist" referred to someone as a helpful guide through life's difficulties. Unfortunately, Miguel did not hear it that way. His "unsaid" context and meaning was completely different.

Miguel's friendly demeanor quickly dissipated and in an angry voice he accused me of sending him off to be brainwashed. He said, "I don't want to end up in a mental straightjacket, while they experiment with mind control pills. First they lay you down on what appears to be a comfortable couch and then the next thing you know you are a blank slate. They'll extract all of your most personal thoughts against your will." My offer was based on the work we had accomplished together through outreach counseling. However, I soon learned the Miguel viewed the word "counselor" in a very different way from "therapist." Apparently, counselor was welcomed onto our playground of language, while therapist was not. He further explained to me that even in the spelling of the word one can see trouble: "the-rapist."

This type of thinking (cultural bias?) is rampant among people experiencing homelessness. You often have two very different houses of language between those who have experienced homelessness and the culture of a mental health clinic. Miguel had spent several years on the streets and living on the fringes of our society. He highly valued safety, and trust did not come easily for him. He had become accustomed to meeting his immediate needs for survival.

Due to a history of layered trauma, which may have included bad experiences within the mental health system, Miguel was naturally suspicious of others and often feared the worst, while being highly appreciative of small things like a pair of socks or a good meal.

On the streets, it is not unusual to call someone crazy, while in the world of mental health clinicians, this term is frowned upon. The mental health clinic provides services that are focused on the language of treatment," which is in itself an unfriendly term to most of us. Other common terms that one will experience while in the office or on the grounds of a mental health clinic are "mental illness," "suicide," "psychotropic medications," and an assortment of diagnostic terminology and acronyms such as "schizophrenia," "depression," "PTSD," and "anxiety." It maintains an office culture that values people making appointments and arriving on time, while showing respectful manners within the waiting room area. There was an evident cultural divide between Miguel and the Mental Health Clinic where I hoped to refer him.

The question became: Is it worth trying to bridge these two different houses of language, and if so, then how? The very next day I apologized to Miguel for my insensitivity, and thankfully he accepted. It was necessary to re-engage before resuming my attempt to refer him to outpatient counseling services. In preparation, I asked his opinion on the most important characteristics of a good counselor. Miguel viewed our relationship as a positive model for counseling practice, and was able to reflect on the value of meeting with someone who really listened and cared, while helping him to get housed.

Upon hearing his description, I reconstructed my offer based on that fact, while being careful not to use the word "therapist." I said, "It seems like what we accomplished through outreach counseling has made a positive difference in your life. Maybe we could find you the right match for counseling at a local clinic, and it could help you to progress even further. Together, we could attend your initial appointment and share your success story with the counselor." Miguel was receptive to this reframe of my initial offer, and so we were back on track.

More work still needed to be done to successfully develop a pretreatment pathway to the Mental Health Clinic. This included actually finding a culturally sensitive therapist who was willing to respect Miguel's need to call him a counselor. Fortunately, I was able to access a local clinic that specialized with the Latino community. Further, I followed through on my promise to support his transition with personal introductions, and shared our work with the new clinician, which helped Miguel to give voice to what he valued. Namely, this consisted of a goal-driven, person-centered relationship with a real interest in his world.

In the end, Miguel formed a meaningful relationship with his new counselor, and slowly but surely experienced greater stability. Over time, Miguel was then able to form an extensive community support system through his therapist, senior services and the local Mental Health Clubhouse, which in turn helped him to remain housed.

The Mental Health Clinic is just one example of the many houses of language we come across in our daily work. Other houses of language include Social Security benefits, which focus on the word "disability," and emphasizes one's ability to work. Another example, among many, is Alcoholics Anonymous (AA), which is a mutual aid fellowship steeped in the words, ideas, and values that reflect getting sober and the twelve steps of recovery with its various slogans such as "one day at a time" to serve as a guide.

Regardless of where we may try to refer a person, the outreach worker is always faced with the task of understanding both the culture and language base of the client and that of the resource or service. Ultimately, we are interpreters who bring two divergent worlds together through the process of engagement and common language development.

Enhancing Communications: Across Cultures and Systems

Beyond outreach activities with clients, we need to create a culture of effective communication and training to better promote our work. Specifically, this means sharing our mission, policies, protocols, and values with representatives of needed referral resources and services. Much of this comes down to implementing engagement strategies with the hope of strengthening our relationships by developing a common language with the liaisons from these different systems of care. Understanding the interests of local providers and utilizing words and ideas that speak to their values, while supporting relevant policies and outcome measures are a necessary part of the process for attaining quality care. Our goal is to not only to facilitate client access to community resources, but also to help these services to be more responsive to our client's needs, or psychologically informed when serving people without homes.

Unfortunately, there remains a treatment bias that promotes a standard of readiness for referral that many of our clients fail to meet. People who experience complex trauma often have difficulty accessing shelter/hostels, housing, and the recovery-based services they most desperately need. We can address this difficulty on three different levels.

- Provide staff training on Pretreatment principles of care
- Facilitate system-wide outreach/engagement trainings that target the providers of our client's most needed resources and services
- Create and develop new programs, such as Housing First residences with integrated support services, which incorporate a Pretreatment philosophy

In practice, we are faced with the task of constructing a common language to improve staff communication and enhance training. In essence, we are in need of a cross-cultural meta-language to facilitate dialogue with our staff and other potential advocates and helpers. I have experienced firsthand the power of utilizing a Pretreatment perspective to improve communication across multiple houses of language. Whether it be outreach workers, clinicians, social justice advocates, representatives from the religious community, or others, Pretreatment principles of care provide a pragmatic approach without conflicting with people's most cherished values.

Further, the principles that underlie a Pretreatment Model draw equally from addictions and mental health practice via Harm Reduction (Marlatt and Tapert, 1993), Stages of Change (Prochaska & DiClemente, 1982), Narrative Psychology (White, 2000) and Ecological Social Work theories (Germain & Gitterman, 1980). Universal aims of Pretreatment are Relationship Formation via stages of engagement, Common Language Construction to improve communication, Supporting Transitions to new environments, Facilitating Positive Change, and Promoting Safety. These have been embraced by others of varying perspectives as an authentic guide for helping people without homes.

The words, ideas, and values of Pretreatment principles and Psychologically Informed Environments (PIE), as reviewed by Robin Johnson in the previous chapter, go a long way toward providing a common language to inform our cross-cultural conversations. The universal principles of Pretreatment can help us to ask the most relevant questions for helping individuals, while noting our progress and/or challenges regarding multiple issues: the Stages of Engagement and Change, Phases of Common Language Construction, Ecological Considerations (transition and adaptation process) and along the harm-to-safety continuum. In this manner, it guides our process of assessment and intervention to better serve people without homes.

Similarly, but on a larger scale, PIE provides an approach for assessing, developing, and designing more suitable environments inclusive of homeless hostels, housing, and human service programs that serve people with complex needs. Our goal and hope is for all interactions with this highly vulnerable population to become more psychologically informed on a system, program, and individual level. Ultimately, it is all about inclusion, rather than exclusion, of highly vulnerable people to critical services and resources. The price of continued exclusion is too high to pay in lives lost, dollars wasted, and an ever-growing insensitivity to those who are most in need.

Transatlantic Conversations on Homelessness

As demonstrated throughout these chapters, cross-cultural dialogue has included transatlantic communications on homelessness between the US and UK. Once again, we are faced with the task of constructing a common language that aids our efforts to learn from one another. While we ultimately share the same mission of ending or significantly reducing homelessness, many of the terms we commonly use to discuss homelessness issues and strategies vary considerably across regions, let alone from one continent to another.

Let's begin with the term "homeless." Some folks who meet the statutory definition for "homelessness" don't relate to the word "homeless," but instead see themselves as campers, travelers, and/or free spirit wanderers, etc. This is particularly evident when working with young adults. Yet, some people insist that they are homeless, while not meeting the statutory criteria of literal homelessness because they are couch-surfing or doubling up with acquaintances. Federal and Local agencies (i.e., US Department of Housing and Urban Development, US Local Housing Authorities, Northern Ireland's Housing Executive Local Offices, and England's Local Authorities) deem these folks ineligible for certain types of housing assistance, though advocates often dispute that claim.

Further disparities in rules, regulations, and definitions exist among these agencies, based on funding sources and the particular subpopulations (i.e., youth, elders, veterans, etc.). There are significant differences in regard to the definition of homelessness, eligibility criteria for housing, and priority populations served within the US (State by State), as well as throughout the UK. These disparities widen when one attempts comparisons from the US to the UK.

Even our most basic words, concepts, and definitions show differences based on the speaker, listener, context, and culture. Commonly used terms, such as "homeless shelter" in the US and "homeless hostel" in the UK have somewhat different meanings and connotations, while also showing internal variations. When providing outreach to people who are unsheltered or sleeping rough in the US or in the UK, it is important to consider that a person's conception of shelters or hostels differs greatly depending upon their direct personal experiences, or what they've heard throughout their social network. Even on frigid nights, it is not unusual for people sleeping rough to refuse these options, due to past negative experiences.

However, the outreach worker may be able reframe the use of shelter or hostel by describing alternative environments that differ greatly from one another in size and in other important ways such as having friendlier staff. Sometimes a turn of phrase or a reinterpretation of a term by expanding one's characterization of shelter or hostel can provide a person with a sense of ambivalence and perhaps a willingness to visit a local shelter or hostel as part of a reevaluation process. When we address people with complex needs in an authentic and caring manner through a common language, a positive outcome consisting of new options becomes possible.

I am fond of saying that no two shelters are alike, even though the general mission of safely sheltering people and fostering connections to affordable housing remains the same. Each shelter has its own set of rules and culture directly informed by the source of funding and the people who run it. The number of shelter beds ranges from the high single digits in some rural areas to triple digits (100-800 beds) throughout the larger urban centers of America. Some shelters demand sobriety in order to gain entrance, while others admit intoxicated individuals and then utilize behavioral-based measures to determine length of stay.

Some of the notable jargon includes the terms "wet," "damp," and "dry" settings to describe acceptable levels of intoxication ranging from gross inebriation to total sobriety. For instance, my outreach team(s) provide counseling services at a sixteen-bed double-decker home (shelter) located amongst the hill towns of Western MA, while also providing outreach to much larger facilities consisting of more than one hundred shelter beds in the cities of Springfield and Worcester, MA.

As a result of the diversity of environments that shelters represent, shelter guests have a great array of responses largely dependent upon their direct experiences with shelter staff and to the degree that a particular shelter actually met their psychological and immediate needs for safety and assistance. Their perceptions are also impacted by the shelter stereotype(s) built from other people's stories, as well as the homelessness mythology common to their particular cultures and communities.

Generally speaking, the larger shelters in urban centers are prone to warehousing, due to being understaffed and attempting to manage hundreds of individuals in tight quarters with an eye toward basic security for both staff and shelter guests. Similarly, no two homeless hostels in the UK are the same. Generally speaking, hostels have much more in common with transitional housing programs in the States, rather than the large urban shelters previously discussed. Hostels are smaller in size, time-limited, and provide individualized case management services.

Interestingly enough, the trend in the States has been to develop more permanent housing options via Housing First programs, while in the UK there has been a greater focus on transforming hostels into Psychologically Informed Environments. In England, Commissioners of Homelessness Services have instituted hostel staff trainings on goal focused approaches that are strengths based, while developing peer support services and a greater sense of community with residents. However, it is also true that some smaller shelters in the States have developed into transitional housing programs, while successful Housing First programs have been propagated and researched in the UK. Nevertheless, there is a difference in emphasis, which provides a chance to learn from one another in terms of our successes and continued challenges.

Despite these initial differences, terminologies and approaches to helping, we are also keenly aware of our similarities. We encourage the sharing of ideas, innovations, research, and stories from both sides of the Atlantic. What's needed is an open dialogue that fully examines our many different descriptors and approaches to the phenomenon of homelessness, as well as a place to jointly explore our experiences.

Fortunately, Robin Johnson has developed such a place on the internet called PIE-Link (2015). It is located at www.pielink.net and it is a worldwide network for addressing homelessness issues with like-minded people through multi-media presentations, live video conferencing, and exploring an extensive library of information. This provides the forum for thoughtful discussion, and the examination of new ideas on homelessness beyond the confines of geographical limits. In the next chapter, John Conolly of Central London continues our exploration by introducing a hybrid of Pretreatment, PIE and Trauma-informed therapies.

Fig. 3-1: Stages of Common Language Development[2]

Stages	Goals & Interventions
Understand Language	Attempt to understand a homeless person's world by learning the meaning of his or her gestures, words, values and actions. Interventions include observing, listening, reflection, and directly asking what particular words and phrases mean, as well as learning what is important to the client.
Utilize Language	Promote understanding by developing and using a mutually agreeable set of terms. Build, modify, and use gestures, words, and phrases from the playground of common language based on the client's cues. Interventions include utilizing common language to ask client questions, explore the outreach worker's role, verbalize client's aspirations, and jointly define goals.
Bridge Language	Connect and integrate the common language developed between client and worker with other systems of language as defined by available services and resources (i.e., housing authorities, Social Security, medical services, mental health clinic, self-help groups, vocational programs, etc.). Interventions include connecting resources and services directly to client's goals, reframing commonly used words and phrases by targeted resources and services to be consistent with the playground of language developed by worker and client. Preparing for interviews via role play and accompanying the client may also be helpful. Prepare intake personnel of needed resources and services for the language that the client speaks. If certain phrases or terms may trigger a negative reaction, reframe and redefine these terms whenever possible, or seek accommodation.

Originally published: Levy, J. S. (2013). *Pretreatment Guide for Homeless Outreach & Housing First: Helping Couples, Youth, and Unaccompanied Adults*

---

[2] The process of Common Language Construction is based on ideas and concepts drawn from phenomenology and Narrative Psychology. Heidegger's book *On the Way to Language* (1971), as well as Epston & White's selected papers (1989-1991), among others, influenced the formation of the above table.

References

Epston, D. & White, M. (1992) *Experience, contradiction, narrative, and imagination: Selected papers of David Epston and Michael White, 1989-1991.* Adelaide, Australia: Dulwich Centre Publications

Freedman, J. & Combs, G. (1996) *Narrative therapy: The social construction of preferred realities.* New York: W. W. Norton Company, Inc.

Germain, C. B. & Gitterman, A. (1980) *The life model of social work process.* New York: Columbia University Press

Heidegger, M., (1971) *On the way to language.* trans. Hertz, P. New York: Harper & Row

Levy, J. S. (2013) *Pretreatment guide for homeless outreach & housing first: Helping couples, youth, and unaccompanied adults.* Ann Arbor, MI: Loving Healing Press

Marlatt, G. A. & Tapert, S. F. (1993) Harm Reduction: Reducing the risks of addictive behaviors. In J. S. Baer, G. A. Marlatt & R. J. McMahn (Eds.). *Addictive behaviors across the life span: Prevention, treatment, and policy issues* (pp. 243-273). Newbury Park, CA: Sage

PIElink (2015). PIElink Website: http://pielink.net/

Prochaska, J. O. & DiClemente, C. C. (1982) Trans theoretical therapy: Toward a more integrative model of change. *Psychotherapy: Theory, Research, and Practice.* 19(3): 276-288

4 Pre-treatment Therapy: A Central London Counselling Service's Enhanced Response to Complex Needs Homelessness
John Conolly

Many people who experience long-term homelessness are hesitant to trust others and have found a sense of meaning that reflects their culture, individuality, and homeless circumstance, while upholding their personal values and need for freedom and safety. These survival strategies, meaning making, and clinging to strongly held beliefs and values form an integral part of the adaptation to the traumatic experiences of homelessness.

— Jay S. Levy (2013)

Introduction

I remember that when I first took up my post as "Lead Counsellor" at the Westminster Homeless Health Service, in the heart of London, I just wanted to run away. Homeless people broke all of my professional expectations. They wouldn't attend when I expected them at their appointment times, and when they did attend, they would be drunk or on drugs, or they would be argumentative, hostile and aggressive. Some would self-harm in the waiting room.

When I tried referring people to addictions services, these would demand a fixed address, and even if a temporary (hostel) address was accepted, the person would miss their set appointment. There seemed to be no basis upon which to build a "therapeutic alliance," where both parties could agree upon the nature of the problem(s) and how to move forward.

One reason I didn't run away was that, as I listened to their stories, I gradually realised how frequently early and middle childhood abuse,

deprivation and neglect appeared in peoples' life narratives. With my
clinical training, this pointed me towards a diagnosis of personality disorder
(or what I now understand as people suffering from a "traumatised personality"), and so I went on a training seminar for people wishing to deliver the
KUF[3] — a personality disorder awareness raising programme, accredited by
the Department of Health.

One of the key features of KUF training is service user involvement. I
count myself very lucky to have met Paul Ashton there. Paul is a former
homeless and mental health service user of some twenty years, (see his story:
Ashton 2011), and we decided to collaborate in offering homeless people of
central London a service more suited to their needs (Conolly & Ashton,
2011, 2013, 2014, 2016). Here, individual and group "drop in" sessions
were offered alongside appointment-based sessions, and people could make
use of these as and when they needed. No appointment or referral was
needed, and there was no expectation of regular engagement. Furthermore,
in times of crisis, telephone and/or email support was available in between
sessions.

Shortly after meeting Paul, my friend and colleague Robin Johnson
introduced me to Jay Levy's "Pretreatment Guide" (Levy, 2013), and I
immediately perceived how Pretreatment principles could be adapted and
applied in my service. I call this Pretreatment Therapy; and what follows is
a description of how, in the face of such multiple, complex needs and
trauma, the Westminster Homeless Health Counselling Service (or HHCS)
developed its Pre-treatment therapy approach as developed from Jay's
Pretreatment principles but now extended and applied to counselling and
psychotherapy.

To illustrate this multi-facetted approach, I will adopt Jay's narrative
approach, using scenarios from the work with particular clients, inter-
weaving these with Jay's Pretreatment principles as outlined in his books,
and also adding my own broader concepts and insights both on the real
nature of personality disorder (PD) and the shortfall of conventional
"mainstream services" in addressing these needs.

---

[3] KUF stands for the Knowledge and Understanding Framework, a National Mental
Health work force training program funded by the Department of Health and the
Ministry of Justice in 2007, developed and delivered by the Open University, the Mental
Health Institute at the University of Nottingham, and the Tavistock & Portman NHS
Trust).

Clinical Intervention

One of the key features of PD is a difficulty in maintaining relationships. The American Psychiatric Association defines PD as:

> relatively stable, enduring, and pervasively maladaptive patterns of coping, thinking, feeling, regulating impulses, and relating to others (cited in Bleiberg, Rossouw and Fonagy, 2012).

However, I have come to understand PD as a condition whereby people suffer from a *traumatised personality*. That is, as the personality was developing in the face of prolonged and sustained traumatic experiences, the natural trauma response, both psychological and physiological, became incorporated into its very development. Hence, baseline physiological arousal is extremely high for people with PD. Their trauma response is very easily triggered, and prolonged, for some lasting over a period of days, making the person prone to re-triggering — and seeking self-medication as an aid to all too temporary coping.

People with Personality Disorders have increased risks of suffering additional mental health problems such as anxiety, depression, substance misuse disorders, recurrent deliberate self-harm, brief psychotic episodes, and eating disorders (Kane, 2006, NICE Guideline 78, 2009). 77% of suicides have PD (DOH, 2009), and people with PD make heavy demands on local services, which are usually ill-equipped to deal with them, and have frequent, escalating contact across a spectrum of services including mental health, social services, Accident and Emergency (A&E) Departments, primary care GPs , and the criminal justice system (NIMHE, 2003).

Early intervention has been highlighted as crucial in preventing major deterioration in PD, which can result in a career as a "professional patient," or lifelong mental health service user, criminality, vagrancy or even premature death (Haigh, 2006). However, mainstream services and treatments assume that patients have a fixed abode — a private safe space in which to recuperate, relax, collect one's thoughts, problem solve, etc., and the psychological resources to engage with and sustain a treatment relationship.

Homeless People with PD, especially "rough sleepers," are disqualified from the above, and are constantly exposed to the retriggering of their trauma reactions, and will therefore turn to self-medication, deliberate self-harm, and emergency care. Even specialist PD services usually require a stable address and patients to be addiction-free, or at least to be managing their substances problem. They offer on average a two year treatment programme consisting of weekly individual and group counselling sessions alongside structured activities.

McDonagh (2011, p. 12) makes the point that homeless people with complex needs can be exposed to further exclusion from services, which feel that they do not meet their criteria:

> In practice, the interplay between the complex needs that go hand in hand with deep social exclusion is often taken as evidence of "chaotic behaviour" and does not generally trigger any differentiated or enhanced response from service providers.

As early as 1968, sociologists such as Erving Goffman wrote how certain groups not appearing to live up to social norms could become stigmatised and their identities invalidated, especially if their "condition" was visible, prevented them from contributing, and was not understood. This stigma unfortunately then became internalised as a "negative identity" and further feelings of deep and intense shame arose as a result.

In research conducted with PD patients on their experience of recovery and the factors associated with it, Costillo (2016) stresses the development of a sense of safety and trust, feeling cared for, and an ability/willingness to learn boundaries as the fundamental conditions to enabling psychotherapy. Paradoxically, mainstream mental health services expect people to have the ability to comply with boundaries before trust has been established, and this when most PD sufferers have had no opportunity to learn or respect boundaries, either due to their caregivers' neglect, and complete absence of guidance, or due to their abusive reactions to their very least of transgressions.

Pre-treatment Therapy

Psychotherapy, amongst other things, is about accepting some responsibility for one's problems. Pre-treatment therapy is then about establishing the circumstances and relationships conducive to this happening. Pre-treatment Therapy aims at developing psychological resilience, but taking into account the chaos of homelessness. It is trauma-informed and is mindful to avoid reactivating trauma reactions; it pays particular attention to attachment and style of relating, (Attachment Theory: Bowlby, 1997, 1998a, 1998b; Danquah & Berry, 2014). It is also very respectful of ex-service user views and perspectives on "recovery."

Pre-treatment Therapy has several features. It accepts people's overwhelming and debilitating distress, and their inability to acknowledge, let alone accept any responsibility. It allows for their desperate search for some form of self-soothing and comforting, however self-destructive. At the same time, it offers the opportunity for a relationship conducive to therapeutic conditions to emerge. It also provides the foundation from which the individual can at last begin to face the pain and challenges of therapy, not least the grieving for a life lost. It leads to the acknowledgement of what could have been, but wasn't, and how best to move on and rebuild, or even simply to build, a new life, more pain-free and satisfying.

This is very much based on Levy's Pretreatment approach where "The relationship is the foundation of pretreatment work, while common language development is its main tool. It is from the safety of a trusting relationship and the development of a common language that it becomes possible to offer potential resources and services that resonate well in the world of the homeless person (Levy, 2013, p 32)."

This bears a remarkable similarity to Attachment Theory's "Secure Base" (Holmes, 2006) and:

> ...which is when someone, a counsellor, a therapist, a friend, has become a safe haven for someone, a trusted comforting person from whom one can derive the confidence to face the world and make new relationships. It is also somebody one can turn to in difficult times. Eventually this becomes internalised and becomes part of the person's mental makeup. An internal resource someone can draw upon in times of stress and by which the person can soothe and calm themselves, manage and regulate their emotions. (Conolly, pending 2018)

Pretreatment as the Framework for Pre-treatment Therapy

The following is a description of Pre-treatment Therapy, couched now in the terms used in Levy's Pretreatment principles (Levy, 2013).

1. **The establishment of safety** — where meeting the safety needs of an individual in crisis is used as an *opportunity* for further engagement and work.

At the Homeless Health Counselling service (HHCS), individuals present in crisis. They may have heard of the service from a friend, their GP, a nurse, their caseworker, etc. Usual crisis intervention models (Roberts' seven stage model, cited in Roberts & Jaeger 2009; CORE, Mellor-Clark et al., 2001), are not used in that for most people presenting, their crisis will be the end result of several previous crises, and coping strategies need to be taught rather than reactivated. Most will be isolated and lack support networks to call on. Furthermore, many will be actively dependent on drugs and/or alcohol.

Thus, in the "Drop in" individual sessions, no history is taken so as not to retraumatise the person, by asking them to narrate and thereby relive the traumatic events of their past or indeed current life, especially if sleeping out on the street. Instead, emphasis is put on making a warm empathic connection, offering them a hot drink, and putting them at their ease. The focus here is to get the person to return, to ensure that the person gets something positive from the interaction. A quick risk assessment will be made some way in the interaction, and will be very much in a conversational style and "signposting" will be offered if needed/wanted.

Ted's Story

For example, Ted — a small, wiry Irishman with dead gray/blue eyes walked in my room recently, the worse for alcohol. I asked him why he had come to see me. His caseworker at the hostel had sent him, he said, because he was concerned about him. I asked him why his caseworker was concerned.

> "Mental health issues, I was discharged from hospital two months ago."
> "Mental Hospital?"
> "Yes."
> "Why were you in hospital?"
> "Because I tried killing myself — I keep wanting to die — I've tried many times."

This was said in such a deadpan voice, my heart sank. Here I was talking with someone who was drunk, and who appeared to be chronically suicidal. The thought crossed my mind that possibly he wanted to scare me, keep me at a distance. I had come across another man some years previously, who in our first encounter with me had related the most horrendous, forlorn and hopeless of stories, something I had come to realize had been his way of managing his anxiety of being with me at that time. Unfortunately he went on to say, "Next time, I'll put stones in my pockets, I know what to do now."

Yet his attempts had not been successful so far, and he had followed his caseworker's instructions, he had come to me. So, there was a chance that his self-harming behaviour could be cries for help, the last ditch attempt at self-regulating inchoate and unbearable feelings. Nevertheless, this man presented a risk.

I decided to try and instill some glimmer of hope, demonstrate that he was important to me and that I cared about him, and to focus on getting him to come back as soon as possible.

I told him I was very interested in his story and I wanted him and me together to find a way of making it possible for him to live with less pain and that I wanted to see him three times a week in order to do this. At this he showed some surprise, but also expressed his gratitude. He went on to say how unhelpful hospital had been. They hadn't been interested in him, only pumping him full of drugs.

We agreed the days and times he would come back, which he did.

2. **The development of a trusting relationship** — For Levy, this entails the promoting of "trust, safety and autonomy while developing relevant goals" (Levy, 2013, p 5), taking into account the "stages of change" (Prochaska and Norcross, 2003).

At the HHCS, we have found this to be absolutely fundamental. Nothing is possible without the prospect of trust gradually emerging. Many long-term homeless people and people suffering from traumatised personalities have experienced what I have come to call Toxic Help, a history of hurt, being let down, disappointed, blamed and turned away, even from professionals designated and entrusted by society to help them. The most usual form this takes is when the person is blamed for the treatment not working, and they are then dismissed as "untreatable," or "noncompliant."

This accumulated history of rejection and failure, confirming the most deeply held conviction of being "different," an outcast, and hopeless, then needs to be overcome. Trust has to be earned over time, and worked at very hard. It cannot simply be assumed and expected, as mainstream services generally do and can do with members of the general public.

Budd's Story

Budd, a man in his late 40s, homeless since his teenage years and attending one of the Anger Support and Discussion Groups, is very proud of his "authority problem," and wears this as a badge of honour. He has invariably been banned from all of the local homeless services for his "attitude problem" and violent behaviour. Gradually, bits and pieces of his story have emerged in the group. He was an orphan, and the little he knows of his parents was that they had never wanted him. After many foster families, he had eventually been placed in a care home where he had been sexually abused by staff there. Budd has a fierce love for his independence and has achieved some status in the street community. He is big, burly, forthright, and physically devastating in a fight, something evidenced by his stays in prison.

At first he presented to the group drunk. The group agreed to leave him be, as long as he was not disruptive. Over some months, his drinking lessened, but he was keen to hold the group's center of attention and hold forth on a liturgy of grievances against the system, "which is out to get you." His whole attitude could be summed up with the following: "You have to get them before they get you." However, with great delicacy, the group and its co-facilitators (including Paul) were able to wean Budd off from hogging all of the attention. Gradually, Budd was able to tolerate listening to other members' tales, and what they revealed about human vulnerability and the need to bear their loads.

A breakthrough occurred when Budd was summoned to court for having hit a hostel resident, after yet another attempt from Budd to leave the streets and engage with the rehousing system. He asked me if I would write a report for the court. I said that I would. He then asked me if I would go to court with him. Again I said that I would, and I did.

From that moment on, I believe Budd felt that he could trust me that I cared about him, and would do what I could for him. A step had been taken towards me becoming his "safe base". The court took into account my report and was lenient. He was not taken into custody. He continued attending the group and began to reveal the development of a more tender side to his nature, his growing dedication to his grownup children and granddaughters "so that they never have to suffer what I suffered." He continued his attempts to engage with the rehousing system, and was able to sustain an 18 month tenancy for a flat. However, he missed the streets, had to sleep out two or three nights a week, spend the odd week with his children in Kent, actions the housing association struggled to take at face value.

The situation finally broke down when he was assigned a young graduate female caseworker whom he felt just didn't have enough life experience to understand and respect him, and when after a three week visit in Kent, he was accused of sub-letting. Budd walked out. But not from the group; he continued to attend, he vented his anger, frustration, grief, but after some time, also his acceptance of limits, his own, and more importantly the limits of others, the limits of systems, the limits of authority.

After 40+ years, Budd is beginning to glimpse the possibility of a more benign side to authority, which needs managing and negotiating with.

Throughout this time, since his latest court appearance, Budd's behaviour underwent a marked change. He is no longer physically threatening. Gradually, his verbal threats have also decreased, he walks away from trouble, and has come to realise that he could choose the timing and the nature of his fights. Budd has attended the group for some five years now.

He has been in a shelter some months and has avoided physical confrontation with both residents and staff there. He has been very unhappy with the staff attitude and behaviour, but has resisted confrontation. He has decided to move to another hostel he believes may be more suitable for him. He has also visited his family more frequently, and the subtlety of his relations with them has increased; something he transfers to other relationships and which he displays in the group.

Arguably, Budd could be diagnosed with the label of anti-social personality disorder, yet patient, respectful, caring and supportive concern are going some way towards undoing decades-worth of pain, grievance, hurt, betrayal, suspicion and hostility. It is a slow but immensely important journey.

Ineffective Treatment

Toxic Help need not be as extreme as that experienced by Budd in his care home. There can be several different kinds: *Ineffective treatment* contributing to an ever increasing sense of hopelessness and despair; *Therapeutic dissonance,* where the treatment actually makes things worse for the person; and *Social dissonance*, where the different social worlds inhabited by care provider and care receiver make for a practice of exclusion rather than inclusion.

Unfortunately, this seems to be especially prevalent regarding Personality Disorder (PD), maybe because effective treatment was only developed in the 90s (Linehan,1993a; 1993b), and is overlaid by a plethora of severe physical symptoms, which get treated, without the underlying psychological condition ever being recognised and addressed.

Sam's Story

Sam was a man extremely quick to anger, and I could hear him shouting in the waiting room even before I set eyes on him. As I was walking down the corridor to fetch and accompany him back to the counselling room, staff were rolling their eyes at me and otherwise letting me know that here indeed was "a character," and my hands would be full.

In that first session and also subsequent sessions, I sat quietly through Sam's anger, without trying to argue with it. I let it blow itself out, only then to acknowledge my recognition of the immense frustration he must feel, and that I empathised with him, about just how difficult it must be for him to have his needs met. This surprised Sam, and he went on to tell me just how arrogant, ineffective and humiliating most mental health workers had been to him, especially psychiatrists. This had been a major factor in his not engaging with them, and blaming himself for his deterioration.

When over the next few weeks I explained to Sam about PD, I saw a flash of recognition light up behind his eyes, and he exclaimed out loud that yes, this was it — this had been his life, bouncing from one crisis to another, his alcohol abuse, his self- harming, all attempts to calm himself down, to shut off his "overheating brain." He then asked why nobody had even mentioned PD to him, none of the psychiatrists who had seen him? Why had they only given him antidepressants, which had stopped helping after awhile?

My tolerating and containing Sam's anger allowed us the beginnings of an exchange that felt worthwhile for him, in that amongst other things, it allowed him to reframe his life journey differently, in a less hopeless, self-blaming, and self-hating way.

The next breakthrough occurred when the crises in Sam's life were beginning to threaten his progress. Housing issues, debts, court appearances, etc. were all beginning to impact on his self-harming and drinking rate. When he first presented he was self-harming three to four times a week, and this dropped to about once every three weeks. However, in my concern to maintain this in the face of growing crises, I suggested to him that I would see him three times a week, and I also gave him my work mobile telephone number, as well as my work email address, explaining very carefully the limits of my availability on these, and to expect some time lapse in my responses.

Sam's face changed, he fell silent and looked at me very intently.

> "I know you mean it now."
> "What do you mean?"
> "Nobody else has done that, none of the other mental health lot have done that, I know that you really care, I know that I can trust you — I've never been able to trust anyone. My father used to beat me to a pulp."

From that moment on, Sam has shown great interest in engaging with PD support treatment, as well as alcohol support services. His self-harm rate dropped to zero, while his alcohol consumption markedly reduced, together with the extent and intensity of his anger outbursts; all this in the face of major life stressors.

I believe that I became a secure base for Sam when he recognised, believed in and trusted my commitment to him. Remarkably, though, he has never made use of non-face-to-face contact with me.

Therapeutic Dissonance

Therapeutic Dissonance occurs when there is a mismatch between the understanding of the patient as articulated by the counsellor/therapist, and the patient's own understanding of themselves. People with PD usually have a very diffuse sense of self due to dramatic and frequent changes in mood, thinking pattern and behaviour. It can thus be extremely confusing when a counsellor suggests an image of Self to someone whose own sense of Self is extremely tenuous (Bateman and Fonagy, 2006). The person can then find themselves conflicted between trying to live up to the counsellor's image of themselves, especially if they like and respect this person, and their own inner sense of chaos, confusion, and inadequacy. This can then lead to a worsening of symptoms and a negative therapeutic reaction expressed by dropping out of counselling, and most tragically, blaming oneself for it, thereby confirming a deeply held sense of failure.

Michael's Story

It took a long time for Mike and me to understand why Cognitive Behaviour Therapy (CBT), hadn't been of help to him. Michael had had quite a bit of previous counselling. He was a man in his 40s, tall, muscular and fit-looking. He presented well enough, articulate, well-groomed and seemingly not in a crisis. He had sought counselling with me, because he got incredibly frustrated with the "rehousing system." He suffered from insomnia, and his previous counsellor had recommended he attend a CBT programme to help him manage it and his anxiety. However, he had dropped out, simply unable to comply with the homework. He had never been any good at school, and had put it down to his own lack of mental ability.

After many months of banter and chatting, Mike's life story began to emerge in dribs and drabs. He had been separated from his mother in early childhood when his parents divorced, and his father had been severe, harsh, undermining, and physically abusive.

We came to realise that Mike expected to be undermined by any authority figure, and didn't trust them one inch. His only repertoire was flight or fight. However, he had become attached to his previous woman counsellor and blamed himself for not having been able to carry through her suggestions. He blamed his inability to focus, and his poor memory, basically believing himself to be mentally inept.

I fed back to him that this certainly hadn't been my impression of him, that in fact I had found him to have a bright, alert and interested mind, when not clouded by lack of sleep or alcohol. What eventually emerged was that Mike was in a constant state of crisis, of physiological and psychological arousal, due to his having been raised in terror of his father. This had prevented him progressing at school and had set in place the vicious spiral of underperformance. He maintained a credible façade (*False Self*[4], Winnicott, 1965), but this quickly disintegrated under stress, and Mike could become very angry and physically threatening, alternating with periods of overconsumption of alcohol and soft drugs.

It had taken at least a year of my mainly following Mike's lead in our conversations for him to reveal enough of his story to throw a different perspective on his dropping out of his previous treatment programs. It subsequently emerged that Mike also had dyslexia.

The Pre-treatment Therapy approach enabled me to give Mike control over the content and pace of our conversations. I was not bound by having to focus in on symptoms and their immediate relief, or keeping an eye on the date and number of sessions, like in most other mainstream treatment programs. By focusing solely on conversations allowing the emergence of a secure base, a safe and trustworthy attachment, Pre-treatment Therapy enables a fuller understanding of Self and its very special needs and adaptations to emerge.

Social Dissonance

> One's personal history and unique life experiences will influence the extent to which we want to occupy and feel able to occupy particular positions within interactions... The therapist could not play a completely professional role unless the person became a complete patient. (Burr, 2015, p 133-4)

Assuming the "patient role" means the relinquishing of control, complying with the implicit and explicit norms of interaction and behaviour for that specific context; entrusting somebody else, a complete stranger, with

---

[4] First developed by Donald Winnicott (1965). A "false self" consists of a "defensive structure created to master trauma in a context of total dependency" (Fonagy and Target, 2003, p. 26). It is a façade developed to pacify a hostile interpersonal environment at the cost of true feelings, the expression of needs, joy and spontaneity. This often leading some people feeling quite empty emotionally.

one's body, allowing them to get close, even possibly to touch. All of this is in somebody else's territory, which might be unknown, unpredictable, unsafe, and where possible escape routes have not yet been mapped out.

Usually, when people enter someone else's territory, especially that of a stranger, there is some kind of acknowledgement of the mutual unease and potential threat this entails, and there are rituals to manage and regulate this; there might be the bearing of gifts, or the making explicit of a welcoming stance, with the offer of food and/or refreshment.

Levy has drawn our attention to how many chronically homeless people have survived their traumatic circumstances by strongly clinging to their individuality, their personal values, culture, and need for freedom and safety, and we have also seen how many homeless people have experienced a history of toxic help. Yet, many health professionals assume that their expectations of the general public can also be applied to homeless people. When, naturally, these expectations are confounded, rather than critically examine them, it is the homeless person who is pathologised, stigmatised, and rejected or incarcerated.

I remember an extremely agitated colleague approaching me about a new case, a man who had just been referred to his service. He was convinced that this man was totally "mad," and beyond his service's capacity to help. He had taken the man over to a hostel and his behaviour there had been "quite mad." He had pulled his hair, and had started slashing his arms and chest. My colleague really felt that he needed to be sectioned (involuntarily detained into mental hospital). Apparently, he talked to a dead relative every day, etc, etc.

Josh's Story

When Josh was finally persuaded to see me a few days later, he was so anxious that he vomited in the room. Over the next few visits, his anxiety gradually receded and his story began to emerge. He had been a political activist in a country ravaged by war, had been imprisoned and tortured, but only after having been forced to watch his family being tortured and killed before his very eyes.

He had come to the UK seeking political asylum, but this had been turned down due to a lack of corroborating evidence, and he had been reduced to surviving hand to mouth on the streets. He was once a dancer, now reduced to scavenging, begging, and drinking alcohol, after all that he had suffered. He saw no point in life, he had lost everything and everyone of value. He had tried to kill himself in public and had been hospitalised. He was discharged to my colleague's service, which is tasked with accommodating people on medical grounds.

He had "lost it" when being told at the hostel that this accommodation would only be temporary. He agreed to my phoning the hostel, to inform them I was seeing him several times a week, and also inform them a little about trauma and self-harming behaviour, as well as offering them some self-reflective practice (although they accepted this, they never took up the offer).

Josh regularly came to see me three times a week. I suggested alternatives to self-harming, which he adopted and found helpful. His self-harm ceased, and we harnessed his natural coping mechanisms instead. This consisted of his dancing for tourists, and the playing of very simple musical instruments, which I made available to him. He wanted to contribute to others, and to feel he was of some value, and despite everything, to have a sense of some self-worth, however fleeting. He was able to manage a subsequent change in his accommodation without mishap.

Positive Psychology

Pre-treatment Therapy takes its lead from Levy by first and foremost interacting with people as human beings. We know from Seligman (2011) that we all need the following in order to maintain our mental wellbeing:

i.   **Positive emotions** (on regular basis)
ii. **Engagement** (to be completely absorbed in something, lose self-consciousness, a hobby, an activity, a film)
iii. **Relationships** (positive ones)
iv. **Meaning** (belonging to and serving something bigger than the self)
v.   **Achievement** (accomplishment, expertise, sense of mastery and control)

It is surely no coincidence that one of the strongest themes to emerge from the mental health recovery movement based on former service users' accounts of meaningful recovery in the late 90s (Faulkner, 2012) was: "that self-agency in recovery had to be allowed for by services and that individuals had to be seen beyond their diagnosis and related to as a whole person." (Castillo, 2016, p 36)

In this respect, the importance of the Psychologically Informed Environment approach, PIE, simply cannot be overstated. Its equipping of staff with the relevant psychological understanding and people skills, for those who have been traumatised and who may be suffering from mental health issues, is crucial. (Keats et al., 2012; Pielink.net).

3. **Common Language Construction** — For Levy, this entails the understanding of the homeless person's world by learning the meaning of their gestures, words, and actions.

A Scottish man, Jim, came to me with a diagnosis of paranoid schizophrenia. Apart from his conviction that the day of judgment would be upon us soon, I found him to be perfectly functional, and we had many a scintillating conversation. He had been hospitalised for violent outbursts of anger accompanied by threatening behaviour while in possession of potentially lethal weapons. But he had been recently discharged from mental hospital to a hostel for the homeless, and experienced severe panic attacks. He wanted help to manage these.

I remember well the session when I tentatively suggested that maybe his experiences of divine revelation had been brought upon by altered states of consciousness. This released a torrent of invectives against psychiatry and the mental health system. However, because over several weeks we had been able to establish a good rapport, we were able to "agree to disagree." I respected that, for him, his experiences had felt so immediate and so momentous that he had no option but to believe that they had been real, and that he had been especially chosen. In return, he perfectly understood that, given my training and my role, I was bound to believe that he had experienced some kind of drug-induced breakdown.

Because our chats were perfectly respectful and non- judgmental, and both of us were keen to understand each other's perspective, they were pleasant and mutually instructive. With time, his anxiety dissipated, and he came to feel that he had his anger under control. He eventually went on to become self-employed.

4. **Facilitate and Support Change** — Very much like Levy's Prereatment, at the HHCS the processes, stages and levels of change are taken into account, and it is recognised "that particular processes are more useful during particular stages of change[5]" (Prochaska and Norcross, 2003, p 525). Thus, relapses are very much seen as part of the recovery journey, and to be learnt from rather than stigmatised.

---

[5] See chapter 5 for Jay S. Levy's detailed discussion of the stages of the change model.

Schema Therapy and Mentalization

Schema Therapy (specifically developed for the treatment of personality disorder by Young et al., 2003) very much sees treatment as progressing through the following three stages:

1. Bonding and emotional regulation
2. Schema[6] Change
3. Autonomy

"Limited Re-parenting" allows the client to fill in critical early gaps in emotional learning via secure attachment, and accurate mirroring, leading to feeling valued and worthy, often for the first time. Thus, this is very much used in the first stage of treatment, and might involve supporting the person to do things he/she doesn't feel able to do independently at that time.

It is very important not to set people up to fail by setting them tasks beyond their abilities. This is something "independent living" care organisations can be at risk of doing. We shouldn't allow allow people to helplessly flounder around, when blatantly, they do not have the resources to do otherwise at the time.

Fonagy and colleagues have shown how childhood trauma impacts on psychological development, especially "Mentalization." This is "the ability to see and describe oneself and others as thinking, and feeling beings whose actions reflect intentions and plans" (Daniel, 2015, p 19). "...a key psychological function which develops throughout infancy and childhood and which allows the representation of emotional states allowing for their regulation; the development of symbolic thought, memory, comprehension and communication and, the development of a core sense of selfhood, self-worth, and self-reliance." (Fonagy and Target, 2003, p 254) However, individuals with weakened Mentalization will be prone to reverting back to "pre-mentalization" states under stress, those states the child works through before achieving Mentalization.

One such state is The "Teleological" mode, where children, and later adults, can only trust actions, but not words, as a means of communicating intent. This is possibly due to a history of caregiver actions contradicting their words. Therefore, someone prone to teleological thinking will not be able to trust any helper's words, unless these are demonstrated via actions. In this case, Limited Re-parenting becomes extremely important.

---

[6] Schemas originate in childhood and are elaborated through a person's lifetime. They are comprised of: memories, bodily sensations, emotions, and cognitions. Maladaptive schemas result from interactions of unmet core childhood needs, innate temperament, and early environment.

Anne's Story

Anne is a middle-aged, diminutive mouse of a woman, whose small, careful, mincing steps seemed to scream the need not to be seen, not to be heard, not to exist even. She was on the streets and desperate for shelter, yet also terrified of this. It emerged that she had a history of chronic depression interspersed with numerous suicide attempts. It seemed that once her basic survival needs were met, she suffered the unbearable awareness of her crushing loneliness, lost past, and hopeless future putting her most at risk.

Anne was accommodated, and duly supported through her suicidal phase, from which emerged long-standing issues of severe and debilitating performance anxiety, which had led to numerous job losses and increasing self-isolation. I offered Anne concrete, material assistance in getting copies of lost/stolen identity papers, filling in all of the required forms for a transfer to sheltered housing, and her mood gradually lifted. She became more hopeful, more confident, and more invested in the possibility of her future.

In the past, approaching others for help would have rendered her incoherent with anxiety, and the help would inevitably prove to be inadequate. Anne had needed the patient, painstaking, caring, yet boundaried "Limited Re-parenting" approach. This taught her that help could be asked for and be forthcoming in the way that she needed. Anne went on to face and solve many other bureaucratic challenges independently, returning only to give quite self-satisfied feedback!

5. **Cultural and Ecological Considerations** — For Jay, this is to prepare and support the person for successful transition and adaptation to new relationships, ideas, services, resources, treatment, and accommodation. This very much acknowledges the concept of a journey, and it consists of different stages.

This is very much acknowledged at the HHCS, and in its attempt to offer people a secure base., Very much like our own families, whose doors are always open to us, HHCS's doors are never closed to its ex-service users, although most move on out of Westminster. It is made clear to them that they are always welcome to touch base, if in need.

Conclusion

Robin Johnson has suggested (personal correspondence) that the field of homelessness seems to throw up the most cutting-edge thinking currently re developments in care, and it seems to me that Jay Levy has done just that. Already in the 50s, Carl Rogers launched the person-centered counselling movement, by putting people at the centre of professional encounters, and Jay has thankfully extended this to the most excluded of groups.

Pretreatment and Pre-treatment therapy are terribly exciting developments in that they offer a key to enabling a greater range of excluded groups in through the door. It wouldn't at all surprise me for further Pretreatment derivatives to emerge, such as Pre-treatment Schema Therapy (for PD), or Pre-treatment CBT (for anxiety and depression), or Pre-treatment Interpersonal Therapy (for depression), or Pre-treatment Eye Movement Desensitisation Therapy (EMDR, for PTSD). The list goes on and on...

The foundations of selfhood and its emergence are very much dependant on the caring-attuned mirroring of caregivers. It is a testimony to the resilience of the human spirit, and to the dedication of a few brave souls, that deficits in early life need not necessarily result in a lifelong journey of exclusion.

References

Ashton, P. (2011) Paul's journey, *Housing, Care and Support*, 14(4): 142-144

Bateman, A. & Fonagy, P. (Eds) (2006) Mentalizing and Borderline Personality Disorder, in *Handbook of mentalization-based treatment* (eds J. G. Allen and P. Fonagy), John Wiley & Sons, Ltd, Chichester, UK. doi: 10.1002/9780470712986.ch9

Bleiberg, E., Rossouw, T. & Fonagy, P. (2012) Adolescent Breakdown and Emerging Borderline Personality Disorder. Chapter 18, pp. 463-509, in *Handbook of mentalizing in mental health practice*, A. Bateman & P. Fonagy, (Eds). Washington DC, London England: American Psychiatric Publishing, Inc.

Bowlby, J. (1997) *Attachment*. London: Pimlico

Bowlby, J. (1998a) *Separation: Anger and anxiety*. London: Pimlico

Bowlby, J. (1998b). *Loss: Sadness and depression*. London: Pimlico

Burr, V. (2015) *Social constructionism*, 3rd Edition. New York, NY: Routledge

Conolly, J. M. P. (2016) *Pre-treatment Therapy For Multiply Excluded Homeless People in Central London*. Masterclass Presentation delivered at the Royal College of Physicians, in Ireland, Dublin, September 2016

Conolly, J. M. P. (2018, pending) A Pre-treatment Therapy Approach for Single Homeless People — The Co-construction of Recovery/ Discovery. Chapter 8, in *The Psychology of Social Exclusion and its Treatment*. Ed, Cockersell. London: Jessica Kingsley Publishers

Conolly, J. M. P. & Ashton, P. (2011) Staff and ex-service user co-working: a counseling service's enhanced response to multiple exclusion homelessness, *Housing Care and Support*, 14(4): 134-141

Conolly, J. M. P. & Ashton, P. (2013) *Homelessness and Personality Disorder —A Journey towards Co-production*, Presentation delivered at the 1st International Homeless and Inclusion Health Conference, London, March 2013

Conolly, J. M. P. & Ashton, P. (2014) *Anger Discussion Group: A New Approach to Engaging Rough Sleepers Towards Working Together Towards Solutions*, Presentation delivered at the 2nd International Homeless and Inclusion Health Conference, London, March 2014

Conolly, J. M. P. & Ashton, P. (2016) *From Symptoms to People, A Counsellor's Enhanced Response to Multiply Excluded Homeless People*, Presentation delivered at the 4th International Homeless and Inclusion Health Conference, London, March 2016

Coid, J., Yang, M., Tyrer, P., Roberts, A. & Ullrich, S. (2006) Prevalence and correlates of personality disorder in Great Britain, *British Journal of Psychiatry*, 188(5): 423-431.

Costilo, H. (2016) *The reality of recovery in personality disorder.* London: Jessica Kingsley Publishers

Danquah, A. N. & Berry, K. (2016) *Attachment theory in adult mental health.* New York, NY: Routledge

Department of Health (2009) *Recognising complexity: Commissioning guidance for personality disorder services.* London: HMSO http://www.dh.gov.uk/en/Publicationsandstatistics/Publications/Publicat ionsPolicyAndGuidance/DH_101788

Department of Health (2010) *Healthcare for single homeless people.* Office of the Chief Analyst. London: HMSO

Faulkner, A. (2012) Participation and Service User Involvement, Chapter 4, *Qualitative Research Methods in Mental Health and Psychotherapy.* D. Harper & A. R. Thompson, Eds. Chichester, UK: Wiley-Blackwell

Goffman, E. (1968) *Stigma: Notes on the management of spoiled identity.* Harmondsworth, Middlesex: Penguin Books

Haigh, R. (2006) People's Experiences of Having a Diagnosis of personality Disorder, Chapter 8, pps-161-179, in *Personality Disorder and Community Mental Health Teams — A Practitioner's Guide.* Sampson, M., McCubbin R. & Tyrer, P. Chichester, UK: John Wiley & Sons, Ltd.

Healthy London Partnership (2016) *Healthy London Health care & people who are homeless* — Commissioning Guidance for London. https://www.healthylondon.org/latest/publications/homeless-health-commissioning-guidance

Holmes, J. (2016) *The search for the secure base — attachment theory and psychotherapy.* 5th ed. New York, NY: Routledge

Homeless Link, (2016) http://www.homeless.org.uk/factshomelessness-in-numbers/rough-sleeping/rough-sleping-explore-data

Kane, E. (2016) Personality Disorder: New Initiatives in Staff Training, Chapter 1, pps 3-20, in *Personality disorder and community mental health teams — a practitioner's guide.* Sampson, McCubbin and Tyrer. Chichester, UK: John Wiley & Sons, Ltd

Keats, H., Cockersell, P., Johnson, R. & Maguire, N. (2012) *Psychologically informed services; good practice guidance.* London: Department of Communities and Local Government. Retrieved from http://www.southampton.ac.uk

Levy, J. S. (2013) *Pretreatment guide for homeless outreach & housing first: Helping couples, youth, and unaccompanied adults.* Ann Arbor, MI: Loving Healing Press

Linehan, M. (1993a) *Cognitive–behavioral treatment of borderline personality disorder.* New York, NY: The Guildford Press

Linehan, M. (1993b) *Skills training manual for treating borderline personality disorder.* New York, NY: The Guildford Press

Maguire, N. J., Johnson, R., Vostanis, P., Keats, H. & Remington, R. E. (2009) *Homelessness and complex trauma: a review of the literature.* Southampton, UK, University of Southampton. See http://eprints.soton.ac.uk/69749/ cited in *Healthcare for single homeless people (2010)*, p12, London: Department of Health, Office of the Chief Analyst

McDonagh, T. (2011) T*ackling homelessness and exclusion: Understanding complex lives.* York: The Joseph Rowntree Foundation

Mellor-Clark, J., Connell, J., Barkham, M. & Cummins, P. (2001) Counselling outcomes in primary health care: a CORE system data profile, *European Journal of Psychotherapy and Counselling,* 4(1): 65-86

Moran, P., Jenkins, R., Tylee, A., Blizard, R. & Mann A. (2000) The prevalence of personality disorder among UK primary care attenders. *Acta Psychiatrica Scandinavica,* 102(1): 52 –57

NICE clinical guideline 78 (2009) *Borderline personality disorder, Treatment and management.*

NIMHE, National Institute for Mental Health in England (2003) *Personality disorder no longer a diagnosis of exclusion.*

Psychologically Informed Environments Website: http://www.PIELink.net

Roberts, A. R. & Yeager, K., R., (2009) *Pocket guide to crisis intervention.* Oxford, England: Oxford University Press

Seligman, M. (2011) *Flourish.* London, Boston: Nicholas Breadley Publishing

St Mungos Community Housing Association, (2016) *Stop the Scandal.* London: St. Mungos. Retrieved from https://www.england.nhs.uk/wp-content/uploads/2016/07/stop-the-scandal.pdf

Winnicott, D. W. (1965) Ego distortion in terms of true and false self, in *The Maturational Process and the Facilitating Environment: Studies in the Theory of Emotional Development.* New York: International Universities Press, Inc, pp 140–157

Young, J., E., Klosko, J., S. & Weishaar, M., E. (2003) *Schema Therapy.* New York: NY: The Guildford Press

5 Working with Meaning and Riding Transitions
Jay S. Levy

I hail from New Hampshire, whose state motto is 'Live Free or Die'. When death comes my way, I hope to have a beer in my hand. — Butch

I am an ultimate fighter, so people would be wise to fear my wrath! — Tex

The search for meaning is alive and well in homeless circles. The only question is how did human service professionals ignore the obvious for so long? Steeped in our clinical language, we often overlook the power of our stories, traditions and values. In short, we risk losing our humanity in exchange for problem-centered work and diagnostic formulations. Many people who experience homelessness have and will choose their dignity over this outdated brand of help.

The following stories remind us of our mission to foster meaningful connections and to tap into the strengths of the most vulnerable in an effort to facilitate positive change and perhaps even adventure down the path of recovery.

Butch's Story: The meaning of loss revisited

My first book (*Homeless Narratives & Pretreatment Pathways*, 2010) introduced us to a solitary woodsman named Butch. I was first alerted to his presence by the combination of the remnants of a campfire and the stale scent of alcohol wafting through the air. The smell led directly to Butch, who was seated and enjoying a dinner, compliments of the local community meal program located in Western MA. Butch was a white male in his early fifties. He was about 5' 5" tall and appeared rather thin under multiple layers of clothes. He had long, gray hair, and a scraggly mustache and beard. He spent his days riding his bicycle from place to place in order to make money by collecting cans. He was pragmatic about his canning routine and even developed a handy device, which amounted to a pole with a hook at the end for snatching cans out of the trash.

Above all, Butch saw himself as a survivor who embraced his hard-earned independence. In fact, when I first met Butch, he said to me, "I have a site (campsite). I was out last winter and I'll do it again this winter. I like doing my own thing!" His autonomous bearing was reflected by his refusal to be bound by the rules at the local shelter, while imbibing multiple beers on a daily basis. Butch proudly shared, "I hail from New Hampshire whose state motto is 'Live Free or Die'. When death comes my way, I hope to have a beer in my hand." Butch made it very clear from the get go that he was not interested in sobriety, and for the most part, he remained dedicated to drinking (change model stage of pre-contemplation) throughout our working relationship.

During the next several weeks, as autumn leaves began to display their vibrant colors, Butch and I continued to chat at the local soup kitchen. It became clear that Butch was very proud of his campsite and his abilities to withstand harsh New England winters. Nevertheless, I couldn't resist encouraging him to consider some housing options from a list of local landlords. In hindsight, this went against the grain. It may have been a better approach to join with Butch and listen to more of his story, while being receptive to his tutelage on how to best manage a campsite. Nevertheless, I was not too pushy, and showed respect for his autonomy and knowhow, which strengthened our engagement. While Butch wanted nothing to do with my list of resources, he was excited to be my teacher, and I recalibrated in time to be an eager student. Butch then said, "You should see my site! I got a nice tent set up by the river... Jay, it's a nice quiet space where nobody bothers me... maybe one day you'll come check it out?" Happy to hear his offer, I immediately agreed. Shortly after the meal, we made our way over to the campsite.

Upon our arrival, I was struck by the planning and organization that Butch had achieved to meet his daily needs. His campsite was impressive. It was located in an open area surrounded by trees and just a stone's throw from the Westfield River. At the center of the site was a rock-lined fire circle with a tent near each end, close enough to benefit from the radiant heat. One tent was strictly for supplies, and the other served as Butch's sleeping quarters. Within ten yards of the tents was a designated area for chopping wood with an accompanying wood pile covered by a tarp, as well as a clothes line nicely situated to catch the afternoon sun.

After Butch gave me a tour, he pointed to the nearby river and stated that this was a sacred place. Butch said, "A buddy of mine drowned in these waters and this is his resting place... It's a burial ground that I watch over!" Close by, I saw his buddy's name, Jeremy, emblazoned on a sign that hung from a tree branch right over the path that opened to his campground. Butch shared, with tears in his eyes, that Jeremy had lived with him at this very place and that the tent that held his supplies was Jeremy's. Suddenly, I was transfixed as Butch's meaning came into view. He saw himself as not only an accomplished woodsman, but also the guardian of his buddy's memorial site.

This experience, among many others, transformed my initial question of how to help someone who initially refuses our offers to the significance of understanding a person's sense of meaning and purpose. Once we established a sense of trust, Butch shared his world with me. His sense of meaning and values shed light on how my words and actions that focused on housing lists must have resonated. Any offer of a room or even an apartment paled in comparison to the duty he had to his departed friend and his purpose and mastery of outdoor survival. In response to the challenges of homelessness, trauma, and loss, Butch had constructed an identity as a woodsman and protector of his friend's sacred resting place.

Tex's Story: ultimate fighter vs. ultimate victim

During the spring of 1994, I did outreach at a shelter just outside of Boston where I encountered a young, tall, thin, white male in his early 20s. He called himself Tex. He was fond of introducing himself to others at the shelter by slowly saying with a southern drawl, "I am Tex from Texas... where everything is big!" I first met Tex at an overflow shelter that served folks when other local area shelters were filled to capacity, but also was a refuge for people who were barred everywhere else. This was generally an overcrowded setting with more than 130 people in a restricted space filled with army cots. It was not unusual for shelter guests to get into fights due to large numbers of people living in such close quarters, while often intoxicated and/or highly symptomatic of mental illness.

When I first met Tex, he apparently had a need to show some swagger. He said, while staring off into the distance, "I am an ultimate fighter, so people would be wise to fear my wrath!" The disconnect between his vacant stare and charged words made me wonder what he had gone through before ending up in an overflow shelter away from his hometown. It soon became evident that Tex's cold stare was reflective of a childhood marked by trauma and rejection. He eventually spoke about his difficult upbringing, which included both the abuse he encountered at home and the transience of moving to and from multiple foster homes. As a young adult, he was left with a deep sense of feeling victimized and unwanted.

Tex's declarative statement of strength and anger made a great deal of sense within the context of his youth, abuse history, and the challenges of a highly charged shelter environment. In many respects, it was much better for a young man living under such harsh circumstances to be an ultimate fighter, rather than an ultimate victim. In fact, one of his favorite movies, The Karate Kid (Weintraub & Avildsen, 1984), is about an adolescent boy who learns self-defense through martial arts in response to being bullied.

Developmentally speaking, young adults often overestimate their abilities and take unnecessary risks, while being strapped with the task of learning their limits. Yet at the same time, Tex's idealism, or more specifically his self-inflation, can provide the hope and confidence needed to strive for his goals, as well as adapt to threatening situations such as living in a homeless shelter. I therefore tried to hear and respond to his bravado without adding to his experience of fear and alienation. This was a bit tricky, because he demanded respect and seemed in need of reassurance, rather than experiencing the shame and anger that may result by my direct confrontation of his aggressive stance. Instead, I gently shared my concern that his talk of being a fighter may impress some, but also will cause others to flee his company, or potentially lead to a violent conflict that could put his shelter bed at risk. I highlighted this point, while showing my concern by stating, "I know that's the last thing that we would want to see happen!"

More importantly, my simply being there, listening, and not cutting off our conversation, passed his first test, and so we successfully engaged in a non-threatening manner. Our initial progress of relationship formation was evidenced by Tex's willingness to initiate further conversation during my very next visit to the shelter. The topic of our second meeting very quickly moved from his preliminary show of strength to communicating a need to find an income and get a roof over his head.

The question raised by our first couple of meetings was how to join Tex's sense of meaning as an ultimate fighter or perhaps as an independent and powerful young man, while working together on his goals of getting settled with an income, and housed.

Working With (not against) Meaning

Viktor Frankl (1985), the creator of Logotherapy/existential analysis, states that "Despair is suffering without meaning." Both Butch and Tex adapted to the inevitable trauma and loss that homelessness brings and, instead of despair, they came out of it with a new sense of strength and dignity. The question is, how does the outreach counselor work with, not against, a person's sense of meaning and purpose?

Through my working relationship with Tex, I was careful not to mirror his childhood dynamic of rejection and abandonment (McManus & Thompson, 2008), while understanding and upholding his value of strength and independence. I therefore began "where he was at" by exploring what qualities were important to ultimate fighting. Tex enthusiastically shared his admiration for Karate as a martial art and Bruce Lee as its ultimate practitioner. He then said that Bruce Lee was his role model on how to care for his body, while mastering ultimate fighting skills. One of many positive ramifications of Tex's interest in the martial arts was that it encouraged him to be very careful about nutrition, as well as to avoid the intake of drugs and alcohol. Tex explained his understanding of Karate as the need for disciplined preparation through exercise and building a foundation of combat skills.

In response, our work focused on the development of a workout schedule, which included enrollment with a local gym. I also encouraged him to learn the philosophy that underlies Karate, and martial arts in general. During our next meeting, I provided Tex with a book on martial arts for us to jointly study. We discovered that true Karate is based on Bushido, which is influenced by Zen Buddhism, as the strength of a samurai is dependent upon serenity and wisdom. The author, Soke Behzad Ahmadi (1996), said,

> "A Martial Artist may become a professional fighter but not every fighter is capable of becoming a Martial Artist. Martial Arts are about restoration of physical and spiritual balance and fluidity; they are about observing restraints and 'setting example.'"

We learned that in true Karate, the harmonious joining of mind and body is all powerful. Together, we read several chapters and discussed the challenges of managing conflict, while living a more balanced and peaceful life. Over the next couple of sessions, we bridged our playground of language from Karate and Zen Buddhism to the impact of past traumas and the Buddhist/existential teachings of being mindful and in the "here and now." Much like the samurai's quest for spiritual balance, the practiced technique of mindfulness could help Tex to better manage past regrets and future anxieties, while helping him to tap into the power of being present-minded. This disciplined technique could provide a calming influence and thereby help him to focus on important life goals, while understanding both his strengths and limitations.

As part of our discussions, I often referred to Bruce Lee's statement (1975), "You must accept the fact that you are capable in some directions and limited in others, and you must develop your capabilities." Tex took Bruce Lee's quote to heart, and so we wrote it down on an index card that he carried in his wallet as a reminder.

In the end, connecting to Tex's meaning as an ultimate fighter unexpectedly brought us down a productive avenue for addressing his sense of mistreatment and anger by adding daily structure via an exercise program, as well as jointly contemplating and developing a connection with the historical philosophy and values of Karate. Over time, Tex became less combative, and showed progress in managing powerful emotions such as fear, shame, guilt, and anger. Most notably, I managed to gain entrance into Tex's world (House of Language) and thereby developed a person-centered relationship.

When working with young adults who have experienced abuse and neglect by parental figures, one of the many challenges is how to provide a present-day meaningful connection with a caring adult. In a manner of speaking, we are attempting to provide a corrective re-parenting experience. In Tex's case, this was accomplished by my becoming a trusted guide to Soke Behzad Ahmadi and Bruce Lee's teachings and wisdom. This enabled Tex to accept my compassionate overtures, rather than trigger trauma-induced fears, suspicions and rage.

This set the stage for our contract for services. Once Tex felt safe and respected through our therapeutic relationship, he very quickly became focused on the best ways to generate income, so he could eventually get housed. Together we decided that the best path to achieve this was to apply for Job Corp services, which provides young adults with education, job training, and dorm. Soon thereafter, Tex was accepted and moved in. This was a welcome change from the stressful adult shelter environment to a more developmentally appropriate placement that was in line with Tex's stated objectives.

Tex's openness to outreach counseling based on pretreatment principles of care had effectively prepared him to contemplate and eventually accept a referral for mental health counseling via a local family and children clinic that specialized with young adults. Tex now understood that his work with a therapist could help him to better manage his stress and anger, resolve interpersonal conflicts, while supporting his transition into adulthood. Our delving into the philosophy of Karate served the dual purpose of establishing a trusting relationship, as well as constructing a support network and meaningful activities within the local community that aided Tex's quest for housing, stability, and independence.

Butch's Pathways: meaning and crisis

In order to be successful with Butch, I needed to "begin where he was at," not where I wanted him to be. This meant entering and accepting his world, so we could establish trust and a common language that reflected his words, ideas, and values. Butch's house of language (Levy, 2010) was built upon his survival as a woodsman and the loss of his good friend Jeremy, which fueled his purpose as a caretaker for consecrated ground. With this in mind, the natural place to start was to hear his stories that highlighted adventures with his friend and how they overcame the outside elements. In many respects, Butch felt that he already had a home among the trees and rivers of Western MA.

It seemed that the only way to productively talk about the option of getting housed was to find a place to fit into his narrative of survival and loss. In a very real sense, our meetings served the purpose of helping Butch to both commemorate the life and mourn the death of his friend. Over time and with my acceptance of his meaning as a caretaker, Butch was able to ponder future-oriented questions such as how would Jeremy feel about him continuing to be at risk during the harsh New England winters? Or, was there a way for him to get housed, while still being a caretaker to this sacred place?

As autumn turned to winter, Butch complained more about the assorted aches and pains that the colder weather inevitably brings, and I was not shy about wondering whether or not Jeremy would have encouraged him to pursue a safe place for the winter. These in-depth conversations on survival, loss, and safety set the stage for the crisis that shortly followed. It came in the form of a massive blizzard.

The weather forecast predicted a huge snow storm and so I forewarned Butch and offered placement at the local shelter, but he refused. However, he was agreeable to a safety plan between him and the local shelter enabling access at any point during the night. As predicted, high winds and blinding snow pounded Western MA. Butch showed up at the shelter after midnight, and was desperate to get inside. Unfortunately, the overnight staff did not read the safety plan and refused him entry due to the late hour. This resulted in Butch spending the entire night walking through snow and doing his best to seek safety under the doorways of local businesses. The next morning, he showed up at the shelter and his mental status was clearly compromised. Butch was in a state of delirium and was showing signs of hypothermia and frostbite on his feet and toes. I immediately called for an ambulance and he was transported to the hospital for emergency care and further evaluation.

Butch was admitted for several days and was truly fortunate not to lose any toes to frostbite. This crisis gave us the opportunity to observe Butch's functioning when sober. He clearly presented with complex trauma, as evidenced by PTSD from years of childhood abuse and extensive homelessness, Traumatic Brain Injury, coupled with ongoing medical concerns due to the ill effects of living outside coupled with his years of addiction. His inpatient stay afforded us time to successfully apply for benefits, while working on an alternative plan to living in the woods or at the shelter. He became contemplative and even entered an action stage of change in regard to getting housed, because he experienced difficulty walking and his feet were hypersensitive to the cold. His quick return to his campsite in the woods was no longer an option.

We therefore planned out a rehabilitative placement at a local rest home, while continuing to work on getting him an apartment that was in walking distance of his former campsite. Butch's alcoholism remained active, but reduced due to the rules at the rest home and him living primarily indoors, though he still remained adamant about his right to drink. Eventually, Butch moved into an affordable apartment. I provided support services and continued to visit him on a weekly basis. Together, we often returned to his former campsite to pay homage to Jeremy and further process his long journey from homelessness to housing and beyond.

Butch's path from homelessness to getting housed was far from linear. His full story, including his post-housing trials and tribulations, can be found in the book *Homeless Narratives & Pretreatment Pathways (2010)*.

Riding Transitions

When one considers people's journeys in and out of homelessness, it affords us the opportunity to cue into multiple transition points along the way. When we truly listen to people's stories, transitions are more easily identified, because we get a greater sense of life's ebb and flow. One of the main themes to Tex's narrative is the developmental challenge of entering adulthood. Young adults are in the midst of change on so many levels, so it is wise and warranted to offer assistance along the way. These transitions (Erikson, 1968; Kegan, 1982) consist of developing a sense of community or belonging with others, identity issues ranging from gender and sexual preference to personal and cultural identity, achieving education/work related goals, striving for independence and living on one's own, as opposed to with parents, doubled up, on the streets, or in a homeless shelter, as well as one's search for greater meaning, among others.

Through the process of outreach and engagement, we are able to build trust, while providing opportunities for persons without homes to share their stories and journeys. The more people share, the easier it becomes to offer needed assistance in a common language that resonates in their world. This is illustrated by my joining Tex on learning what life lessons martial arts have to offer in an effort to strengthen our relationship, while supporting his adaptation to a chaotic shelter environment.

Another example of working with transitions includes my discussions with Butch, which highlighted the coming of cold weather, and us joining one another in the development of a safety plan. An additional way to frame this challenge is to think ecologically. This means that we support the process of transition and adaption to new environments, or in other words, the person finding a better sense of balance or equilibrium in any given environment, situation, or challenge.

The beauty of a Pretreatment perspective is that it enables us to see that transitions are happening all around us, so there are plenty of opportunities to offer assistance. Many examples abound, such as a person entering a shelter for the first time, or orienting to new people, ideas, or even adapting to a change in the weather. The more we join and support people in transition, the greater the level of trust, because we are "meeting people where they are at" and addressing a current life challenge, or difficulty. I call this *riding the transition bus*.

Pretreatment Strategies for Facilitating Change

The question for us to ponder is how best to support transitions. Individualization is the key, so our understanding of a person's world or perspective is an essential element of developing transition plans. That being said... there are some general approaches for supporting the process of transition and adaptation that bear further discussion.

First, it is essential to develop a client-centered relationship that respects people's autonomy by reinforcing that persons are experts on their own worlds. This embraces Jean Paul Sartre's declaration (1956) of the inescapable connection between freedom and responsibility. Upholding choice within the presence of a safe relationship ensures that people are more likely to own their successes, while also being open to review their missteps or mistakes with someone who engenders their trust. In this manner, client-centered relationships empower people to learn the valuable life lessons of what works and what doesn't work, and thereby help them to make more responsible choices. This is in accord with a solution-focused approach to helping (Walter & Peller, 1992), which emphasizes our ability to construct present day resolutions to problems based on what's worked, while letting go of strategies that have not panned out in the past or present.

Second, it is important that we understand the power of joining a person on their quest for change, rather than allowing people to feel alone, isolated, overwhelmed, and powerless. This means actively offering to accompany people to attend critical appointments, jointly filling out needed paperwork for housing and other resources, and being there to review their strengths, challenges, and barriers to change. We can further facilitate the change process by getting feedback from the client on the rate of transition, so we don't make the error of moving too quickly based on our own need to promote a change agenda. In fact, many people without homes have complex trauma concerns. They can benefit by being introduced to things slowly, which provides a type of desensitization by gradually increasing exposure over time to new environments.

How we orient people to service and resource opportunities is of critical importance. This means truly understanding a person's words, ideas and values, while speaking a common language that fosters an ongoing connection. We hope to establish a feedback loop that speaks to people's current concerns, as well as their identity, culture, and aspirations for a better future. In order to do this well, it is necessary to reflect on our own blind spots, so we can step away from personal biases and intervene in a manner that is supportive to the client, as opposed to simply meeting our own needs. It is therefore essential to facilitate reflective practice through the provision of 1:1, group, and peer co-vision (supervision) meetings.

Third, we can help people prepare for life transitions by stating an objective, and then jointly breaking it down into a step by step process of achievable goals. It is important that our work becomes goal-centered and optimistic, rather than problem-centered and defeatist. This is in agreement with psychiatric rehabilitative principles of care. Psychiatric Rehabilitation (Anthony et al., 1990) is goal focused and thereby defines barriers to change, while understanding the importance of developing and/or enhancing skills, the importance of building a strong support system, and modifying the environment as necessary in order to achieve one's goals.

Prochaska and DiClemente's Trans Theoretical Model of Change (1982) is an important guide. It breaks down the change process into distinct stages to help guide interventions:

- **Pre-contemplation:** Prior to the development of understanding that change is needed

- **Contemplation:** Awareness of problem; ambivalent feelings about change

- **Determination:** Initial movement away from ambivalence and toward action resulting in preparation for change

- **Action:** Attempts toward achieving change; Implementation of action plan; Steps are made to attain goal(s);

- **Maintenance:** Sustaining the change accomplished by previous actions

- **Relapse:** Previous problem behaviors are repeated

It is important to note that relapse is an expected part of the change process, and so a client's movement through these stages is often not linear. Further, someone can be in different stages of change in regard to different types of problems or need areas. I find it particularly useful to think in terms of five different major domains from which to consider what Stage of Change someone currently resides in, and thereby intervene accordingly. They are Addiction, Mental Health issues, Medical concerns, Income, and Housing. For example, a person can be in the Action Stage of Change in regard to Income and Housing, while still Pre-contemplative in regard to Addiction, and Mental Health issues, and perhaps Contemplative for Medical concerns. The key is to facilitate a person's movement through the stages of change by beginning where they are at and providing the right environment (physical and social) to enhance motivation.

Motivational Interviewing is a well-researched, effective counseling approach that is sensitive to "where people are at," and joins with the person toward addressing the need and strategies for change. In this manner, it is person-centered and helps facilitate people's movement through the Stages of Change. The hope is to help our clients to enter the "action stage" of change and to eventually achieve and maintain positive life change. The "action" embarked upon by a person experiencing homelessness can range from something as basic as connecting with a nurse for foot care to beginning Mental Health and/or Addiction treatment or filling out housing applications.

Five general principles guide the practice of *Motivational Interviewing* (Miller & Rollnick, 1991, pp. 55-62) as follows:

> **Express Empathy:** Skillful reflective listening and joining with the person in need is fundamental. Accept and understand a person's perspective without necessarily agreeing with it. Identify ambivalence, and explore the different parts of the person by giving voice to inner conflict.
>
> **Develop Discrepancy:** Reflecting on discrepancy between present behavior and a person's stated goals, values, or wishes can motivate change. The client can develop an improved awareness of actions and related consequences, thereby reinforcing personal responsibility for meeting one's goals, or re-evaluating what they need to work on.
>
> **Avoid Argumentation:** Avoid power struggles. Arguments are counterproductive. Describe rather than label, understand resistance, but don't fight it.
>
> **Roll with Resistance:** The client is the key resource for creating solutions. New perspectives are jointly considered but never imposed. Resistance is a signal to change strategies.
>
> **Support Self-Efficacy:** Our counseling approach should be optimistic. Belief in the possibility of change and restored or newfound hope are important motivators. We know that it is beneficial for people to take ownership (personal responsibility) of the change process by actively participating and planning future steps.

These theories (Change Model & Motivational Interviewing) can guide human service workers by providing stage-based interventions to facilitate the change process. The change model and motivational interviewing are pretreatment approaches that can help a person move from *precontemplation* toward *action* in order to become an agent toward creating positive change. Stage based interventions include, but are not limited to, providing education, facilitating ongoing self-inventory at every phase, and developing structure to support change (e.g., relapse prevention). Further, this approach shows that pointing out discrepancy and thereby creating ambivalence and/or awareness of internal conflict (*contemplation stage*) are important positive steps toward addressing issues of denial, or minimization of problems. Therefore, counselors should carefully facilitate some exploration of ambivalence, rather than avoid this issue.

Trauma, Homelessness, and Pretreatment

This chapter reviewed general and specific Pretreatment interventions for assisting people who experience trauma and homelessness. It should be noted that Pretreatment is a Trauma Informed approach. It respects a person's autonomy and sense of internal control throughout the counseling process, while maintaining a focus on personal safety. This is further reflected through the outreach worker's sensitivity to a client's values, meaning and purpose in an effort to support the journey from homelessness to housing. In other words, it is a person-centered approach that is founded upon a strong engagement process, developing a common language that resonates with the client, and becoming goal driven, rather than problem centered, while promoting safety.

Pretreatment principles of relationship formation, common language construction, ecological considerations, facilitating change, and promoting safety all speak to the issue of working with a person's sense of meaning and facilitating transitions. Common Language Construction, which was discussed at length in chapter 3, includes the art of Bridging Language between the worlds of people without homes with available resources and services. This was exemplified through my efforts to transition Butch and Tex to housing and support services. I worked with their meaning, while bridging their world of trauma, loss, and survival to the safe confines of an apartment or Job Corp residence.

For Butch, this specifically meant helping him to grieve the loss of his friend, Jeremy, while understanding that Jeremy would want him to be alive and safe. This resonated in Butch's world because it was responsive to his narrative. Common language construction set the stage to extract opportunity from the ensuing crisis of a New England blizzard. Ultimately, Butch not only got housed, but received necessary medical follow up, while establishing a home in his community.

Similarly, Tex was able to utilize the life philosophy and values of Karate to help bridge his worldview with the need for greater compassion and discipline. This set the stage for addressing his anger in a more productive way, while opening him up to the benefits of counseling and placement at a Job Corp residence.

In this manner, and there are countless examples, a Pretreatment approach puts into motion simultaneous processes that facilitate positive transitions to housing and healthcare for the most vulnerable in our society.

In the next chapter, Ray Middleton takes the ideas of engagement and common language development a step further. He introduces the concepts

of Open Dialogue and the psychological model of Ladder4Life, as a means
of promoting the development of Psychologically Informed Environments
throughout all relevant systems of care.

References

Ahmadi, S. B. (1997) Legacy of a Sensei. Mahrang Publishing (Mahoyya print)

Anthony, W., Cohen, M., & Farkas, M. (1990) *Psychiatric rehabilitation*. Boston University: Center For Psychiatric Rehabilitation

Erikson, E. H. (1968) *Identity: youth and crisis*. New York: Norton

Frankl, V. E. (1985) *Man's search for meaning*. New York: Washington Square Press

Kegan, R. (1982) *The evolving self: Problem and process in human development*. Cambridge, MA: Harvard University Press

Lee, B. (1975) *Tao of Jeet Kune Do*. Edited by Caldwell, L.L. & Johnson, G. Valencia, CA: Black Belt Books

Levy, J. S. (2010) *Homeless narratives & pretreatment pathways: From words to housing*. Ann Arbor, MI: Loving Healing Press

McManus, H. H. & Thompson, S. J. (2008) Trauma among unaccompanied homeless youth: The integration of street culture into a model of intervention. *Journal of Aggression, Maltreatment & Trauma,* 16(1): 92-109

Miller, W. R. & Rollnick, S. (1991) *Motivational interviewing: Preparing people to change addictive behavior*. New York: Guilford

Prochaska, J. O. & DiClemente, C. C. (1982) Trans theoretical therapy: Toward a more integrative model of change. *Psychotherapy: Theory, Research, and Practice.* 19(7), 276-288

Sartre, J. P. (1956) *Being and nothingness*. New York, New York: Washington Square Press

Walter, J. & Peller, J. (1992) *Becoming solution-focused in brief therapy*. Chicago: Brunner/Mazel

Weintraub, J. (Producer) & Avildsen, J.G. (Director). (1984) *Karate kid* [Motion Picture] United States: Columbia Pictures Corporation

6 Ladder4Life: Developing Dialogical PIE
Ray Middleton

Sooner or later what is heard and actively understood will
find its response in the subsequent speech or behavior of
the listener.

— Mikhail Bakhtin

I currently work as a freelance PIE consultant and trainer and also as a
System Broker (and "Work Force Development lead") for Mental Health
Concern and Fulfilling Lives in the North-East of England. This non-profit
programme works with 115 people who have "complex needs." We define
this as combinations of mental health, substance misuse, homelessness, and
offending, where mainstream services then experience difficulty engaging
effectively with the individual. Fulfilling Lives in Newcastle and Gateshead
is funded by the Big Lottery and is one of twelve such programs running
between 2014 and 2022. In our program, we had two research and
evaluation staff, three "system brokers," a team leader, and twelve
"navigators."

Currently at Fulfilling Lives, our staff employed as navigators attempt to
build relationships of trust with clients in flexible ways and then attempt to
"navigate" the client into existing services. Inevitably, this presents clients
and staff with many difficulties as existing services have historically
developed into silos of professional training and different ways of thinking
about, and working with, this group of people. Bakhtin (1981) would call
these ways of thinking/working *professional genres,* distinct from our
clients' everyday genres of ordinary life.

Three of the navigator posts were ring-fenced (earmarked) for people with lived experience of complex needs so we had a good mix of backgrounds within the team. Part of my ongoing motivation for working in this area for over 20 years now is that I used to have complex needs myself in the 1990s, and attracted seven different mental health diagnoses during seven inpatient admissions to the psychiatric hospital. Personally, I did not find the mainstream response from services very helpful, partly as in the 1990s, services were stuck in a medical model way of thinking which does not fit well when people have more than one need.

We have found that traditionally organised and offered services tend to exclude those most vulnerable and in need in our society. That is, the people with the most complex needs, which have often developed in reaction to complex trauma histories, are not offered an effective service. For example, in the UK, statutory mental health services are divided into primary and secondary (specialist) care, where people with more serious and enduring mental health problems are supposed to be treated by secondary mental health services. Yet our data showed that 98% of our 115 clients had serious mental health issues but only 20% were receiving a secondary mental health service (see: www.fulfillinglives-ng.org.uk).

There are many problems with, and reasons for system failure — why professionals in traditionally offered services think and act in ways that do not meet the needs of the most vulnerable in society with complex needs. These are systemic problems and the primary task we have been given at Fulfilling Lives is to take our research findings and the experience of frontline workers and clients, and somehow help the system of services to reflect on itself, see its failings, and so help change the system to improve the lives of people who don't fit service providers' expectations.

If I am honest, I felt a significant degree of challenge, anxiety and hope, starting this journey in 2014, because having "change the system" on my job description seemed an ambitious task! This was particularly felt as our program was relatively small in relation to the significantly more powerful and larger resourced set of statutory services (such as the local Mental Health Trust, the Council (local government), Substance Misuse services and Criminal Justice departments.

In addition, we had no formal authority or power to change these large service sectors, so any influence would need to be earned by building relationships of trust and/or the tactful presentation of evidence as we encouraged large organisations to reflect on:

1. What they currently do well and

2. Where they currently fail people with complex needs, and therefore

3. What could they do better /differently?

My colleagues and I have tried a number of different approaches to changing the system. This chapter outlines the story of just one of these — how we have developed Psychologically Informed Environments or PIEs in our local area, in response to the research findings around systemic failure and neglect of people who are too chaotic to benefit from traditionally offered services.

Developing PIE as a Way to Change the System

When we reviewed the early quantitative and qualitative data from the experiences of our clients, we were struck by the contrast between our client group's having 98% serious mental health problems but only 20% accessing mental health services. Whatever the underlying reasons, this appeared to be a clear example of severe and enduring system failure.

I undertook a review of the national and international literature in this area. A number of studies showed clients with complex needs had more than the average levels of trauma and neglect in their childhoods, and less than the average level of skills to deal with life's adversities (e.g. Livesley, 2003, Bramley, 2015). Thus, complex needs appear to develop *in reaction* to this combination of trauma, neglect and lack of skills combined with the kind of society someone is living in (e.g. the type of housing, community groups, employment, etc. on offer locally).

This kind of explanation is supported by the research findings showing higher rates of complex needs in the Northern post-industrial towns of England compared to more affluent areas — because people with complex trauma histories will likely experience a different biographical trajectory for their life-journey in a context where there are high levels of unemployment and poor housing, compared to a social context of high employment rates and good housing options (e.g. see Bramley, 2015).

A report published by the U.K. government and the National Mental Health Development Unit (DCLG & NMHDU, 2010) had already showed that homeless people with complex trauma histories experience systemic neglect from traditional mental health services. This report offered good practice guidance on how best to meet the psychological and emotional needs of homeless people. Central to this report's argument was that it was homeless services that were engaging and working with people with complex needs in contrast to secondary mental health services, which predominantly were not.

However, staff in these services often felt overwhelmed by their task, and tended to lack training around complex trauma and mental health needs. Thus it made sense to put the resources, training and support into those frontline services that were working with the client group already, predominantly those homeless and accommodation based services. But this guidance also included many examples of services that were working constructively with these issues; and for that it adopted a term that had only very recently been coined — a Psychologically Informed Environment, or PIE (Johnson & Haigh, 2010).

By 2014, the good practice guidance ideas of 2010 had evolved further and been elaborated into a fully-developed "framework" of key issues to refer to the core areas a "psychologically informed" service would want to consider when developing its practice. This all pointed to the PIE approach being a good innovative strategy for our task of system change. A PIE aimed at building skills and knowledge of frontline staff to work better with people with complex needs by helping professionals to think about the psychological and emotional needs of homeless people. So, the PIE idea was an example of "bottom up" strategy — different from a "top down" approach to system change (such as changing government policy or by commissioning of services).

When I spoke with homeless services in the locality, I found there was a general lack of knowledge about where to or how to start developing along a PIE framework, but often a willingness and enthusiasm to do so, and an acknowledgement of the need for their service to embark on a PIE journey. I then found a wealth of further information in the PIElink (see: www.Pielink.net), a community of practice website that one of the authors of the two guidance documents, Robin Johnson, had set up to promote this way of working. It was helpfully free to join, and so its information was not hidden behind an academic institutional paywall. As it happened, I had met Robin Johnson when I previously managed a Personality Disorder Accommodation Service in Leeds, showing him around services we used there, during some of his research which led eventually to the DCLG/ NMHDU report. Thus we started a dialogue about how best to encourage the development of PIE in our locality, given limited resources.

Having reflected on the evidence, we decided to enable and encourage services to develop PIEs locally as one way to enable better journeys through the system for people with complex needs. Given our limited resources, we decided on a strategy with two work streams. We would rely on new digital technology to promote the idea of PIE, and use it as an educational platform to explain what the idea of PIEs was about, and encourage dialogue on the opportunities and challenges it raises. The second strategy was to role model good practice by setting up PIEs in three frontline services and then research and evaluate its effect.

Our Philosophical Approach to PIE: "Journeying" and "Dialogue"

From the outset, we have promoted taking a dialogical approach working with people with complex needs, philosophically drawing on the work of the Russian literary theorist Mikhail Bakhtin (1981, 1984, 1986). Bakhtin is perhaps best known for the story of an ethical dilemma he faced when he ran out of cigarette papers during a siege of a city he was stuck in. He decided to tear up his only copy of his thesis to roll his cigarettes to enable him to enjoy smoking whilst he awaited his fate and the outcome of the siege. His story illustrates his dialogical principle that knowledge is "unfinalisable" and we only ever partly know a thing in dialogue with others, so we ought not be so attached to our current ideas that we cannot let them go up in smoke.

I became familiar with dialogic approaches, but am particularly indebted to a family therapist Val Jackson for introducing me to the application of these ideas through the "Open Dialogue" approach pioneered by Jaakko Seikkula (2006) near the Arctic Circle in Western Lapland. I was fortunate to chair a working group piloting an open dialogue approach in an Early Intervention in Psychosis service in 2013, where I worked alongside and learnt a lot from Val and the client we were working with. In developing "Dialogical PIE," I had to adapt and simplify some of the ideas from Open Dialogue due to the resource constraints.

"Open Dialogue" was originally pioneered around psychotic experiences in crisis situations. Other dialogical approaches are available, such as anticipating dialogue (see Seikkula, 2006). The statutory mental health service in Western Lapland abandoned the medical model as evidently ineffective in the 1980s. England is a little slower in reflecting on the evidence of the ineffectiveness of the medical model for entrenched systemic reasons. Western Lapland developed open dialogue as a needs-adapted alternative to the medical model. The results have been outstandingly impressive and well supported by research (Seikkula, 2006), with rates of people previously diagnosed with schizophrenia who return to education or employment raising from below 10% to over 85% since this approach was adopted in the 1980s — with low or no anti-psychotic medication.

However, without the resources and experience of Western Lapland, and acknowledging the limits of what we can do, we have adopted a modest approach by applying three principles from Open Dialogue and added some principles drawn directly from Bakhtin's writings. At Fulfilling Lives, we have also been applying a dialogical approach to problematic habits of people with complex needs, which are commonly associated with the diagnostic threshold for a personality disorder. This has produced an approach to complex needs that could be called "*Journeying Dialogue*" — if it needs a name.

These are the principles we applied in terms of taking a dialogical approach:

1. We accept we only ever partly know what is going on (Open Dialogue express this principle as "tolerating uncertainty")

2. Therefore, we value and open up a dialogue between different ways of seeing an issue (an open dialogue principle)

3. We understand that human beings make sense of our journey through life via narratives and the stories we tell each other

4. It is possible to change the narrative within which we orientate (to "re-orientate") our bio-graphical life-trajectory (at any point we may change our philosophical, spiritual, faith, self-help, educational, employment, health/illness narratives we orientate our lives within)

5. Sometimes we "journey" alongside others for awhile, some of whom experience very troubled journeys through life.

6. In our work, we accept our un-finalised personalities in an unending dialogue with other un-finalised personalities.

7. We understand that we see the expressed experience of people with complex needs in the relatively remote context of our own life experience (Bakhtin, 1986)

8. We take responsibility for our role, resources and limits (boundaries) within the social network — another open dialogue principle (see Seikkula, 2006)

Such a dialogical approach agrees with Professor Livesley (2003), that an oversimplified categorical personality test such as the current DSM-5 (2013) diagnostic criteria for Personality Disorder have no therapeutic use in helping to plan someone's support.

Psychiatry's failure to reform itself in line with scientific findings over decades (See Livesley, 2012) is a symptom of a deeper systemic problem that the medical model approach to mental health often rejects working with people with complex needs — directly due to the monopoly of its modernist and positivist categorical approach. Systemically, the roots of this problem lie in psychiatry's financial relationship with *Big Pharma* (see Whitaker 2010; 2017). Even a past chair of the DSM Task-Force now argues against the increasing medicalisation of "normal" life by the APA, and DSM-5 being driven by its financial relationship with the pharmaceutical industry (Frances, 2013a; 2013b).

My view is that categorical models such as diagnosis are an outdated modern clinical tradition, increasingly irrelevant to the lived lives of people with complex trauma histories, who live in a post-modern world (Bracken, 2005). The future is dialogical. Dialogical approaches offer an alternative to meeting complex mental health needs, with a more balanced power relationship between professional and patient, because both parties are considered as unfinished personalities who only ever partly know what is going on.

Dialogical approaches appear to be both more realistic and more helpful for frontline staff in building relationships of trust with people with complex needs. Categorical personality tests like DSM-5 Personality Disorder definition (DSM-5, 2013) or other similar approaches to personality, like the Voigt-Kampff test (Dick, 1999), tend to be harmful, because of the uses they are put to by the relatively powerful professionals on behalf of the State, and their failure to assess the assessor in the dialogic exchange.

How We Developed the Original PIE Pilots

We piloted developing PIEs in three frontline services. There was a homeless drop-in day centre in Gateshead (run by Oasis Aquila Housing) and two residential mental health rehab and recovery units (run by Mental Health Concern.)

The aim was to develop in six key PIE areas, as they had been described in the earlier operational guidance and various presentations since then, which are:

1. Reflective Practice (to develop skills, maintain mental/emotional wellbeing)

2. Using a Psychological Model (to better understand ourselves and the client group)

3. A Focus on Building Relationships of Trust

4. Training and Support for staff re complex need (e.g., being trauma informed)

5. Developing the Social and Physical Space

6. Evidence Generating Practice

What we actually did in each PIE area was:

Reflective Practice

I visited each service every four weeks and facilitated a 90 minute group reflective practice session with the staff. I also promoted understanding and practice of reflective practice through the complex needs training. The evaluation of this aspect found a significant increase (31%) in use of personal reflective practice amongst staff following the training.

A Psychological Model

I designed and wrote a psychological model, Ladder4Life (Fig. 6-1, p. 95), in line with the advice from Professor Livesley (2003), who says any such model should be "in plain English" and avoid psychological jargon. I took the emerging international evidence around the social and psychological problems people with complex needs experience, and converted these into a simple narrative story about someone walking up a hill with obstacles to overcome that can be seen in that same figure.

In this narrative, a staff member, or a person struggling with multiple issues, could see themselves on a journey through life as one of the characters depicted. They may be journeying alongside someone. The desired improvement in their life Direction is represented in picture language as the top of the hill. This could be any idea someone has about the "good life" they value and wish to lead in the future (see Taylor (1989) for a discussion of the good life concept). The desired good life may include having a house, a job, a relationship, or any other-future that is better in some way. This gives the opportunity to open up dialogue about someone's *motivation* to work towards this good life.

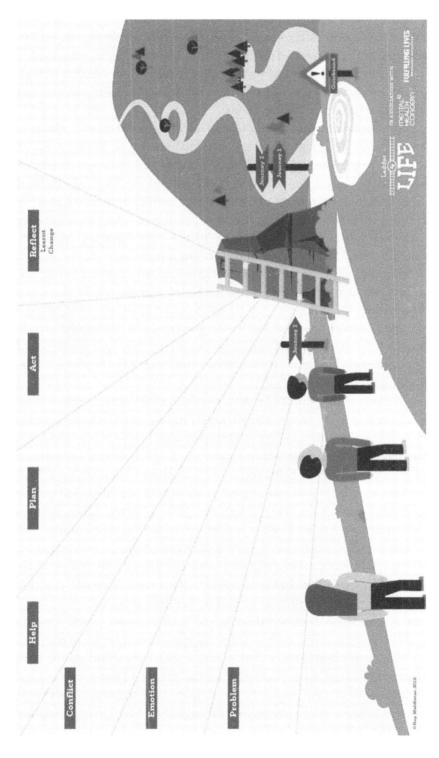

Fig. 6-1: Ladder4Life

For people with complex needs, Direction and Motivation are key difficulties linked to forming a sense of identity. In this framework, people are invited to see themselves on a Journey through life to get to the good life at the top of the hill. This draws on narrative ideas, which see that human beings primarily experience life through the stories we believe and tell ourselves and others (e.g., White, 2000).

On our journey through life we can all get side-tracked, which is represented by the dead end that leads into the blue forest. We can also all get stuck in unhelpful habits of thinking, emotions and/or actions, and this is represented visually by quicksand at the side of the path. (Unhelpful habits that stop us progressing on our journey could be anything such as self-harming, substance misuse or anxious avoidance.) Any problems we experience that prevent us from getting to the better life we desire are represented by the "Rock" in the middle of life's path.

The strengths, skills or good habits of thinking, emotion and/or action that we practice to overcome life's problems are represented by the seven rungs of a Ladder4Life. People with complex trauma histories tend to have less than the average level of skills (or good habits) to handle strong emotions such as anger, guilt, shame, low mood, joy, fear and anxiety, so I have represented skills in this area by the second rung of the ladder — skills in "Handling Emotion."

The second general point to be drawn from reviewing the international literature is that people with complex needs have more than the average amount of difficulty in managing relationships, so I have represented this with the rung of the ladder which opens up a space to dialogue about "asking for Help" and the third rung which is about "handing conflict." People with complex trauma or neglect tend to find interpersonal power relationships difficult. For example, they may have difficulty functioning in social relationships due to being too submissive or too dominating. The rung around conflict is a space to allow a dialogue to open up to reflect on how people tend to react when the inevitable conflict of wills crops up on their journey through life. Bakhtin reflects that our will passes through zones involving other people's wills, and is therefore refracted.

There is also good evidence that people with complex needs struggle with problem solving skills, such as assessing the size of a problem realistically, planning a solution (rather than acting impulsively), putting the plan into action, and reflecting productively on the plan, so I put four rungs of the ladder to allow a conversation to open up on how someone tends to be in these areas while they are journeying through their life. Three figures are represented, because people with complex needs are more sensitive to their social context than the average citizen, so they tend to end up in poor housing or abusive relationships where they can be retraumatised, but equally, moving to a more positive supported accommodation or building positive trusting relationships with staff can have a positive influence.

Thus, I have tried to sum up key social/psychological points in understanding people with complex needs, or ourselves as staff, into a simple story about going on a journey up a hill and overcoming some problems on the way. I then interview clients and/or staff on this 10 point framework and open up a dialogue about the *helpful habits (skills) and unhelpful habits* in each area to reflect upon.

I introduced the framework to staff teams to help them reflect upon themselves and their clients. I also used the framework to interview experts by experience, and produce PIE training films. I produced an animated film explaining these key points (Middleton, 2017 b).

Training and Support

In addition to the ninety-minute group reflective practice sessions every four weeks, we co-produced and co-delivered a training course using the Ladder4Life resources, using a reflective practice approach. Research was then undertaken to evaluate the effect of this approach on staff. The evaluation found worker's knowledge and skills around complex needs improved 36%, their understanding of a psychological relationship improved 25%, and their personal reflective practice increased by 31% as a result of the complex needs training (see: www.fulfillinglives-ng.org.uk).

By reflecting on the international evidence, and in the light of my own practice in working with people who are homeless with complex needs, I concluded there were five key skills worth focusing on initially in training. I remembered these through a mnemonic A, B, C, D, E:

- **A = Accepting and Engaging** people as they are (e.g., Listening and Validation skills)

- **B = Believing** they can Get Better (e.g., Motivational Interviewing skills)

- **C = Collaboration** (e.g., co-production in helping overcome obstacles on the journey)

- **D = Develop Trust in Relationship** (e.g., be reliable, consistent approach, communicate clearly)

- **E = Establish your Role and Boundaries** (e.g., manage realistic expectation of what you can do)

Building Relationships of Trust

In the training, in the resources, and in the reflective practice sessions, particular emphasis is placed on the value and importance of building relationships of trust — both between clients and staff, but also among staff within the service who are doing a very difficult and challenging job. The building up of trust took time, but it could be seen in the reflective practice sessions as attendees felt able to disclose more of the uncertainty of the work and the emotional wear and tear it provokes trying to build relationships with people who understandably find relationships difficult. The high levels of trauma and neglect in people's lives directly links to this need to develop trust in relationships as people have often many experiences of their trust being broken and let down, including from services.

Social and Physical Space

Services were invited to reflect on how the physical and social space could be improved. Often there were resources limitations to what could be done, but Oasis Aquila Housing did change their space significantly, and the manager, Phil Conn, reflects on this in a film interview "What it is like implementing PIE on the frontline to improve services?" (Middleton 2016x).

Action Learning and Evidence Generating Practice

The original PIE pilots were evaluated (Boobis, 2016), and the findings fed back for all to reflect upon. The complex needs training course was evaluated separately. The "Training the PIE Facilitator" course for frontline staff is currently being evaluated and its publication date is pending. There has been considerable interest in these PIE pilots, and so two further research projects are underway to evaluate these pilot PIEs. We have declined further evaluation requests so as not to overwhelm the staff with being evaluated around PIE!

The first national PIE evaluation and practice conference was in January, 2017, and we were pleased to be invited to present the initial evaluation by Sophie Boobis. It was good to learn from what others are doing around evaluation of PIE, as this is an emerging field, hence the phrase "evidence generating practice," which seems appropriate to innovative work that is breaking new ground.

New Work Requires New Genres

Formal research evidence, though useful and informative, is only one manifestation of a wider culture shift many people are trying to create around working with people with complex needs. This shift is towards developing *the learning organisation* and creating a culture of inquiry. Techniques such as action learning sets, staff developing PIE reflecting and learning together about what works and what is difficult and challenging, are an essential part of this wider culture shift working with this client group.

I think dialogical concepts drawn from Bakhtin can contribute to this wider culture shift as dialogism is essentially an epistemology — where the truth is created in a dialogue between unfinished personalities who only ever partly know what is going on. I think this way of being, ontologically, better resonates with how most staff feel working in the health and social sector with people with complex needs with its inevitable emotional wear and tear.

Using New Digital Technology

To promote the idea of PIE using new technology, I searched the internet and found a live-streaming app, called Blab that allowed me to run live chats online where people from around the world could join in and ask questions about PIE. I realised the challenge of the medium was to create great content from the shows, which had real value for staff in frontline services.

I recorded the shows as PIE training films, and saved them to You Tube in case the startup for the live-streaming app went bust — which it did! Initially I created a series of PIE training films and made them freely available online, such as interviewing Robin Johnson as the originator of the PIE concept to explain what it was about to a wider audience (Middleton 2016a).

Via Robin, and by experimenting with live homeless talk-shows formats, I met Jay Levy from the USA. (An example of this genre is Middleton 2016b.) I was impressed with Jay's ideas in his books, outlining his five principles of pre-treatment. So, I invited him to be interviewed live and online from the USA, to promote his ideas about engaging rough sleepers (Middleton 2016c).

Originally, I started making actual films on my iPad in response to a manager who said they struggled to free up stretched frontline staff to attend my PIE training, so I reflected — dialogically — that if I put some of the key ideas into films and made them freely available online, would that adapt what I offer enough to meet the needs of the service? And they thought it would be very helpful as staff could more easily have thirty minutes free to watch a training film and then reflect with colleagues on the content over a cup of tea.

The first of these films received positive feedback, and had over 1,000 frontline staff watch it (Middleton 2016c). However, I found it difficult and stressful at times as I had to teach myself a new set of skills, using Doctor "Google," around hosting talk shows and making films. It helped that my employing organisations and line manager were supportive of my trying innovations, even when it could be hard initially to see the value of them, and which involved new work practices such as occasionally having a sign on my door, which read, "Please do not disturb — live-streaming blab talk-show in progress!"

In addition to demonstrating the value of interviewing experts like Robin and Jay, we wanted to demonstrate valuing the voice of "experts by experience," so we produced a series of films interviewing a group of people we were working with from among our clients, for example, asking them why (Middleton 2016d) asking for help is difficult. Feedback from staff on our Ladder4Life PIE training course was very positive about hearing the voice of experts by experience, so we did a further set of longer in-depth one-to-one interviews with two of our current clients (an example of which is Georgia's Journey: Middleton 2016e).

We have also started working on a new innovation in PIE, which we are calling Digitally Enhanced Reflective Practice (DERP) with Newcastle University's Human-Computer interaction research group, Open Lab (openlab.ncl.ac.uk). We are really pleased to be working with Doctoral Researcher Jay Rainey from Open Lab to co-produce with our experts by experience audio technology that will allow people with complex needs, staff and PIE facilitators to reflect on their experiences — recorded on an app on a smart phone (currently in a Beta testing phase).

The aim is to use new audio technology to create reflective learning communities around people with complex needs. We hope to create new knowledge dialogically by listening to and valuing the stories of people with lived experience, and enabling people to connect and reflect on their own narratives. This can then be produced into content for training staff to increase their skills.

Scalability: The Next Steps

After reflecting on the research evidence from the initial PIE pilots, we decided to write and deliver a "Training the PIE facilitator" course and then pilot it at ten services. Ten frontline staff from services were invited to attend a one day Ladder4Life PIE facilitator training course. They were then asked to develop PIE in another service. Specifically, they were asked to visit another service within the ten pilot sites to run ninety-minute reflective practice sessions every four weeks.

They were asked to swap with another service so they would become an external facilitator not working with the service day to day. They did this, using the resources developed such as the Ladder4Life framework and films. They often showed one of the films co-produced with experts by experience for twenty minutes at the start of each session, and then facilitated the staff team to reflect on what they had listed to using the framework. Some facilitators built their confidence up using this approach to the point they felt able to ask the staff team to reflect on their work with clients without showing a film.

Part of the thinking behind developing this "Training the PIE facilitator" model is the belief that it is good to build the skills and capacity of frontline staff rather than paying for a clinical psychologist to visit the service once a month. Also, few services can afford to buy in specialist facilitators, and so it seemed wise to build up a model that could be sustainable in the long run at low cost. This Ladder4Life PIE pilot is now being assessed by three independent researchers to evaluate its effectiveness. An evaluation from Fulfilling Lives will be soon published. Informal feedback from the staff involved has been very positive in terms of building the skills to work with people with complex needs, and their capacity to reflect productively.

Since then, interest in PIE has been building momentum and been given further impetus by local commissioners increasingly requesting services demonstrate how they are developing as PIEs. In London, Westminster City Council, having experienced the value of PIE, asked Clare Ritchie to write an implementation and assessment guide (Ritchie, 2015). In the UK, commissioning of new services now often uses this Westminster guidance as the basis for asking for evidence that services are developing PIEs. Here at Fulfilling Lives, we were pleased to be consulted on the drafting of the document. Within the Westminster PIE Guidance (tinyurl.com/ladder4pie), the Ladder4Life PIE is referenced as an example of good practice.

Opening dialogue, to see issues from many new perspectives, is helping to transform the way we understand the real work of homelessness services in the UK, and inform the development of our PIEs. So I'd like to think that this book, by opening a new dialogue between the US and the UK, will have a part to play in helping us understanding homelessness and complex needs far better, and especially, in finding better responses.

References

American Psychiatric Association (2013) *Diagnostic and Statistical Manual of Mental Disorders: DSM-5.* Fifth Edition. Arlington: American Psychiatric Association

Bakhtin, M. M. (1981) translation by C. Emerson & M. Holquist, (editor) *The Dialogic Imagination: four essays.* Austin: The University of Texas Press

Bakhtin M. M. (1986) translation by V. W. McGee, C. Emerson, & M. Holquist (editors) *Speech Genres and Other Late Essays.* Austin: University of Texas Press

Bakhtin M. M. (1984) translation by C. Emerson (editor) *Problems of Dostoyevsky's poetics.* University of Minnesota Press

Bramley G. & Fitzpatrick S. (2015) *Hard Edges: Mapping Multiple and Severe Disadvantage.* (England) Lankelly Chase Foundation http://lankellychase.org.uk/wp-content/uploads/2015/07/Hard-Edges-Mapping-SMD-2015.pdf

Boobis, S. (2016) *Evaluation of a Dialogical Psychologically Informed Environment (PIE) Pilot,* Ann Arbor, MI: Loving Healing Press Inc.

Bracken, P. & Thomas, P. (2005) *Postpsychiatry: mental health in a postmodern world.* Oxford University Press

DCLG & NMHDU, (Department of Communities and Local Government and the National Mental Health Development Unit (2010) *Meeting the psychological and emotional needs of homeless people.* available at http://pielink.net/the-idea-2/

Dick, P. K. (1999) *Do Androids Dream of Electric Sheep?* Orion Publishing Group

Frances, A. (2013 a) *Saving Normal: an insider's revolt against out-of-control psychiatric diagnosis, DSM-5, big pharma, and the medicalization of ordinary life.* New York: William Morrow

Frances, A. (2013 b) *Essentials of psychiatric diagnosis: Responding to the challenge of DSM-5.* New York: Guilford

Johnson, R. (2016) *Is the PIE evolving?* (summary) available at: http://pielink.net/is-the-pie-evolving/

Livesley, J. (2003) *Practical Management of Personality Disorder.* The Guilford Press

Livesley, J. (2012) Tradition versus empiricism in the current DSM-5 proposal for revising the classification of personality disorders *Criminal Behaviour and Mental Health* 22(2): 81-90

Middleton, R. (2016) Ladder4Life [graphic] *Narrative social-psychological framework.* Newcastle, England: JUMP

Seikkula, J. (2011) Becoming Dialogical: Psychotherapy or a way of Life? *The Australian and New Zealand Journal of Family Therapy.* 32(3): 179-193

Seikkula, J. and Arnkill, T. E. (2006) *Dialogical Meetings in Social Networks.* H. Karnac (Books) Ltd.

Taylor C. (1989) *Sources of the Self: The making of modern identity.* Cambridge University Press

Whitaker, R. (2010) *Anatomy of an Epidemic: Magic Bullets, Psychiatric Drugs and the rise of Mental Illness in America.* New York: Broadway Books Crown Publishing Group

Whitaker, R. (2017) *Mad in America: Science, Society and Social Justice* [website] https://www.madinamerica.com/ accessed 03/01/2017

White M. (2000) *Reflections on Narrative Practice: Essays and Interviews.* Adelaide: Dulwich Centre Publications

Film references:

Middleton, R. (2016a) PIE training Film: Interview with Robin Johnson: *What is PIE (Psychologically Informed Environment)?* [video] https://youtu.be/NKrFI5Bvndg

Middleton, R. (2016b) Film : *International Chat Show: Improving Homeless Services.* [video] https://youtu.be/nHw1XK7exEI

Middleton, R. (2016c) PIE training Film : *International Exchange of ideas — Interviewing Jay Levy from USA about his 5 principles of Pre-Treatment* [video] https://youtu.be/_lJ-QzdyC6g

Middleton, R. (2016d) Film: *How to combine two innovations — Open Dialogue ideas from Western Lapland (i.e., Bakhtin) and PIE.* retrieved from https://youtu.be/bYWXWfVAcEM

Middleton, R. (2016e) *Discussion with experts by experience with complex needs: Why is asking for Help hard?* [video] https://youtu.be/XTDAbF6qLac

Middelton , R (2016x) : *Interview with Phil Conn, Manager of Homeless Day Centre in Gateshead.* [video] https://youtu.be/4ruu5fwmKS4

Middleton R. (2017 a) *Learning from Georgia's journey through homelessness, mental health & addiction* [video] https://youtu.be/J6MHidZCAmI

Middleton R. (2017 b) *Episode 1 Trauma Informed PIE (Psychologically Informed Environment) Ladder4life* [video] https://youtu.be/nTAcv7GOuv4

Organisations:

Fulfilling Lives is a non-profit programme working towards system change for the benefit people with multiple and complex needs: http://www.fulfillinglives-ng.org.uk/

Mental health Concern is a mental health charity
http://www.mentalhealthconcern.org/

Oasis Aquila Housing is a homeless Charity:
http://www.oasisaquilahousing.org.gridhosted.co.uk/

Open Lab https://openlab.ncl.ac.uk/about/ is a human-computer interaction, social and ubiquitous computing research group in the School of Computing Science at Newcastle University.

Pielink www.pielink.net is an online community of practice for those interested in developing Psychologically Informed Environments (P.I.E) as a way to develop better services for people with complex needs.

7 Peer Advocacy: Here, There, and Everywhere
Jay S. Levy

Today, we will put aside the word "treatment," and instead talk about "healing"… we will not speak of "counseling," but rather of "consoling;" we will not speak of "illness," but rather of "woundedness".

— Pat Deegan (1986)

One of the most exciting recent developments in human services throughout the US and UK is that the Peer Movement has steadily grown and has become a widely accepted best practice. It has taken root, and there is no turning back!

Ray Middleton, who is an "expert from experience" and a doctoral student in Social Psychology, has facilitated the transatlantic dialogue between his British colleagues and me via the internet, which led directly to this project. It was through his and Robin Johnson's efforts that we began to contrast and compare the elements of PIE with the principles of Pretreatment.

One of the benefits of our dialogue was the discovery of how our thinking had converged in regard to Ray's use of "Open Dialogue" and the development of Dialogical PIE with my writings and ideas on "Common Language Construction." These concepts are central to our attempts at bridging the cross-cultural divide between staff and clients.

In fact, Peer and non-Peer workers alike benefit from the integration of these concepts into their practice. This is not only true in our efforts to directly reach out and engage people without homes, but also in our attempt to form a team approach to helping based on a common language of words, ideas, and values that can provide a guiding humanistic philosophy to our work. Further, these same concepts can be used to help cross the cultural divide that may exist between team members inclusive of, but not limited to, bridging the differences between Peer and non-Peer Team members.

Peer Advocacy and Outreach in NYC, Boston, and Western MA

I began working in the field of Homeless Services back in 1988. My first job was with the Manhattan Bowery Corporation providing homeless outreach via the bus terminals, subways stations and streets of NYC. When visiting places like the Port Authority, Penn Station, Grand Central Station, and Central Park, we proceeded with caution. Safety was highly valued both by us and the people we were attempting to serve.

In order to stay safe in these chaotic and highly stimulating environments, we almost always worked in pairs. We often did outreach by having one team member approach the person who appeared to be homeless, while the other team member stayed back to observe the surrounding environment and assure that it was free from any evident threats before joining in with the conversation. The team members who usually served as our initial check on safety were bi-lingual (English/ Spanish or Street Slang) and in recovery from addiction, as well as formerly homeless. They were known as Peer advocates and they were a vital part of our team outreach approach to homelessness.

We worked in multidisciplinary teams composed of social workers, nurses, and peer advocates. It was the peer workers who knew the streets, the best haunts of where people without homes gathered, and were adept at introducing us to some people who would not readily engage with us otherwise. My memories of those days were colored by the strong sense of companionship I felt with all team members. While I am sure that there was a sense of hierarchy when it came to certain clinical considerations, I also know that we respected the opinion of our workers who had firsthand knowledge of homelessness and the recovery process. They were our "experts from experience."

During that same time period, I visited Fountain House in NYC. It's a special place where people who experienced mental health issues could gather and give voice to their needs, wants and aspirations. It is a bottom-up model where the members essentially organize and run the club. Fountain House was known as a social club or clubhouse model that served to empower people with mental illness by stepping away from clinical jargon and/or medical language and thereby embracing people on a more humane level by speaking in human terms.

As Psychologist and Peer advocate Pat Deegan (1986) said, "Today, we will put aside the word 'treatment', and instead talk about 'healing'... we will not speak of 'counseling', but rather of 'consoling'; we will not speak of 'illness', but rather of 'woundedness'..." It is where empathy and the good work begin.

Fountain House was the first establishment of the clubhouse movement that now has a significant national and international presence in North America and Europe. This movement very quickly showed that people can achieve their potential through the power of group acceptance and the formation of a caring community. Over the past 30 years, I have worked closely with clubhouses in NYC, Boston and Western MA, and I am thankful for their critical role in helping people who have experienced homelessness, trauma and loss. Throughout our many outreach journeys, the clubhouses have been there time and time again to be a welcoming and accepting place for people without homes who present with complex needs.

Over the past several years, one of the exciting new developments across Massachusetts has been the introduction of Recovery Learning Communities (RLCs) for people with mental health concerns. An RLC is a safe and accepting place where people with mental health concerns can gather and share their stories, as well as attend groups and learn about alternative ways of helping one another. The RLCs encourage Open Dialogue approaches (Bakhtin, 1981; Siekkula, 2006), as discussed by Ray Middleton in the previous chapter, such as Hearing Voices groups and psychosocial methods to support recovery, rather than restricting one's options to psychotropic medication and other traditional medical model treatment approaches.

The Hearing Voices group is a prime example of this philosophy in that it supports exploration, rather than labeling, targeting, and diminishing symptoms with psychotropic medications. An Open Dialogue approach welcomes the opportunity to understand the "voice" as part of the person and to thereby explore what it means to the person, rather than simply trying to extinguish it through prescribed medications. Open Dialogue approaches encourage people to consider viable roads for recovery, whether it be traditional or non-traditional methods, in a non-hierarchical manner. There is no upfront preferred approach, though success is ultimately rooted in providing the client choice of psychosocial considerations, medical model and/or traditional methods, or a combination there of, as well as the maintenance and development of helping networks to promote recovery, among other options.

More recently, Peer-run recovery drop-in centers have flourished in Massachusetts as part of the response to the opioid epidemic. Building off of the Peer/self-help concept of AA, this model has expanded its reach to include people who may be contemplative of change, but are actively using. It is based on a harm-reduction philosophy, so sobriety is not a preliminary requirement. The centers are conveniently located and welcoming to people who are in need of warmth, companionship or just a place to feel safe. Peers or "experts from experience" reach out to those in need and can offer case management services, recovery groups and access to detox facilities, among other services and resources.

Nationally, there has been a federal initiative to integrate Peers with our PATH (Projects Assisting Transitions from Homelessness) Outreach Teams. I manage several PATH outreach teams across Massachusetts and have had the pleasure of hiring, supervising and overseeing the integration of Peer Specialists with existing clinically trained team members.

This is not as distinct as it sounds, as I have always been in favor of hiring team members who are both clinically trained and had developed an expertise through firsthand experience. This has resulted in many staff members utilizing their personal recovery from mental health concerns, addiction, and/or homelessness to inform their day-to-day work. It also means that self-care and providing a culture with staff that promotes this value is critical to our success.

Whether it is Peer or non-peer staff, staying emotionally centered and healthy is a key component to providing quality outreach services, and therefore must be formally addressed by providing opportunities for reflective practice and adequate support and supervision of staff. Our challenge as a diverse team with multiple personal experiences, differing levels of education and different areas of expertise has been to find a common language to inform our mission of outreach and engagement with people experiencing homelessness. Coming together around our joint mission in support of one another is an empowering experience. A Pretreatment approach as a guide for informing staff supervision, client assessment and enhancing communication between staff members through a common language has served this purpose.

Sharing Stories

Drawing from my own experiences of outreach in a variety of settings ranging from the streets of NYC to the woods and riversides of Western Massachusetts, I have come to believe in the power of narrative, and this is reflected throughout my writings. Telling stories is an all too human way of communication, which has served us well through the ages. We have come to understand the *Power of Myth* (Campbell, 1988), whether it be in written form or part of an oral tradition of storytelling, to help put forth and preserve our sense of culture, values and important lessons learned. The wisdom we can garner is often best communicated in the form of a story or narrative.

Similarly, Michael White (2000), the founder of Narrative therapy, views our life journey as something that can be understood as a story and can thereby be examined and reframed by its author. Epston and White (1992) state, "In striving to make sense of life, persons have the task of arranging their experiences of events in sequences across time in such a way as to arrive at a coherent account of themselves and the world around them... This account can be referred to as a story or self-narrative."

The Peer movement is informed by the personal stories of its members and has much to teach us, as long as we are willing to listen. Their success and recovery are in many ways dependent upon the construction of a narrative, and yet we won't have the privilege to hear it if we intrude with our treatment-based language and program-centered agenda. We would be wise to respect that people are the authors of their own stories (Epston & White, 1992; Freedman & Combs, 1996).

We can create the opportunity for people to construct their own narratives by providing client-centered relationships that encourage people to find their "voice," and thereby get perspective on their journey. Our role is to encourage Open Dialogue and foster a Common Language to spur a Being Here connection (Levy, 2010). A Being Here connection is best exemplified when both the client and worker establish a common frame of reference, sharing the same house of language, so issues can be jointly explored and new narratives can be formed, while always respecting the autonomy of the person. This invariably strengthens the client-worker relationship and future dialogue. It is through this dynamic process that we can begin to hear one another and consider different points of view. Our task is to ultimately help the people we meet to share their expertise with themselves and others, or as Ray states in the previous chapter, "The future is dialogic."

The Peer Movement Dilemma: Many Houses of Language, but too few Playgrounds

Over my many years of bearing witness to the Peer movement, as well as through my direct involvement working with "experts from experience," I have observed a great variety of approaches to helping. Of course, a similar tale could be told about traditional service workers as well. In many respects, the Peer movement is a relatively recent occurrence and still coming of age. Nevertheless, some confusion abounds as to who is actually a peer and what should be part of a standardized Peer training to promote the many roads to recovery.

After all, there have been many formulations of Self-Help organizations, ranging from Alcoholics Anonymous (AA) to Recovery Learning Communities (RLCs). In regard to each organization and the culture (House of Language) it imparts to its members, the notion of who is a peer and how to support the recovery process varies. Through my own work, I have struggled with the question of who is a Peer. For instance, I employ staff who are veterans or ex-military service members, or others who are in recovery from addiction, while others who have experienced poverty, mental health issues, trauma, homelessness, or who identify as a member of a minority group. In fact, in many respects, I play the role of Peer for the people I supervise, because I have a form of "lived work experience" from my many years of outreach counseling. All of us view our work through a Pretreatment lens and draw from our own life experiences, as well as our own developed personal, educational and work expertise to help each other and the people who we serve. At the same time, we respect and invariably remind one another that there is not one right road to recovery.

From the standpoint of our PATH Homeless Outreach contract, as well as from the viewpoint of Peer Certification trainings, the Peer role is quite distinct from a clinical role. It is often defined by a particular set of life experiences (trauma, systemic frustrations, disempowerment, situational concerns, etc.) and one's recovery mixed with engagement and advocacy to help promote acceptance, safety and empowerment for people with complex needs. In many respects, the Peer is the client's liaison who supports transitions into chosen systems of care, while also identifying the barriers to membership and advocating for policies that support inclusion and empowerment. The Peer movement stands as an important check, illuminating the critical parts of the system that is currently insensitive to people's needs, as well as helping us to formulate needed systemic change.

A few years ago, I participated in a planning committee with "experts from experience" in order to facilitate a Community Conversation on Mental Health and Homelessness. Early on in the planning process, the sensitivity to language was raised by people with "lived experience" to demonstrate the built-in cultural bias and stigma people with mental health concerns face. They then suggested better ways to make folks more comfortable in discussing Mental Health topics. This is an important educational piece that experts from experience can share with others.

After all, we are people first and should not be identified by our diagnosis, because such labels as "schizophrenic" or "manic-depressive person" are oppressive in that they discount our dynamic nature and can negatively impact our identity. This is not just true in regard to the Peer movement, but is also part of the development from Existentialism (Sartre, 1956) to Postmodernism (Derrida, 1976) and how it characterizes the human condition by understanding our 'being' as inseparable from action (e.g., To Do is to Be). In other words, we are always "becoming," and in that respect undefinable. We are thereby dynamic beings who can never be wholly labeled by one specific trait, action, or diagnosis.

Our conference planning committee ultimately had longer discussions about banning certain phrases or words from the Community Conversation on Mental Health and Homelessness. This included commonly used phrases such as "mental illnesses," or more specific diagnostic terms such as "schizophrenia." This seemed a bit ironic considering that there are many roads to recovery, as espoused by the Peer movement, and that one of those roads includes the acceptance of mental illness and some traditional treatment methods.

The planning committee struggled with this point of contention through many meetings. In the end, much credit can be given to all involved as we were able to work out a "common language" and understanding among ourselves that promoted community conversation without any phrases being prohibited from the dialogue. We found a balance by constructing a "safe space" for dialogue that welcomed all points of view, while encouraging sensitivity and respect to others throughout the community conversation.

Within Peer communities, conflicts have sometimes arisen and continue to cause some confusion, such as over the names/labels of organizations. For example, the National Alliance for the Mentally Ill (NAMI) has recently gone through some upheaval and conflict with its members. Historically, this organization was first developed by family members of people diagnosed with mental illness, but has now evolved to people with mental health concerns directly advocating for themselves along with family members and other advocates. In turn, this brought up the issue as to whether the name of the organization is outdated because it uses the term "mentally ill," as some of its members have understandably raised concerns about the effectiveness of the medical model of mental health and its role in stigmatizing or perhaps even propagating oppressive practices. This conversation continues.

All of this is part and parcel of an advocacy-social justice movement and people finding their own voice, as well as freely expressing the trauma and anger that they have and often continue to experience at the hands of so called "professionals," or even allies who have not kept pace with newly accepted practices.

So here we are — left with the complexities of the Peer movement and its several formulations, not unlike traditional approaches to addiction and mental health. There are many Houses of Language, and so it is hard to fully understand its development and how it can become representative of all involved. Perhaps different approaches for different types of concerns and experiences are an inevitable part of the beautiful tapestry of advocacy and recovery. Nevertheless, I can't help but wonder about the need for more "safe spaces" where we can form "playgrounds of common language" that welcome discussions of our differences, commonalities, and all the approaches that abound toward helping one another.

Only, now it can and should be done by hearing and listening to the many voices of the people who are experts from their own life experiences. The Peer movement has moved forward with establishing best practices, and a unified approach via Peer Certification trainings and instituting innovative creative dialogue approaches such as Intentional Peer Support (IPS).

Shery Mead (http://www.intentionalpeersupport.org/what-is-ips/), the founder of IPS, states,

> As peer support in mental health proliferates, we must be mindful of our intention: social change. It is not about developing more effective services, but rather about creating dialogues that have influence on all of our understandings, conversations, and relationships.

What is of paramount importance is that we continue to find ways that encourage dialogue and exploration, rather than shutting it down.

We Are All Peers — No more us and them

For the first time in many years, I recently attended the National Health Care for the Homeless Conference in Washington, DC during June of 2017. I was awestruck by the degree of integration the Peer network had achieved with all of the daily activities of the conference. Whether it was leading presentations, co-presenting, asking questions and sharing comments from the audience, receiving awards, running booths, or leading protests across from the White House, the Peer community participated with both grace and confidence, while putting forth a powerful message for all to consider.

The Health Care for the Homeless Conference was both planned and enhanced through the contributions of these experts from experience, and all of us benefited. Hearing their stories was a powerful and moving experience. It enabled us to get a better understanding of the multiple paths to recovery, and several ways that human services can play a critical role by establishing person centered relationships that help people give voice to their homeless plight, goals, and aspirations for a better future.

The Peer movement, like any movement, is part of a process with a beginning, middle, and end. It has evolved, and over the last several years it has risen to new heights. In many respects it has become an integrated part of our daily practice in both the US and UK. I can imagine a time when our continued dialogues will help to create a different reality.

Perhaps, a time will come when there will be no more "us" and "them." Human service providers and participants will join on a more human level through a new human service culture that upholds and values people's experiences, stories, and the many roads to recovery. We will realize that we are more alike than different, and will inhabit the same house of language… one that we have developed together to inform better practice.

Both Pretreatment and PIE are based on what has been learned by directly listening to people without homes, as well as to the staff who have worked alongside them. Both of these approaches can provide a new lens for exploring and understanding effective ways of helping. PIE and Pretreatment, through the integration of Open Dialogue, Common Language Construction, and "getting where people are at" value first and foremost the development of trusting relationships that are respectful of people's autonomy, while tapping into their culture, language, strengths and aspirations. Or as Ray Middleton states in the previous chapter,

> My view would be that categorical models such as diagnosis are an outdated modern clinical tradition, increasingly irrelevant to the lived lives of people with complex trauma histories, who are living in a post-modern world. The future is dialogical.

Our mission is cross-cultural in the sense of integrating the peer world — words, ideas, and values — with the world of non-peer staff, and our efforts to form a common language to have a team approach to helping those in need. Our journey continues in the next chapter where Suzanne Quinney introduces us to the language of Appreciative Inquiry and how it can tap into people's strengths through the transformative process of dialogue.

References

Bakhtin, M. M., (1981) translation by C. Emerson, & M. Holquist, (editor) *The Dialogic Imagination: four essays* Austin: The University of Texas Press

Campbell, J., with Moyers, B. (1988) *The Power of Myth*. New York, NY: MJF Books

Deegan, P. E. (1986) Excerpts from *Accepting the challenge to care*. Presented on 5/8/86 at Metropolitan State Hospital, Waltham, MA.

Derrida, J. (1976) Of Grammatology, trans. G. C. Spivak. Batimore: The John Hopkins University Press

Freedman, J. & Combs, G. (1996) *Narrative therapy: The social construction of preferred realities*. New York: W. W. Norton Company, Inc

Levy, J. S. (2010) *Homeless narratives & pretreatment pathways: From words to housing*. Ann Arbor, MI: Loving Healing Press

Mead, S. (2017) Intentional Peer Support (IPS) website: http://www.intentionalpeersupport.org/what-is-ips/

Sartre, J. P. (1956) *Being and Nothingness*. New York, New York: Washington Square Press

Seikkula, J. (2011) Becoming Dialogical: Psychotherapy or a way of Life? *The Australian and New Zealand Journal of Family Therapy*. 32(3): 179-193

White M. (2000) *Reflections on Narrative Practice: Essays and Interviews*. Adelaide: Dulwich Centre Publications

8 Telling a different story: Appreciative Inquiry's Contribution to Creating Dialogue and Psychologically Informed Environments
Suzanne Quinney

You can enlarge the conversation by taking your focus off the negative and noticing all the things that are going right, taking a stand for the goodness of humanity.

— Pam Grout

Part 1 - Learning and Building on strengths — Appreciative Inquiry and Psychologically Informed Environments

What if we (the public, and staff delivering services) related to hostel residents by learning more about their strengths and how to build on those? This was the question I asked myself, and which started my work with the staff and residents at King George's hostel and subsequently with staff and residents at other Westminster hostels in London. This work is described in detail in two articles I wrote with Leo Richardson for *Housing Care and Support* (Quinney & Richardson, 2014, Vol 17, Numbers 2 & 3) but here I want to tease out the wider picture, and connections.

It was partway through this work that I came across the concept of a PIE, and saw immediately how Appreciative Inquiry (AI) fitted into it and supported it. Here I would also like to contribute some examples from AI work that I am doing to support learning and strengths in other sectors, and then to indicate some of the overlap that an AI approach has with some of the strands mentioned in previous chapters, and indeed some of the reason why AI is such a good fit with a PIE.

That first question was prompted by conversations with hostel staff and residents, which mentioned the frequency with which a resident made progress, but then when faced with a setback, they responded by going back into addiction/chaotic behaviour and losing some of the progress they had made — the "revolving door." Staff from some of the hostels I knew made reference to people being tired of telling, and being identified by, the story of their problems. Thus I was prompted to think about how to encourage the telling, and hopefully the living, of different stories.

Appreciative Inquiry (AI) sprung naturally to mind, since one of the pillars of AI is its use of storytelling, and its explicit recognition that focusing on and telling different stories allows different narratives and outcomes to emerge and develop. Having already used an AI framework to research and write a number of case studies on hostels known for their good practice, I knew that AI was a good fit. I also had a number of conversations with my AI colleagues in the AI network about my approach, as at that time I was not aware of any references to the use of AI in homeless hostels.

One of the things I value about AI is that, underpinned by a deep philosophy, it has a simple framework and set of tools that can be applied to virtually any situation or setting. It offers staff a psychologically reflective model for building wellbeing and resilience, working from their own strengths and those of their clients. It is immensely practical, and although less costly (in time and money) than most therapeutic approaches, it has many evidenced therapeutic benefits. It supports creativity and innovation while building trust and a genuine feeling of "we are working together" between staff and residents.

AI draws on the power of social constructionism (Berger & Luckman, 1966), which describes how our worlds, the stories that we tell about ourselves and our life, and the meaning that we give to things are socially constructed. Once this is known, it is possible to question our construction of a given situation and to co-create different ones. It also allows us to accept and include other people's constructed realities and so to work with a richer view of the world. Harlene Anderson (2001) sums this up:

> We are in continuous conversation with each other and with ourselves. Through conversation we form and reform our life experiences and events; we create and recreate our meanings and understandings; and we construct and reconstruct our realities and ourselves. Some conversations enhance possibility; others diminish it.

The concept of (co-) constructing different stories can be made explicit, or implicitly included in any AI session. In hostels, it can include the staff telling different stories about themselves as workers, and about the role of the hostel, as well as different stories about the residents they work with and those they interact with on an informal day to day basis in the hostel and on the streets. For the residents, it can be about them telling a different story about themselves — their past, their present or their future. This is not about denying the hard elements of their lives, but about shining a different lens on aspects of them. It is also about explicitly elaborating on and amplifying their strengths and expanding awareness of options and possibilities. Attention is both a searchlight and a fertilizer.

After posing that question (above) to myself and to the manager of King George's, we were fortunate to be supported by Westminster City Council to develop this approach. The first step was then to train the staff team in AI and its principles, and to co-design with some of them the process of working with residents. This took a number of different forms or stages, beginning with a three-day residential at a Youth Hostel in North London. This helped us keep costs down and allowed us to go out of the daily atmosphere of the hostel, which is right in the heart of London.

AI is very adaptable to short and longer processes. During the whole programme in Westminster, the staff and I eventually organised a number of events of different lengths — two hours, half day, a whole day — in order to suit the interests of different residents (those with dogs, for example, didn't want to do a residential where they couldn't bring their animals). A second phase was training more cohorts of staff from other hostels so that they could use AI in their own workplace, and they could also attend a residential with residents from their own hostels.

At the time, there were a number of new elements to this way of working, and we felt it was important that residents had a taste of what was to be involved before they signed themselves up, so we ran a short introduction session in the hostel. This included a simple summary of the approach and a practical activity with staff and residents together.

Some of the key elements of the programme were focusing on residents' strengths and encouraging them to think about their own future plans in a creative way, then asking them to decide on small steps towards their goal. The learning environment included concepts and practical tools drawn from Positive Psychology, such as Seligman's PERMA[7], referred to by John Conolly in Chapter 4 and Appreciative Living (Kelm, 2005). We looked at the value of positive emotions in building resources, resilience, connections, and broadening capacity to see more options and possibilities

---

[7] The acronym PERMA stands for *Positive emotions. Engagement, Relationships, Meaning and Achievement.*

(Frederickson's Broaden and Build theory, 2001). While we talked about and encouraged positive emotions, negative ones were not excluded.

The Power of Conversation

> We live in the worlds our questions create—Every conversation is a potential adventure, capable of tremendous results.
>
> – Reginald Somerset-Ward

A core part of any AI process is the appreciative conversation, usually paired, which can last from five to forty-five minutes. So, we first asked everyone to think of a good experience when they helped a friend (or were helped by a friend). Initially, a staff member shared his story by responding to my questions, and this in itself set a very different tone than more routine meetings residents attended. He talked about a story where he had helped someone, which showed a side of him that most had not had a chance to connect with.

Then residents paired up with staff and each shared a story. Again, the residents expressed how nice it was for them to learn more about the staff member. One resident spoke to his newly assigned key worker (case manager) and subsequently shared that he had not been at all keen on the change, but this paired activity meant he learnt things about his new worker that changed his mind. The pairs then identified the key qualities demonstrated in helping their friend.

This provided a natural sequel to identifying some of their strengths (whereas if we had asked them outright an initial question on their strengths, the responses would have been much more limited). From the staff point of view, they could choose the stories they wanted to share, which needed to be authentic but which didn't make them feel that they had crossed any personal or professional boundaries.

Having sown some seeds amongst the residents, invitations for the two days were then sent out to those likely to be interested. Eight to twelve residents usually attended. Some of them would often leave early, having concluded that this approach was not for them. We emphasised that their presence was voluntary. However, the rest all participated fully throughout the two-day programme.

Some key Benefits to Clients of Working in an Appreciative Way

AI's emphasis on strengths offers clients an alternative way of thinking, and a way of moving beyond their painful past. They don't need to feel as though they are a "problem" the service is addressing. Rather, they are individuals with resources of their own. This helps them consider their strengths; it helps them generate a viable vision for their next step, and identify potential sources of help. It supports and enhances their resilience to deal with what life may bring (and in their chaotic lifestyles this is very valuable). The reflective practice it encourages gives clients a tool to process emotions and deal with times when life doesn't seem to go how they want it to. There are parallels here with the work described in many other chapters.

Leo Richardson developed a questionnaire to collect qualitative information on the AI pilot in conjunction with the support staff at King George's hostel. Using a semi-structured format, he asked open questions about the use of AI and its beneficial outcomes, to elicit their personal views and experience of the AI intervention. The interviews were carried out by support workers involved in the project at King George's Hostel, and notes written up in case study format. Leo's dissertation (2012) expands on this work.

Participants described improvements in quality of life, reduction in drug use, move on to independent accommodation, reduction in crime and better financial management.

> Yes, my quality of life has improved. I am living independently with support when needed. This is an improvement from life in a Hostel. (DS)

> So, I stopped using class A drugs. I got in touch with my family and my son. I started a beginner's course in barbering and am now undertaking the advanced barbering course. (LM)

> My life has changed as I have not been in trouble with the Police for a year. I am now thinking of getting a job within a hostel environment. I am thinking of this as I would like to give back into the system that has supported me. (KD).

A number of the participants described transformations that involved a newfound focus on the positive and reflective, using metaphors such as turning the corner. Such events were often associated with the three-day residential trip.

> It was not until we went on the Appreciative Inquiry programme, which was held for three days with other residents and staff. That was when I really turned the corner. I really thought to myself "Enough is enough, grow up and be a man." (LM)

> Without AI, I was in the cycle of borrowing money to use drugs. AI helped to get me out of that cycle. (PB)

> Since I did AI, the way I view negative emotions, negative thoughts has changed, also the role of will power and quality of life. (MT)

AI and Positive Psychology strengthen reflection and emotional intelligence, and participants described increased awareness of their behaviour, thoughts and reactions as being an important part of their progress — such as improving control of impulsive behaviour. At least two of them were still journaling two years later and telling their friends about the benefits. Seeing the value they found in journaling prompted us to design appreciative journals to be used in subsequent training (Slack, 2011).

> I can use the techniques of self realisation to show myself that there are angles that I cannot see of myself that others can. AI has restricted my impulsive behaviour and made me think twice about my actions. (DS)
>
> I am writing now in my diary of people who are the problem. In the past I would have reacted in a bad manner, but now I must have chilled because I do not over-respond to the situations as I once would have done... I think more about situations rather than jumping straight in. (KD)

The structured conversations at the heart of AI strengthen relationships — new connections were formed with other residents and staff, and choices made to change friendships.

> I just went on the AI trip but had a good relationship with staff who went with us. The staff I went with were able to support me in my goals. (CH)
>
> I have disconnected myself from my old hostel and friends and in the area where I now live I keep myself to myself and I have chosen not to give my address to anyone (PJ). (Staff saw this as a good step as they felt that the relationship with one of his friends had been unhelpful.)

Residents also valued the chance to tell a different story about their workers, for example after one paired conversation between a resident and a new locum worker who had only recently joined the hostel, the resident told the larger group that after having heard her story he felt proud of his new key worker. Having conversations with staff as peers meant that the residents felt more trusted, and this was a powerful boost to their confidence in themselves.

This summary from a staff member who attended indicates the benefits to both staff and residents.

> The workshop was very well structured for the 3 days with the entire team going through a journey of self realization by exploring the nuances geared towards self actualization. The atmosphere was congenial and generative hence engendered lots of positivity. The engagement levels were very high and free flowing with all the participants making an attempt to get a lot of issues of the past from their system to ensure a sturdy transition of life's challenges... Personally I learnt to prioritize my objectives working towards self realization and to enjoy myself and celebrate life.

Some outcomes from the work in Westminster were: reduced substance use, health improvement, engagement with services, development of reflective practice, improvement in managing their emotions, reduction in anti-social behavior, improvement of relations with family and friends, and successful move on to independent living. The deputy manager of the hostel observed that participants had made more progress in a two-day residential than in two years of key working (personal communication). This progress was particularly noteworthy, given that all participants had a formal or informal diagnosis of personality disorder.

At that time, resources did not permit an in-depth quantitative cost-benefit analysis, but in a single case study, one individual cost £14,960 for the year before the AI intervention. This was for Arrests, Prison Stay, Probation curfew (tagging), ASBO (anti-social behavior order), and Failed Detox. This was reduced to £0 for the year following the AI intervention.

Part 2 — So, What is Appreciative Inquiry? And how does it contribute to reflection and dialogue?

Much of my professional career was in the aid world overseas, and each time, I came to the end of a contract feeling profoundly dissatisfied with the way this kind of work was structured and the way in which it involved defining local people as being in profound need of external help. I returned to UK and studied to see if there was a different way, and then went out again on another job. In the end I stopped this work completely, but I think if I had discovered AI then I would have continued doing it longer — primarily because of the way in which AI brings people into conversation as peers, and the way in which it can facilitate genuine co–creation and co-production, and also because it doesn't start with a problem! Problem-solving paradigms work well when dealing with non-human systems like fixing a car, but when people are viewed as problems to be fixed, they are unlikely to be inspired and engaged in a co-creative way.

Appreciative Inquiry (AI) is unique in being an Organisational Development (OD) approach that supports organisations while at the same time having an excellent record in supporting personal development. Cooperrider, Whitney, & Stavros (2003, p. 16) describe an organisation as "a mystery that should be embraced as a human centre of infinite imagination, infinite capacity, and potential." I and other AI writers also feel that this definition can apply to individuals.

AI offers a *generative* alternative to asking questions such as "What are the problems?" "What's wrong?" or "What needs to be fixed?" As an "asset-based approach," it starts with the belief that organisations, and everyone in those organisations, have a positive core, which can be built on and amplified. To do this, AI asks questions like "What's working well?" "What's good about what you are currently doing? How can we do more of it?" It seeks to renew, develop and build on this positive core. From this point of view, it could be posited that perhaps identifying people by their needs is ultimately something to move away from.

AI, combined with learning from Positive Psychology, allows the concept of a "negativity bias" to be raised, explored, and then methods offered to counter it. This bias refers to the fact that our brain seems to have a predisposition to pay attention to the negative, to give negative facts more weight, and to retain them for longer. Something positive will generally have less of an impact on a person's behaviour and cognition than something equally emotional but negative. Things of a more negative nature (e.g., unpleasant thoughts, emotions, or social interactions; harmful/traumatic events) have a greater effect on one's psychological state and processes than do neutral or positive things. Rick Hansen (2016) describes the brain as like "Velcro for negative experiences but Teflon for positive ones." Barbara Fredrickson says, "The negative screams at you but the positive only whispers (2009)."

AI focuses on reframing issues into words that are more inspiring and more likely to generate interest, engagement and action. It also acknowledges difficult situations, history and exclusion. As Sharp, Dewar & Barrie (2016), among others (Grant and Humphries, 2006; Duncan and Ridley-Duff, 2014), express clearly:

> A number of authors suggest that in complex situations of human dynamics and community power, AI can help to highlight issues of power, develop critical thinking and actions, disrupt self-

limiting and taken for granted assumptions and be an "act of transgression" that can change habits of deference.

Jay's conversation with Miguel (chapter 3) and the various ways they find to rename "elder housing" are lovely examples of reframing.

Benefits for staff and the organisation

AI provides a way of engaging with people as equals and encouraging them to share valuable information and experiences in a positive framework.

Positive Core – individual, team & organisational wealth, wellbeing & energy

Successes

Peak experiences

Key learning

Every organisation & person has a positive core

Best practices

Strengths

Fig. 8-1: Positive Core elements

It allows a way of meeting challenges and of reframing them where appropriate. It supports team building. It unleashes creativity. Recent Organisational Development research and writing confirms the benefits of this approach to coping with personal and organizational uncertainty and change — highlighted by book titles such as *Appreciative Inquiry: Change at the Speed of Imagination* (Watkins et al., 2011). People and organisations become more resilient, and able to harness and grow their strengths, fostering wellbeing and morale. They can work more effectively and take more informed decisions about personal futures (Lewis, 2011). AI offers a way of systematising and embedding strengths based reflective practice — required for a PIE.

The appreciative approach can be applied to many parts of an organisation's work — e.g., supervision and coaching, teambuilding, and meetings. An "appreciative voice" provides safety for others to speak their truths. It is invitational and watchful. An appreciative voice is unhurried and patient. It can reframe situations to be helpful and resourceful. It is flexible. The appreciative voice is inclusive. It acknowledges diversity and identifies opportunities to offer possibilities to hold the space for transformational shifts to emerge. (Stratton-Berkessel, 2017)

AI is founded on a number of profound philosophical underpinnings. Jackie Kelm has written two books (Kelm, 2005; Kelm, 2009) about these. For this article, I will elaborate on the three most important principles.

The Social Constructionist Principle: Words create worlds

Multiple interpretations of what is real co-exist — we're constantly co-creating our reality with every conversation and social interaction. We create stories to make sense of things, but our stories are not the truth, just one perspective and interpretation. The language we use and conversations we take part in all contribute to how we construct our world and the world of those we talk to. Other people's language and images/ metaphors in conversations reveal elements of their construction.

Each person's reality is subjective. There is no right or wrong reality — just a difference of interpretation. I love Ray's comment in Chapter 6, "We only ever partly know a thing in dialogue with others, so we ought not be so attached to our current ideas that we cannot let them 'go up in smoke'." We **are never neutral observers** — aptly summed up by Jay in chapter 3: "Language creates the world in which we communicate and live," and by his quote from Freedman and Combs" "Speaking isn't neutral or passive. Every time we speak, we bring forth a reality."

Social constructionism allows us to engage in reframing both the past and present in a way that they become the building blocks for a newly possible seen future.

In *Stuart: A life Backwards* (Masters, 2005), Stuart was very clear how he wanted Alexander to tell his story. Stuart himself suggested the format for that book. "Do it backwards, like a murder mystery," he said. "How did I get to be like this? What murdered the little boy I was?" And it's interesting to discover that a life told backwards can be so much less confusing than a gruesome death told forward (Guardian review 2007).

The Simultaneity Principle: Inquiry is change — and the first question is fateful...

The moment we inquire, or ask a question, we initiate a reaction at many different levels of our consciousness. The language, tone and intention of the question determine the direction of the conversation. This principle connects with a quantum physics concept that there are no neutral observers. Heisenberg said that atoms or elementary particles are not real; they form a world of potentialities or possibilities rather than one of things or facts. Observation creates the reality being examined. Mind can be thought of as a bridge locating us within a particular community at a particular moment.

The way an observation is set up determines what will be observed. Rather than a neutral observer and observed, the questions we ask determine the answers we get. Niels Bohr indicates we cannot know the quantum world; we can only know our description of it. Our experienced world is a construct, operationally necessary, but a construct nevertheless. Rather than assuming that we can know reality in any definitive and unquestioning way, practical realism pursues truth as an ongoing opportunity. So when you create your questions, consider what you're really seeking to learn more about, and how you can encourage the respondent to reflect on what is valuable and important. The moment you ask a question, you've started a narrative journey. (*Taste of AI 2.0,* 2017)

The Anticipatory Principle: Image inspires action

We all live in a future state to some extent. We constantly look forward to what might be, prompting us to make decisions that influence our present condition and actions. Our future is a constructed reality, created by our present thinking and imagery. When we create positive, uplifting images of our future, we're more likely to make decisions and act to help us reach that desired future. When we anticipate the worst, we fill ourselves with a sense of foreboding, fear and limitation; we hold back and don't embrace opportunity, sending a powerful negative message to our minds. The placebo affect is a good demonstration of what is called the Anticipatory Principle in AI.

This quote from Viktor Frankl (1985, p. 86) in *Man's Search for Meaning* illumines a profound application of the essence of these principles—"Everything can be taken from a man but one thing: the last of the human freedoms—to choose one's attitude in any given set of circumstances, to choose one's own way."

In many contexts, it may not be appropriate to go into the principles in any depth, but the essence of them can be touched on by explaining these powerful underlying assumptions:

1. In every situation, something works… find it and let it flourish.

2. What we focus on becomes our reality… if we focus on possibilities, we find possibilities, if we focus on problems, we find problems.

3. There are always multiple realities — different ways of seeing.

4. The way we ask questions either creates or denies possibilities. So, be mindful how we do this. The questions we ask affect the emotional state of the person we are asking them of and the ongoing, ever-changing image they have of themselves, the organisation and the process of change.

5. The language we use creates our reality.

6. When we carry some of our old ways forward to the future, they should be the very best of our old ways.

7. Value differences — diversity nourishes creativity and resilience — seek it out and welcome it.

The Transformative Power of Appreciative Conversations

Appreciative conversations on their own have a transformative power:

> Evidence from a steel mill trying to improve safety performance underscores how organisations go in the direction of what they ask the most questions about. Conversations dramatically shape individual and collective behaviour. The conversations were designed and facilitated to prepare for an AI summit; however the safety improved soon after the conversations started, and including nearly all voices in the system led to generative connections and significant behaviour changes. (Ron Fry, 2012)

AI offers a light touch framework for eliciting stories of strength and good experiences, and of deeply listening to them. The very fact that it is a framework offers permission to be persistent in re-orienting and reframing as appropriate, and can support people from being diverted down the well-worn paths of problems. In its option for a genuine paired conversation, it also offers another way for the joining that Jay refers to as one of the Pretreatment strategies. The dream stage of AI is built on the discovery stage, and can offer a fun way to help people develop their personal vision/objective. Out of this, they can design easily achievable next steps. Often, when I train staff, they comment that they were doing much of this anyway but didn't have a name or framework for it. AI offers an easily accessible framework that can be shared with newcomers at any level.

As a Relational Tool, AI is ideally suited to building relationships, and it sits well within the emerging field of relational leadership, dialogic organizational development (Bushe & Marshak (2017) and relational care. My Home Life (MHL) has found that AI works with and for people to change practice in a less threatening way, by focusing on what is currently working well and what more needs to be done to make it even better.

It values all forms of knowing, and crucially, includes connecting with and exploring what others value, respecting hidden stories of experience and personal narratives, and demonstrating sensitivity to feelings. It supports change by establishing trust, authentic connection and a different quality of learning. An evaluation of the programme in Scotland during 2013-15 found consistent results; it developed understanding of how to improve the culture of care, enhanced the engagement of staff and promoted greater leadership and communication skills, with positive outcomes for managers, staff and residents. (Sharp et al., 2016)

AI has a clear philosophy and framework, but because it is generative and co–creative, it includes an element of uncertainty and unpredictable outputs. The term *Chaordic* (Hock, 2000) was first coined by Dee Hock to include a combination of chaos and order. Chaordic organizations must rely on the collective intelligence of their people to create a desired future. Knowledge and information sharing go hand-in-glove. In the Chaordic organisation, power arises from becoming a source of knowledge, and sharing it. It supports experimentation, risk-taking, and failure, and views trial-and-error as a viable process. AI facilitators need to be comfortable with this chaos and uncertainty, and moments where the process might seem not to be working. I think that AI's ability to relate to chaos makes it a good fit in the sometimes seemingly chaotic world of the homeless. It also overlaps with the first of the principles applied by Ray in taking a dialogical approach (chapter 6) — *We accept we only ever partly know what is going on (Open Dialogue express this principle as "tolerating uncertainty").* There are many moments in my work as a facilitator where this holds true!

Part 3 — Wider Dialogues and Contributions to the Field

When beginning to write this chapter, a sentence in Jay Levy's first chapter jumped out at me: *people are experts on their own worlds* (Eptson & White, 1992). This seems to take the concept of "working from people's strengths" that bit deeper, and the fact that AI developed in the UK in dialogue with the originators in the States is a nice link with a purpose of this book — building dialogue between the UK and the States.

With its stress on co-production at an individual, inter-personal level, there is clearly a lot of overlap and synergy between AI and the Pretreatment approach, as described by Jay. In its use of dialogue, there is clearly much in common with Ray Middleton's description of his work with Open Dialogue. Perhaps most of all, in the context of work in the homelessness hostel we have described here, it is clearly one form of positive psychology that can rapidly be taken on board, to create culture change and a whole, positive, psychologically informed environment.

In fact, I have discovered many more examples of AI in use in these kinds of environments — for example, Barbara Thomas, an AI practitioner in the USA describes how

> As director of services, I have experimented in asking appreciative questions and designing appreciative interventions to guide the tasks of serving over 400 homeless people daily. AI has become my leadership model and philosophy, resulting in a highly effective and cohesive team. I also believe that the homeless population of Charlotte, NC is better served because of it. (Thomas, 2016, p.15)

Two of our AI colleagues in the States have developed and worked with Critical Appreciative Inquiry (CAI), which brings together social constructionism, critical theory and appreciative inquiry.

> Asking ourselves whose stories are told and what meaning is given to the stories that an organization shares. Critical theory is a huge field of study but for the purposes of this article it is useful to turn to Stephen Brookfield (2005), who describes critical theory as being grounded in a "desire to fight oppression, injustice, and bigotry and create a fairer, more compassionate world... CAI fosters positive movement in highly complex issues where it is very clear what the problem or issue is but less clear what a future state might look like." (Cockell & Mcarthur-Blair, 2012, p. 53)

Looking wider still, there are many other examples of the power of telling a different story about our realities. A Stanford University study (Zahrt & Crum (2017) reports that simply changing your mindset and perceptions about the health benefits of everyday physical activity (such as walking to the corner store or taking the stairs) could help you live a longer and healthier life. In 1979, Professor Langer of Harvard University was investigating the extent to which ageing is a product of our state of mind.

She devised the "counter-clockwise study:" putting a group of elderly men into the world of 1959. Taking their minds back twenty years had an impact on their bodies. This kind of study has been repeated since with notable results on the faculties of the participants. Hotel cleaners who were told that the activities in their daily job were equivalent to a gym workout lost weight and got fitter, while a control group of workers doing a similar job but without that additional piece of information didn't. Sports Psychology is already using many of these strength-based concepts to great effect. There are many references to examples, such as a team that only reviews its good performance does better than a team that looks at the things it did wrong, and teams that do vision work do better than teams that only train. (AIP, May 2016)

Other Applications of AI: Building Psychological Safety

Learning from Everyday Excellence and what goes well in the NHS

We miss so much by focusing on error and not learning from what is going well. Personal and organisational learning benefits from an emphasis on and encouragement of the positive. Safety is an area where the focus is often exclusively on the negative — Dr. Adrian Plunkett (2016) said that trying to learn about safety from failures is like trying to learn about sharks by studying shark attacks. So, he developed the idea of *Learning from Excellence* — the simple process of submitting an "excellence report" on a colleague/team when a staff member has noticed something being done well. These are then collected and shared — that in itself has a significant impact on staff morale and culture, and reinforces good practice. In addition, the reports are sifted through and one or two identified for learning potential, which could then be shared more widely — AI is the framework for the reporting and the learning. (Plunkett, 2016; Quinney & Slack 2017)

John Conolly (see Chapter 4) on Pre-treatment Therapy talks about relationship being the foundation of pre-treatment work, and the establishment of safety as being the first principle. Levy (2010, p. 15) defines pretreatment more formally as "an approach that enhances safety while promoting transition..."

A PIE is an environment that needs to feel "safe" for both staff and residents. Increasingly, it seems to me that we all need to be more "psychologically informed." There is an interesting overlap with, and some useful research on, the power of psychological safety. The term was coined by Edmondson (2002). Her TED talk covers the importance of "a shared belief that the team is safe for interpersonal risk taking." She outlines three routes for leaders wanting to create psychological safety in their organisations:

1. Framework as learning problems, as opposed to execution problems: "We've never been here before; we can't know what will happen; we've got to have everybody's brains and voices in the game."

2. Make simple statements that encourage peers and subordinates to speak up, such as, "I may miss something — I need to hear from you."

3. Model curiosity by asking a lot of questions.

A further addition to this field is the book *Humble Inquiry*, where Edgar Schein (2013) elaborates on the fine art of drawing someone out, of asking questions to which you do not already know the answer, of building a relationship based on curiosity and interest in the other person. An AI–based approach dovetails naturally with building safety.

Parallels and Insights from other practices: Supporting personal learning

Implicit and explicit in many of the chapters in this book is an understanding of the power of giving someone genuine positive and truthful attention. In my work in other fields (health and community, and organisational learning), I share an increasing number of examples of the power of simple "positive regard" to support learning and change. Two of these examples follow.

Sugata Mitra (2016), in his work with children on the street and in schools, concluded that, given a computer securely held in a hole in a wall, children could teach themselves and their peers how to use a computer and speak English. The only essential factors were being observed (by a camera) and having an encouraging adult on the sidelines (including "grandparents"). Sugata found no limit to children's capacity to learn while unsupervised and working in groups to solve a problem. Sugata's work inspired a novel which became the basis of the Oscar-winning film Slumdog Millionaire.

Video Interaction Guidance™ (VIG) (Kennedy, 2011) is an extremely powerful process where a trained facilitator makes a video and then extracts micro-moments of strengths or good practice to play back to the people they are working with. This shows them their good practice in action (for example to parents who might be at risk of having a child taken into care). They are then able to have a conversation built on this tangible example of strength. VIG engages clients actively in a process of change towards realising their own hopes for a better future in their relationships with others who are important to them. Guiders are themselves guided by the values and beliefs around respect and empowerment. These include a belief that people in troubled situations do want to change, a respect for what clients are managing to achieve in their current difficulties, and a conviction that the power and responsibility for change resides within clients and their situations.

Seeking other strength-based examples to share with clients, I have come across two UK services for and with homeless people. The power of friendship and "relatedness" are at the heart of Camerados — a national movement of people who want to provide a solution to tough times that isn't a service and is simply people helping each other find the two essentials in life: Friends and Purpose. "Camerado" comes from Walt Whitman's poem "Song for the Open Road" where he says that the most important thing on the journey is someone beside you (as also described so vividly by the authors of these chapters!). An example is their drop-in café and lounge area at Blackpool library.

Mayday Trust is an organisation that works with the homeless that threw out its problem-focused rulebook. Instead, it developed a strength-based approach to homelessness. Mayday's innovative, personal transitions service, *Mayday Inspire,* is the first strength-based model for people experiencing homelessness and those going through the toughest of life transitions.

Final Reflections Arising from the Delights of a Psychologically Informed Process

> Cultivating an appreciative voice not only strengthens you and expands your world, it also strengthens others and expands their worlds. — Robyn Stratton-Berkessel (2017)

At its best, AI conversations are genuine dialogues between connected beings where surprising and delightful content might arise — similar to the dialogical approach that Ray describes in Chapter 6. Margaret Wheatley, contemplating the "quantum world view," stresses that there are no independent entities anywhere at the quantum level; it's all relationships, and most systems should be seen as webs of relationships. So in this final section, I would also like to include the topic of deep dialogue or Dialogue in the Spirit of David Bohm (2010) where dialogue can be considered as a free flow of meaning between people in communication, in the sense of a stream that flows between banks. I see this kind of dialogue as an important element of AI and a really helpful element for consideration in the homeless sector. These "banks" are understood as representing the various points of view of the participants.

How would it be, if we considered conversations between staff/professionals and homeless people as conversations between these two banks? In these conversations, we are all "explorers" of meaning and language, and the subtle but profound effects and connections that can occur with ensuring that we converse with the maximum understanding of each other's reality and experience, and the maximum potential of building self-reflection and a sense of authorship of our worlds.

John Conolly's description of his journey with Jim in chapter 4 is a nice example. AI can offer a simple and user-friendly "punt, pole and compass" (in that it offers tools to support interactions, structures, and a philosophical framework) to navigate this journey. It particularly appeals to me in the way it supports "horizontal" conversations, where everyone builds up a language and awareness they can use to help themselves and each other. The dialogue in peer-based learning and small group work makes it cost effective as well.

> ...it may turn out that such a form of free exchange of ideas and information is of fundamental relevance for transforming culture and freeing it of destructive misinformation, so that creativity can be liberated. — David Bohm (2010 p240)

Jane Galloway Seiling (2005) uses the term "collective person" to represent the notion that each of us is a collective product of all our interactions. She uses a metaphor of the Mississippi River to describe the formation of the self — The river begins with droplets from the originating streams and tributaries, and grows with additions from other small and large rivers, fields, and streams. And I love how this remark from Adyashanti extends this metaphor: "Your whole organism is not other than life around you. There's no such thing as a human being without an environment." (From "Contraction to Vastness" Broadcast Aug 2016)

We are like the Mississippi: a collective notion formed and altered through the contacts, experiences, learning, desires, and actions of multiple others. Jay gives us a lovely sense of this in his journey with Miguel, and John Conolly in his with Michael, Josh, Jim, and Anne. Ray Middleton describes his role as a systems navigator, using conversations and dialogue. We are not just being carried by a current, we are all navigators, in home and work life... And knowing this enables us to apply more thought and presence to our own journey, and the times during which we connect with the journey of others. I suggest we can all be fellow explorers on this journey, and want to conclude with a quote from Ray (chapter 6) —

> Drawing on Bakhtin's concepts, I encourage staff to see both themselves and their clients temporarily journeying together, meeting dialogically in overlapping worlds as unfinalised personalities, who can listen to and learn from each other at crossroads on our life-journeys.

Note of Appreciation

Thanks go to Leo Richardson for his dedication to AI, for being wonderful to work with, and for documenting the conversations with some of the residents of King George's hostel. Thanks to the manager and staff at King George's hostel for whole-heartedly joining me in exploring the practical applications of AI in their work, and to Westminster council for commissioning me. And thanks to Robin Johnson for his excellent, patient, generous and "generative" editing.

References

Adyashanti (2011) *Falling into Grace — Insights on the End of Suffering.* Boulder Colorado: Sounds True

Anderson, H. (2001) in D. Cooperrider, H. Anderson, K. Gergen *The Appreciative Organization.* Ohio: Taos Institute Publications

Berger, P., & Luckman, T. (1966) *The Social Construction of Reality.* New York: Doubleday

Bohm, D. & Peat, D. (2010) *Science, Order, and Creativity.* New York Routledge Classics

Bushe, G. *(*2007) Appreciative Inquiry Is Not (Just) About the Positive. *OD Practitioner*, 39(4): 30-35

Bushe, G. & Marshak, R. (2017) The Dialogic Organization Development Approach to Transformation and Change, in *Practicing Organization Development* (4th Edition) Editors: **Rothwell, R. J., Stavros, J. M., & Sullivan, R. L.** New Jersey: Wiley

Cockell, J. & **McArthur-Blair, J.** (2012) *Appreciative Inquiry In Higher Education: A Transformative Force.* San Francisco: Jossey-Bass

Camerados blackpoollibraries.wordpress.com/2016/05/19/camerados-living-room-in-central-library-cafe/

Cooperrider, D. L., & Whitney, D. (2005) *Appreciative Inquiry — a positive revolution in change.* San Francisco: Berrett-Koehler Publishers, Inc.

Crum, A. J., & Langer, E. J. (2007) Mind-set matters: exercise and the placebo effect. *Psychological Science.* 18(2):165-171
    www.ncbi.nlm.nih.gov/pubmed/17425538

Duncan, G. and Ridley-Duff, R. J. (2014) Appreciative inquiry as a method of transforming identity and power in Pakistani women, *Action Research*, 12 (2): 117-135

Edmondson, A. C. (2002) *Managing the risk of learning: Psychological safety in work teams.* Dissertation, Harvard Business School

Epston, D. & White, M. (1992) *Experience, contradiction, narrative, and imagination: Selected papers of David Epston and Michael White, 1989-1991.* Adelaide, Australia: Dulwich Centre Publications

Foot, J. (2010) *A Glass Half-full — How an asset approach can improve community health and wellbeing*
    www.idea.gov.uk/idk/aio/18410498

Frankl, V. E. (1985) *Man's search for meaning.* New York: Washington Square Press

Fredrickson, B. (2001) The role of positive emotions in positive psychology: The broaden-and-build theory of positive emotions. *American Psychologist,* 56(3): 218–226

Fredrickson, B. (2003) *The Value of Positive Emotions. The emerging science of positive psychology is coming to understand why it's good to feel good. American Scientist:* July–August 2003. www.americanscientist.org/template/IssueTOC/issue/394

Fredrickson, B. (2009) *Positivity: Top Notch Research Reveals the Upward Spiral that will change your life.* New York: Three Rivers Press

Fry, R. (2012) Improving Safety in a Steel Mill: Words Really Can Create Worlds! What really causes or creates behavioral change? *AI Practitioner,* 14(2): 51-55

Grant, S. and Humphries, M. (2006) Critical evaluation of appreciative inquiry: Bridging an apparent paradox, *Action Research***, 4(4): 401–418**

Hanson, R. (2016) *Hardwiring happiness.* New York: Random House

Hefferon, K. & Boniwell, I. (2011) *Positive Psychology: Theory, research and applications,* Berkshire, UK: Open University Press

Hock, D. (2000) *Birth of the Chaordic Age.* San Francisco: Berrett-Koehler

Johnson, P. (2007) Transcending the Polarity of Light and Shadow, in *Life and in Practice in Linkage: A journal of creative research, thought and feeling.* Leadership Institute of Seattle www.lios.org

Kelm, J. B. (2005) *Appreciative Living —the principles of Appreciative Inquiry in personal life.* Charleston, South Carolina: Venet Publishers

Kelm, J. B. (2009) The joy of appreciative living: Your 28 day plan to greater happiness in three incredibly easy steps. New York: Tarcher

Kelly, N., Blake S & Plunkett, A., (2016) *Learning from excellence in healthcare: a new approach to incident reporting.* ADC Online First, May 4, 2016 10.1136/archdischild-2015-310021 Produced by BMJ Publishing Group Ltd (& RCPCH)

Kennedy, H. (Editor), (2011) *Video Interaction Guidance: A relationship-based intervention to promote atunement, empathy and wellbeing.* London: Jessica Kingsley

Kretzmann, J., & McKnight, J. (1993) *Building Communities from the Inside Out: A Path Toward Finding and Mobilizing a Community's Assets.* http://www.abcdinstitute.org/publications/

Levy, J. S. (2010) *Homeless narratives & pretreatment pathways: From words to housing.* Ann Arbor, MI: Loving Healing Press

Lewis, S. (2011) *Positive Psychology at Work: How positive leadership and Appreciative Inquiry Create Inspiring Organisations.* Oxford: Wiley-Blackwell

Magruder-Watkins, J., Mohr B & Kelly R (2011) *Appreciative Inquiry: Change at the Speed of Imagination,* 2nd edition. San Fransciso: Pfeiffer Wiley

Masters, A. (2007) *Stuart—A Life Backwards.* London: Harper Books www.theguardian.com/culture/tvandradioblog/2007/sep/24/theweekend stvstuartalife

Mayday Trust www.maydaytrust.org.uk/

Mitra, S., Kulkarni, S. & Stanfield, J. (2016) Learning at the Edge of Chaos — Self-Organising Systems in Education, In *The Palgrave International Handbook of Alternative Education.* UK: Palgrave Macmillan

Plunkett, A. (2016) *Learning from excellence in healthcare: A new approach to incident reporting.* ADC Online First, May 4, 2016
    BMJ Publishing: 10.1136/archdischild-2015-310021

Quinney, S. (2012) *Back on My Feet* from *Innovation & Appreciative Inquiry: Positive Images, Positive Action - special video edition* www.aipractitioner.com/videos www.appreciatingpeople.co.uk/king-georges-hostel-in-westminster/

Quinney, S. & Slack, T. (2017) *Reflections - Realising the Power of Appreciative Inquiry: An Appreciative Journal and Practical Resource Book.* Liverpool: Wordscapes

Quinney, S., & Richardson, L. J. S. (2014) Organisational development, appreciative inquiry and the development of Psychologically Informed Environments (PIEs). Part I: a positive psychology approach. *Housing, Care and Support* 17(2): 95-102

Quinney, S., & Richardson, L. J. S. (2014) Organisational development, appreciative inquiry and the development of Psychologically Informed Environments (PIEs). Part II: pilot study and evaluation *Housing, Care and Support* 17(3): pp. 131-141

Reivich, K. & Shatte, A. (2003) *The Resilience Factor: 7 Keys to Finding Your Inner Strength and Overcoming Life's Hurdles.* New York: Random House

Richardson, L. (2012) *The experience of Appreciative Inquiry for substance misusing hostel residents: A positive approach to working with addiction and homelessness.* Unpublished M.Sc. research project, London Metropolitan University

Schein Edgar H. (2013) *Humble Inquiry. The Gentle Art of Asking Instead of Telling.* Berrett-Koehler Publishers: San Francisco

Seiling, Jane, G. (2005) *Moving from Individual to Constructive Accountability.* Unpublished dissertation, The Netherlands: University of Tilburg

Seligman, M. (2011) *Flourish: A visionary new understanding of happiness and well-being.* New York: Simon & Schuster

Sharp. C., Dewar, B. & Barrie, K. (2016) *Forming new futures through appreciative inquiry.* Scotland: Iriss Insights
www.iriss.org.uk/insights

Sharp, C., Dewar, B., Barrie, K. & Meyer, J. (2017). How being Appreciative creates change – theory in practice from health and social care in Scotland. Action Research,
doi:10.1177/1476750316684002

Slack, T. (2012) *Food for Thought: A Journal for Appreciating Daily Life.* Liverpool: Wordscapes

Slack, T. & Quinney, S. (2017) *Taste of AI 2.0 — An easy to use guide to AI.* Liverpool: Wordscapes

Stavros, J. M. & Torres, C. B. (2005) *Dynamic Relationships —unleashing the power of Appreciative Inquiry in Daily living.* Ohio: Taos Institute Publications

Stratton-Berkessel, R. (2017) www.positivitystrategist.com/what-is-an-appreciative-voice-in-your-world/

Thomas, B. (2016) AI: A Method for Daily Leadership in an urban ministry. *AI Practitioner*, 18(3):15-20

Tugade, M. & Frederickson, B. (2006) *Resilient Individuals Use Positive Emotions to Bounce Back from Negative Emotional Experiences.* www.ncbi.nlm.nih.gov/pmc/articles/PMC3132556/?tool=pubmed

Wheatley, M. (1999) *Leadership and the New Science: Discovering Order in a Chaotic World.* San Francisco: Berret-Koehler

Zahrt, O. H. & Crum, A. J. (2017) "Perceived Physical Activity and Mortality: Evidence From Three Nationally Representative U.S. Samples," Stanford University. *Health Psychology,* published online, July 20, 2017 at
www.psychologytoday.com/blog/the-athletes-way/201707/stanford-researchers-identify-life-changing-power-mindset

9 Ending Homelessness for the Most Vulnerable Among Us
Jay S. Levy

> I am the voice of the oppressed, so don't mess with me!
>
> – Judy

Introduction

Effective Homeless Outreach and housing with support services can play a critical role toward reducing homelessness when integrated with community resources and sound government policy. This chapter begins from our experiences in the field to demonstrate some of the challenges homeless services workers face in reaching out to people with complex needs. It then examines the barriers to accessing essential resources and services, as well as considering helpful interventions on both the direct care and systemic levels, such as implementing Pretreatment strategies or developing a coordinated entry network of services. Larger systemic and cultural issues between the US and UK are also discussed and compared.

The success of homeless outreach is dependent upon the ability to facilitate housing placement, whether it be transitional or permanent in nature. Namely, quick access to housing with support services for people who are struggling with long-term homelessness with complex needs is essential. Unfortunately, for many years the US has been sorely lacking in these housing options for the most vulnerable, until there was some improvement by instituting Housing First (HF) over the past decade or so.

Joe Finn's foreword for this book, as well as Judy's narrative and the discussion that follows, highlight this issue and the resulting change in policy and practice that led to greater access to housing for chronically homeless individuals in the US. HF is not a panacea for homelessness, nor is it intended to be a one size fits all housing solution. Nevertheless, one must understand, and to some degree, experience the real life particulars within the US context to fully appreciate why it came about and how it can be most helpful.

Judy's Story: Survival on the Streets

When I first met Judy, a white female in her early 60s, I was immediately struck by her weathered appearance, strength, and candor. She is among the long-term homeless who frequent several small towns in Western MA. Sadly, Judy experienced early life difficulties, ending up in foster care due to extensive abuse/neglect by her biological parents. During her teen years, she dropped out of high school, contended with alcohol/drug abuse, and was briefly incarcerated for public intoxication and disturbing the peace with loud diatribes about the ills of capitalist society. Since early adulthood, she has spent more than twenty years surviving the outside elements, temporarily staying in shelters, and occasionally ending up in jail for assault and/or theft.

Judy suffers from schizophrenia, which is her principal diagnosis. She also has a history of intermittent alcohol abuse and significant trauma. During the past two years, Judy's functioning has steadily declined as reflected by more frequent verbally aggressive interactions with fellow community members. Unfortunately, this has led to run-ins with the police and an increased number of arrests, as well as an uptick in short-term involuntary psychiatric inpatient stays.

Many times in the past, we have offered Judy both housing and treatment options, which she adamantly refused. Like so many others, Judy does not believe that she has mental illness or substance abuse issues, and so she takes particular offense to anyone who insinuates or even hints at this being a concern. Over the years, Judy has developed an entrenched pattern of telling people who offer help to "screw off!" Other times, she would recite what sounded like her mantra, "I am the voice of the oppressed, so don't mess with me!" In fact, her mantra has only become more entrenched and defiant due to her recent negative experiences with police and involuntary psychiatric hospitalizations. Beyond Judy's anger, there is a sense of meaning in her rage against the machine, which she envisions as capitalism and all those who participate in the economy.

A useful place to begin engagement is to connect with someone's sense of purpose (Frankl, 1985; Levy, 2010), rather than to disregard or challenge it. We sometimes overlook that individuals who have experienced long-term homelessness have gone through a process of transition to the harsh realities of homelessness and trauma, which includes the incorporation of adaptive behaviors and finding meaning in their struggle for survival. Their reaction to homeless outreach is often marked by caution and mistrust, which can be viewed as an adaptive response. It is therefore important that we think of the process of engagement with people who experience homelessness and the effects of trauma in a psychologically informed manner.

My role as regional manager for PATH (Projects Assisting Transitions from Homelessness) includes the provision of clinical supervision for the master's level clinician who serves the local area where Judy often resides. He is a white male in his late 60s, and is an expert from his own life experience of homelessness, college education and outreach counseling. Through his active community engagement, the outreach counselor established a presence at several local stores up and down the town's main street, which includes a local donut shop Judy frequents. This is one of the many businesses where our outreach team has maintained positive relationships within our community.

Our outreach clinician began engaging with Judy by offering needed items such as coffee and a donut at the local shop, while purposely not focusing on housing or treatment options that she had historically refused. Due to the severity of Judy's past traumatic experiences, coupled with psychological distress bordering on paranoid ideation, Judy was only able to withstand ten-minute meetings before becoming unfocused, belligerent, and then abruptly leaving the store. In response, the outreach counselor kept these meetings short in order to make Judy more comfortable, and thereby begin a more productive dialogue.

Pretreatment Strategies

Over time, Judy responded in a positive manner to the offering of needed items, and the consistent non-demanding presence of the outreach worker at the local donut shop. It also helped that the outreach counselor was able to speak Judy's language in a way that upheld her values of a non-materialistic philosophy, thereby meeting the client where she was at. This was an effective strategy as evidenced by Judy referring to others in a judgmental and condescending tone as "the dummies with the money" before turning to the outreach worker and saying, "but you're all right."

The worker's past homeless experience played an important role in his ability to successfully connect with Judy in a compassionate manner.

She now trusted him and engaged more readily, though she hadn't yet agreed to work on specific goals. Our clinical supervision discussions focused on how to frame an "offer" for Judy in a way that might resonate in her world. The outreach counselor shared that Judy had complained on several occasions about her belongings getting stolen, as well as a concern about various rodents — chipmunks and squirrels — rummaging through her bags. We both understood that Judy valued keeping her personal property safe, and so we decided to address these immediate concerns as a potential point of further engagement and contracting for services.

The outreach counselor was advised to offer housing as a means of protecting Judy's bags from the elements, rodents, and others. Judy liked this idea, so keeping her and her stuff safe became our primary focus. However, there were some significant challenges due to her untreated psychiatric issues and baseline behaviors that consisted of loud protests about her homeless plight, while directing blame and anger at anyone in the immediate vicinity. Unfortunately this also included potential neighbors and landlords.

As the winter months approached, we began working with the local shelter and housing provider to consider accommodating Judy. We explained to Judy that if she could stay at the shelter during the coldest nights of winter and thereby stay safe, we would also advocate with the local shelter and housing provider to prioritize her for affordable housing. The outreach counselor joined with Judy through a common language by referring to her strongly held value of safety and the option of affordable housing to keep her belongings secure.

Since we attend weekly provider meetings with shelter staff, we took the opportunity to jointly develop a plan on how to respond to Judy's disruptive behaviors, while allowing her to have shelter access throughout the winter months.

In essence, we developed a plan of *reasonable accommodation* to provide Judy with a renewed and more realistic opportunity to successfully leave the streets during the height of winter to the relative security of our small, local homeless shelter. "Reasonable accommodation" is a legal right in the States for people with disabilities that can be utilized when their particular issues related to disability interferes with access to needed services and/or resources. In this case, Judy had been denied access due to her inability to follow the shelter policy of residing inside for the entire night without leaving.

Instead, we offered the shelter supervisor and Judy an anger management Pretreatment strategy that allowed her to leave the premises whenever she felt over-stimulated or overwhelmed knowing that she was welcome to return upon calming herself down. The outreach clinician reviewed this plan with Judy and worked with her on strengthening coping strategies. This allowed Judy to successfully utilize the shelter on a more frequent basis than in the past. We were therefore able to prioritize her for affordable housing.

However, the housing provider added the requirement that Judy accept Department of Mental Health (DMH) support services in order to be fully considered. This was *not* a Housing First program, so certain preconditions to entry could be instituted.

In the past it has been difficult to attain DMH eligibility for a variety of reasons such as a potential applicant's concern that his or her autonomy and safety may be compromised by state authorities, or due to the stigma of being labeled with mental illness, among other reasons. The stark reality is that Judy was not willing to agree to DMH services and would certainly refuse to sign the application form.

Community Partners and Critical Response Team (CRT)

Judy's inability to access housing and services caused us great concern as her physical and mental health had been deteriorating at a rapid pace. This was evidenced by her appearing much thinner, walking with a pronounced limp, and more frequent conflicts with people visiting the town's business district, as well as a recent arrest by police for assault. Further, our outreach team utilizes a vulnerability index[8] (O'Connell, 2005), which indicates that people over sixty years of age who live on the streets for six months or more are at high risk of death. Therefore, we decided to pull together a Critical Response Team (Levy, 2013) in an attempt to promote eligibility for state services such as Department of Mental Health (DMH), Statewide Head Injury Program (SHIP) and Department of Developmental Services (DDS).

The Critical Response Team (CRT) consisted of various provider representatives who had either directly interacted with Judy over the past decade, or were connected to a service and/or resource that might help to resolve Judy's homelessness and promote her stability. This particular meeting included representatives from Health Care for the Homeless, the local shelter, DMH, Housing providers, me, and the outreach counselor. In order to respect Judy's confidentiality, we limited our discussion to either what we had all experienced and observed in the public arena, or to pertinent safety issues.

We explained to CRT members that at first, Judy was not at all interested in DMH services, though we were able to develop a "common language" that reflected some mental health concerns based on her exper-

---

[8] http://www.jedc.org/forms/Vulnerability%20Index.pdf

iencing high stress, lack of sleep, and difficulty getting along with others, not feeling safe, etc. We (the outreach clinician and I) explained to the DMH liaison at the meeting that we had a client in need of services, but she was uncomfortable with the term "mental illness." Further, she wasn't agreeable to entering DMH property/building, refused sign releases for past medical records, though all of us agreed that she clearly presented with Major Mental Health and medical concerns that warranted DMH housing stabilization services.

The CRT meeting led to the fruitful decision of doing joint outreach by an eligibility specialist and our outreach worker. Shortly thereafter, Judy was found eligible for DMH case management services without signing a single release for past medical records as normally required. This was a successful request for "reasonable accommodation" (exception to DMH eligibility rules/process due to disability) by the Critical Response Team.

Homeward Bound

During this same period of time, we received a community call that Judy was walking in the middle of traffic in the downtown area. We responded by immediately alerting the community police and local MH Crisis team. This quickly led to Judy being involuntarily hospitalized due to her safety being at imminent risk. Her well-adaptive survival skills were compromised by command auditory hallucinations stating that she should share her homeless plight with the oncoming traffic.

While at the hospital, Judy was given immediate access to health care services and they successfully addressed her physical concerns of dehydration, weight loss, and an injured left leg. Since DMH eligibility was recently approved with a new case manager assigned, we were able to jointly visit Judy at the inpatient unit, and made discharge plans that resulted in affordable housing with support services via the local shelter and housing provider. This was now possible because we met the demands of the housing provider by providing support services through the Department of Mental Health (DMH), so in return they made an exception to their entry criteria.

After Judy's discharge from the hospital, she transitioned to her new apartment. She met with a Health Care for the Homeless nurse for follow up on medical issues, and also received transitional support services via our PATH worker. From time to time she still imbibed alcohol, or temporarily stopped taking her psychotropic medications, though with much less frequency. She was very happy to have a place of her own where she no longer had to stand guard over her belongings. This gave her greater peace of mind and she expressed appreciation for her new sense of tranquility. She said, "Now that I have a home... I can finally rest."

Crisis/Opportunity

After three months of being housed, Judy felt stable and no longer saw a need to continue taking her psychotropic medications. Within weeks, her behaviors became disruptive and less tolerable to her neighbors, which resulted in heightened conflicts, threats, and eventual re-hospitalization. This led to a team meeting at the hospital to strategize with Judy on the best ways to support her return to the community. Judy angrily responded, "I don't like institutional food, so the sooner I can get out of here the better. Doesn't anyone understand that all I want is to be left alone?"

This statement captures the frustration of her adult life: pursuit for autonomy never being reconciled with her evident need for assistance. Our discharge plan reflected her values of safety and independence (autonomy), though we still needed to find a common language that would better resonate in her world. The outreach counselor responded to Judy's concerns by stating, "All we want to do is to figure out the best way for you to leave the hospital and return safely to your home!" Judy responded well to the outreach counselor's framing of the discharge plan, but was markedly less enthusiastic about her need for psychotropic medications. She was soon discharged back to her apartment, but remained ambivalent about taking her prescribed medications.

When I heard about this from the outreach clinician, we discussed a pretreatment strategy that could help motivate Judy to follow her treatment plan, while softening the blow to her autonomy. We offered her an incentive consisting of a gift certificate (instead of cash) that could be traded at the local donut shop for "free food" in exchange for every week that she remained out of the hospital, in conjunction with taking her prescribed medication. The careful re-framing of the discharge plan simultaneously upheld Judy's non-materialistic values, while pairing the success of staying out of the hospital with her current medication regimen. This supported her autonomy, daily routine and interests without the need for money, and circumvented a power struggle with support staff.

Further, Judy had a very positive relationship with the Healthcare for the Homeless nurse, so she was encouraged to review her medication and overall progress during their meetings. As Judy became more stabilized in her housing, they discussed the possibility of lowering the dosage of her psychotropic medication. This resulted in the nurse and Judy successfully negotiating with the psychiatrist to slowly reduce the dosage over time as long as Judy remained housed and met with her support team on a weekly basis.

Judy responded well to our proposal, and has since shown up reliably to receive her gift certificate. While more consistently taking prescribed medications and meeting with her support team was only a small part of the plan, it appeared to be a critical piece of the puzzle that led to Judy's success. The positive outcome of this intervention was dependent upon us being open to negotiate with Judy, which included rewarding her for her efforts and providing compassionate housing support services.

As noted by Ray Middleton in Chapter 6, when Open Dialogue (Mackler, 2014; Seikkula, 2011) is utilized as a psychosocial therapy for schizophrenia and related psychotic disorders, the research from Finland indicates that about 20% of the people served are in need of *long-term* psychotropic medications to help stabilize them in the community. A strong case can be made that these medications are over-prescribed in the US and that psychosocial interventions such as developing a Dialogical PIE (see chapter 6) are often preferable. Yet, it stands to reason that some, if not many people experiencing long-term homelessness with major thought disorders can benefit by symptom reduction through carefully prescribed and monitored psychotropic medications. Judy appeared to be among this subgroup.

Over the next several months, Judy was able to connect well with neighbors, and she continued to be an accepted part of the community at the local donut shop. On more than one occasion, we have witnessed her joking with store employees, while proudly stating that she is exceedingly happy to be off the streets and more than ready to lead the revolution so others can be successfully housed. Judy's newfound stability and sentiment to help others led to her participation in the peer network, composed of experts by experience at the local mental health clubhouse, furthering her sense of community and purpose. This also provided her with meaningful structure, and helped to reduce her alcohol consumption to an occasional nip. As of today, Judy remains successfully housed with DMH case management services, though the road there was not without considerable difficulty.

Lessons Learned from Judy's Story — Pretreatment Alternatives

Judy's narrative is a nice example of how an outreach worker who is an expert from experience can remain humane and clinically savvy by partaking in reflective practice of Pretreatment Principles of care. Judy's success was ultimately dependent upon a well-established network of community service and resource providers. This is further proof that it really does take a village, which in this case consists of donut shop employees, Community Police, Shelter and Housing Staff, MH Crisis Team, DMH Case Manager, Critical Response Team, Health Care for the Homeless Nurse, Judy's neighbors and landlord, Inpatient Social Worker and psychiatrist, Peer Network Staff, as well as the PATH Outreach Counselor and Supervisor in order to facilitate a successful outcome.

Judy's narrative gives us a close look at the harsh world of trauma, mental illness, and long-term homelessness. She valued safety and was most at ease when left to her own devices. She saw herself as an advocate for the oppressed, but found it difficult to do this in a socially acceptable manner. Nevertheless, she found meaning in her rage against the system and this provided a sense of purpose and power, as opposed to being despondent and helpless. Judy preferred to be sheltered or even housed, yet could not function on a level that would allow her to independently get off the streets.

Her entrenched adaptive responses of fight/flight (due to life-long trauma) kept her relatively safe from others, but also separated her from needed social supports. In addition, she experienced the detrimental effects of schizophrenia as evidenced by paranoid ideation and difficulty with expressing her wants and needs. She experienced auditory command hallucinations and found it hard to maintain a coherent thread to her communications without drifting into other subject areas or abruptly ending conversations with others. This made it difficult for community members to respond in a helpful manner and only added to her sense of fear, anger, and isolation.

Basic truths that are applicable to both sides of the Atlantic come into view through Judy's narrative, such as the importance of person-centered relationships, joining with a person's sense of meaning, and the need to be trauma informed, as well as the need for access to affordable housing and Pretreatment strategies to help facilitate a pathway to recovery. While we did not have access to a Housing First option, we used effective advocacy and upheld Judy's rights to be housed via the Americans with Disabilities Act's "Reasonable Accommodation" law. However, none of this would have led to placement and stabilization without an emphasis on developing active community partnerships.

We now know that Pretreatment alternatives such as Homeless Outreach and Housing First programs can greatly assist highly vulnerable, unsheltered homeless individuals with a primary diagnosis of major mental illness (e.g., Schizophrenia). In fact, Housing First was specifically developed to effectively serve this homeless subgroup, which has much larger numbers in the US than in the UK. I utilize the term "Pretreatment" to emphasize that none of these approaches require treatment compliance or even an openness to partake in mental health, addiction, or medical services. Nevertheless, when clients connect with Homeless Outreach counselors, Critical Response Team efforts, and/or Housing First Programs, this often facilitates their contemplation of the potential benefits from mental health, addiction and/or medical interventions. The amazing thing is that pathways to recovery can be accessed by people on their own terms, if we are patient and guided by Pretreatment principles of care.

Initial Look at Housing First

Housing First efforts supported by US-HUD funds began during the 1990s with Safe Haven Programs that were designed to house at-risk, unsheltered individuals suffering from severe mental illnesses. The Safe Haven Model is a "low demand" alternative based on harm reduction principles that makes few demands on the tenant, but provides 24/7 staffing support and so welcomes residents who are not yet ready to partake in treatment.

The Pathways to Housing program located in New York City is widely credited as the beginnings of the Housing First movement. During 1992, Dr. Sam Tsemberis designed this program and instituted a research component to formalize best practices. Since then, a variety of Housing First programs with different levels of support have been tried in many cities throughout the US, Canada, and the UK. Multiple studies have confirmed successful outcomes, such as better than 84% housing retention rates, as well as reducing overall health care costs (Bretherton & Pleace, 2015; Common Ground, 2012; Home and Healthy for Good Report, 2010; Stefancic and Tsemberis, 2007; Tsemberis, 2010).

Housing First, as defined by the Pathways to Housing model, does not require that a person partake in mental health, addiction or medical treatment; or that they achieve sobriety prior to being housed. The basic premise is that people should be housed as quickly as possible with support services that can establish pathways and/or bridges to community resources and services. Judy's story demonstrates the long road of effective outreach and advocacy that led to her placement in independent permanent housing with support services.

While this is a success story, one can fairly question why it took so long. System reform is essential. We can do better at directly connecting affordable housing and support service options to outreach teams and shelter or hostel staff, so that assistance can be readily available for persons experiencing long-term and/or chronic homelessness. Housing First initiatives in many towns across the US and UK have achieved this reality. However, we must be careful to assure that Housing First efforts that are geared toward helping people with complex needs provide the level of support services and rapid crisis response that are necessary to best facilitate people's safety and stability with successful tenancies.

Speaking frankly, I have seen and heard of too many Housing First programs in the US being ill-equipped to respond to the level of need of our most vulnerable clients. This is in part due to a Federal (HUD) driven public policy that has reduced funding for support services in favor of targeting the money toward housing resources. However, good public policy dictates that this is not an either/or choice of housing affordability over an appropriate level of quality support services. We ultimately need both to be successful. If we really want to resolve long-term homelessness, then we need to offer accessible, affordable housing alternatives with quality support services.

One local endeavor in Western Massachusetts that's well worth noting for its emphasis on support services, with staff training on Pretreatment practices, is the REACH Housing First model (Levy, 2013). REACH stands for Regional Engagement and Assessment of Chronically Homeless persons. The idea is that if we are going to house people as quickly as possible, then effective outreach strategies are needed within the context of housing to help develop pathways to recovery and thereby support transitions to relevant treatment resources and services.

A key element of the REACH model is that the outreach worker provides ongoing service delivery to vulnerable individuals, regardless as to whether or not the housing placement is successful. The therapeutic relationship flows across homeless and residential environments to promote consistency of care, so that the price of progress or failure is not the loss of a key relationship. Further, a long-term trusting relationship provides a sense of joint witnessing with the client to better understand what works and what doesn't work throughout one's housing experience. When initial tenancies end due to eviction or other reasons, these lessons learned can effectively set the stage for rapid rehousing.

REACH Housing is an integration of both Housing First and Homeless Outreach. Through the years, it has been funded through a mixture of local, state and federal dollars. It began in 2007 and has since successfully served many residents throughout the Greater Springfield Massachusetts region as evidenced by keeping over 85% of its highly vulnerable, formerly long-term, unsheltered homeless participants housed over a five-year time period. This is truly remarkable, considering that folks were placed directly from the streets with untreated illnesses. In fact, 94% of participants struggled with co-occurring issues of mental illness and addiction, as well as major medical issues (tri-morbidity) and averaged more than eight years of homelessness (Levy, 2013).

The key to our success was due to incorporating a Pretreatment philosophy that provided guidance for person-centered work, which in many cases eventually led to needed treatment/recovery services. It should also be noted that what made the success of this program possible was the courage, foresight and hard work of Jerry Ray, David Havens, and their staff at the Mental Health Association. The REACH Housing First initiative has been adopted by the Western MA region (All Roads Lead Home, 2008, p. 23) as a best practice toward ending chronic homelessness. The REACH Housing First Program and the successful housing placement of Judy demonstrates what can be accomplished. It is well worth considering what role the greater community can play in supporting and/or promoting such achievements.

Personal Liberty vs. Community Responsibility

A bastardized myth has been propagated throughout the cities and towns of America. It is based on a kernel of truth from libertarian circles, and the folklore of capitalism: the story of independence and the costs of freedom. It holds that people can move up the economic ladder to success, providing that they work hard and make well-informed decisions. In other words, people get what they earn, so if you are a dedicated worker and make the right choices, you will take part in the American dream of a good paying job and home ownership.

There is also another myth, perhaps a close cousin, and one that is equally broken, that those among the long-term homeless have chosen their fate. The assumption is that poverty and homelessness are directly due to bad choices and a lack of motivation or due to a person's preference for less responsibility. It seems to me that our cultural myths make it too easy for us to write off people who experience the traumatic effects of long-term homelessness as not wanting help. Even worse is the possibility that this way of thinking convinces people who are impoverished and at risk to refuse essential community supports that may otherwise prevent homelessness.

On countless occasions, I have met people who were too proud to ask for help, especially when the assistance offered is based on the person admitting fault and/or promising to do better. The presumption is that the vast majority of people without homes have chosen their fate or that it is a consequence of a personal failing. Conveniently, this relieves our own sense of guilt, shame and community responsibility. Judy's story, and the homeless narratives of so many others, confronts these mistaken beliefs.

Is it really acceptable for an older woman with schizophrenia, or anyone with significant mental health or medical issues, to be among the long-term homeless? Is this truly the price of freedom? If not, surely we understand that there are roles for our communities and governments to play in ending homelessness for the most vulnerable among us.

It is very easy to assume that the Judys of our world are among those who don't want our help and are beyond our service capabilities. In many respects, US culture and commitment laws (Involuntary Commitment for Mental Illness) support this point of view. However, the transatlantic reality is that other societies and cultures can come to different conclusions about how to address these issues. England on a whole rarely has people with untreated schizophrenia among their long-term homeless, while in the States this is a more common experience.

Though the reasons for this disparity are not immediately evident, when we look a little deeper some cultural, societal, and policy differences come into view. English law allows people with untreated schizophrenia to be more easily committed or mandated for treatment by concerned family and community members via a doctor and social worker, when their illness grossly interferes with their ability to function. In fact, many would see doing otherwise as a dereliction of our duty to care for the most vulnerable among us. The criterion throughout the States is much more stringent, and generally defined as a person's safety being at imminent risk due to mental illness resulting in a danger to self, others, or an inability for self-care. The key word is "imminent," which means within a narrow, measurable timeframe. This law is an echo of the deinstitutionalization movement of the 1960s, when people were released from mental health hospitals where they were often provided with substandard or even abusive care, as opposed to trauma-informed care.

The promise of deinstitutionalization was for ex-patients to find a greater sense of independence and functioning through the use of psychotropic medications and follow-up care from Community Mental Health Centers, as well as housing with support services. Unfortunately, the funding for housing with support services was never really fulfilled, and eventually many of these folks stopped taking their prescribed medications, lost contact with Community Mental Health support services, and ended up homeless. Back in the 1980s, I met and did active outreach with many people who were deinstitutionalized during the 60s on the streets of NYC.

Today, this is no longer an issue, though US involuntary commitment laws remain a reflection of our value for personal liberty and hard-earned civil rights for certain oppressed groups, which, in this case, consists of people with major mental illness who were often mistreated in mental health institutions. The result remains problematic, as people with severe, untreated, mental health issues are numerous among the homeless in the States. This is further compounded by the lack of access to *voluntary long-term inpatient stays* when necessary to promote mental health stability and successful community placement. In fact, the length of both inpatient psychiatric stays and detoxification from alcohol and drug admissions shrank dramatically throughout the 90s due to insurance companies instituting cost savings measures in an effort to eliminate waste, while maximizing profits. Arguably, this externalized those costs to the wider society[9].

In contrast, England, through tax funded medicine for all, avoids the conundrum of privatized insurance companies mandating acceptable lengths of stay for inpatient MH and/or detoxification treatment. Health care free from managed care dictates provides space for more collaborative doctor-patient decisions on the course of treatment and the needed length of inpatient stays. This ultimately results in greater individualization and promotes long-term stability. This is yet another reason why it is a comparatively rare occurrence to find someone with a major thought disorder sleeping rough in England.

While convincing arguments can be made and should be considered from the perspective of upholding personal liberty, we still have the community responsibility to provide quality outreach services and accessible voluntary inpatient/outpatient treatment, as well as housing and support services for people without homes who are compromised by major mental health concerns. Many studies on both sides of the Atlantic have demonstrated that significant numbers of people experiencing homelessness, as well as incarcerated individuals who eventually become homeless, are impacted by the detrimental effects of behavioral health issues on a daily basis, stemming from complex trauma, acquired brain injuries, addictions, other severe mental illnesses, and personality disorders.

---

[9] For more information See Chapter 12 - Cross-Cultural Connections: Homelessness, Costs and Interventions

Robin Johnson's chapter, which immediately follows this, argues that this very broad language of "behavioral health issues" may be masking important transatlantic differences. He sees the US addressing untreated major mental illness via Housing First centered policy and programs, as opposed to the kind of problems that they find in the entrenched homeless population in the UK. This, he suggests, may be one of the reasons that Housing First seems so necessary in the US, whereas in the UK, it is seen as one of many useful approaches to a wider range of pressing issues, where different solutions for different problems have been found.

I believe that both sides of the Atlantic could benefit from a wide array of housing options that are inclusive of Housing First. It is important that we do not limit ourselves to one primary option, or one that is emphasized to the point of cutting funding from other models that can be helpful when properly matched to the many sub-populations.

One striking example, out of many, is the need for more transitional housing programs to serve young adults. Developmentally speaking, everything about young adults is in transition, so even the thought of permanent supportive housing (as we call it in the US) doesn't jive well with where they are at. What remains important, whether it be Housing First, transitional housing opportunities, or some other formulation, is that people in need have quick access to affordable housing options with support services and that residential program policies provide the opportunity to individualize the work with residents (even within a group home setting), effectively meeting them where they are at, while incorporating PIE and Pretreatment approaches.

Silo Mentality vs. Triage Response

For too long, the US response to homelessness has been hampered by administratively splitting its causes into specific categories such as mental illness, addiction, medical issues, brain injuries, and developmental-cognitive impairments. In turn, services that matched these designations were supplied from different funding streams such as the Department of Mental Health, Substance Abuse Bureau, or Traumatic Brain Injury Services, etc. This has the dual consequence of shifting our focus away from the broad issue of access to affordable housing that underlies all homelessness, as well as magnifying and reinforcing a silo mentality throughout our service delivery culture.

Further, this leads to the negative consequence of narrow eligibility criteria tests to see who qualifies for services derived from the appropriate funding stream. In retrospect, people who present with an array of challenges have been forced into the dilemma of how to fit into a silo of services determined by primary diagnosis, as opposed to directly addressing their most pressing concerns or needs. This over-medicalization of homelessness went hand-in-hand with a treatment-first philosophy. The idea was to fix the person before the provision of housing. Today it is obvious that this type of approach has multiple failings and not only misses the link between safe affordable housing and better outcomes, but also significantly slows down the helping process by forcing people down separate rabbit holes of eligibility.

At best, people without homes were found eligible for a discrete set of services that may or may not have included affordable housing assistance, or at worst, people were denied eligibility and then redirected to a different rabbit hole where they could start the eligibility process all over again. Instead of a triage approach to homelessness that quickly matches vital resources to those most in need, we ended up playing a very slow and unintentionally cruel game of what we derisively referred to as ping-pong. It consisted of people who were seeking assistance being sent from one place to another and then back again as they were often found ineligible for services, before being redirected to another system of care.

For example, if someone presented with a head injury, mental health concerns, and also addiction, it was not uncommon for the person to fill out three different eligibility applications, only to be denied eligibility to all three, rather than given across-the-board access or integrated care. Such is the absurdity of a silo mentality and the service culture it produces.

In many respects, the Housing First movement can be understood as a triage response to medicalizing homelessness and the systemic barriers created through the separation of human services by diagnosis and corresponding funding streams. Instead of providing treatment-compliance based housing and services with restrictive eligibility standards, the common underlying issue of homelessness is more efficiently addressed by providing permanent affordable housing with flexible support services that respond to a wide variety of people's needs, wants and concerns. This has the immediate effect of melting away the delays of eligibility and lack of integration of services that were inherent to separate bureaucratic systems of care (silos). Over time, the housing support worker can further play the role of fostering communication between silos of care, as well as advocating for targeted services to address treatment issues.

If we are serious about ending homelessness for the most vulnerable, then what is clearly warranted is a triage approach. Housing First principles have been applied to the development of coordinated entry systems to assess, prioritize, and house people as quickly as possible. Even though coordinated entry can be utilized to properly match people to an array of different service and housing options, it is sometimes referred to as *Systems or Strategic HF.* Coordinated entry and vulnerability assessments are not based on silo eligibility or particular diagnostic language, but rather on emergency service usage, safety concerns, level of functioning, and acute needs ranging from income to crisis intervention.

An initial assessment can facilitate the referral to obtain assistance via an array of options. This may include access to shelter, Rental Assistance programs, Permanent Supportive Housing, Critical Response Team, or short-term case coordination paired with funds to divert people from home-lessness to an immediate housing placement, etc. However, in most communities, there is still much work to be done to develop a true triage response. Difficulties persist when considering the reality of large homeless numbers, limited funds, and the expense of housing programs with support staff. Housing people with major functional impairments and significant health risks into affordable units without adequate supports is inefficient. It is dangerous, and apt to result in a reoccurrence of homelessness. Yet, throughout the States, this has become common practice and paraded as Housing First policy. We can and must do better.

Another emerging problem is that the new, coordinated entry systems being proposed and acted upon are more and more centralized, regulated, data driven, and rife with bureaucratic dilemmas. An example can be found in the States due to the Department of Housing and Urban Development (HUD) mandating coordinated entry systems in conjunction with vulner-ability tests to determine eligibility for permanent supportive housing. In our efforts to comply with HUD regulations and to show that we are sufficiently data driven, we have in many cases become too reliant on the numbers scored via vulnerability assessments or too restrictive based on overly specific chronic homelessness criteria, or have deemed those who refuse to sign releases of information (required by us in order to collect the data) as unworkable.

These forms and checklists in regard to chronic homelessness and vulnerability should not be utilized as a substitute for professional assessment and opinion of our most skilled workers, but rather as an additional tool or a crude measure that can inform the triage process. In many ways, the absurdity continues as we give a nod to innovative approaches and rebuild centralized systems of eligibility, while professional opinion is cast aside and many people without homes continue to suffer the frustrations brought about by lack of individualization. I am reminded of the exclamation by the Who (Townsend, 1971) "We won't get fooled again!"

The Need for Pretreatment Strategies and Psychologically Informed Environments

This chapter began with the promise of ending homelessness for the most vulnerable among us and it ends with the reality that there is a lot more work to be done. The key is to remain person-centered even as our systems of care evolve toward data-driven, practice-based on coordinated entry, vulnerability scores and centralized or even decentralized waiting lists that prioritize people most in need for housing with support services (Strategic HF). This needs to be done with a mindfulness toward creating psychologically informed environments driven by the quality of our relationships with each other and appreciation of people's stories, culture, values, challenges and aspirations.

Whether it is coordinated entry, outreach work, or low demand transitional or permanent housing programs, we must begin where people are at and earn their trust, before proceeding toward our mutual goals of attaining a better quality of life that most often includes affordable housing and meaningful connections with others. If we are not careful, we risk the pitfalls that overreliance on formalized assessments and data collection can bring. We must guard against seeing people mainly through the lens of an assessment score or simply as names on a list.

Namely, we risk the loss of the very thing that brought us to this work… our compassion and the belief that we are all in this together. Both Pretreatment Strategies and Psychologically Informed Environments (PIE) provide us with the guidance necessary to remain person-centered, while we continue to use assessment tools and new technologies to facilitate the positive change of ending homelessness for those whose functioning and safety are significantly compromised by disability.

The exploration of HF and its many different meanings, applications, and limitations on program and systemic levels of care continues in the next chapter as Robin Johnson takes us along on his visit to America. Through new eyes, we can learn new things.

References

All Roads Lead Home, (2008) *The Pioneer Valley's Plan to End Homelessness*. Supported by the Cities of Holyoke, Northampton, Springfield, MA. Funded by One Family, Inc.

Bretherton, J. & Pleace, N. (2015) *Housing first in England: An evaluation of nine services*. Center for Housing Policy: University of York

Common Ground Website (2012) Housing First Research. http://www.commonground.org/mission-model/our-results/

Frankl, V. E. (1985) *Man's search for meaning*. New York: Washington Square Press

Home and Healthy for Good Report (2010) Compiled by Massachusetts Housing & Shelter Alliance Staff. Retrieved from website: http://www.mhsa.net/HHG

Levy, J. S. (2000) Homeless outreach: On the road to pretreatment alternatives. *Families in Society: The Journal of Contemporary Human Services*, 81(4): 360-368

Levy, J. S. (2004) Pathway to a common language: A homeless outreach perspective. *Families in Society: The Journal of Contemporary Human Services*, 85(3): 371-378

Levy, J. S. (2010) *Homeless narratives & pretreatment pathways: From words to housing*. Ann Arbor, MI: Loving Healing Press

Levy, J. S. (2011) *Homeless outreach & housing first: Lessons learned*. Ann Arbor, MI: Loving Healing Press

Levy, J. S. (2013) *Pretreatment guide for homeless outreach & housing first: Helping couples, youth, and unaccompanied adults*. Ann Arbor, MI: Loving Healing Press

Mackler, D. (2014) *Open Dialogue: An alternative Finnish approach to healing psychosis*. (Complete Film), http://wildtruth.net/dvd/opendialogue/

O'Connell, J. J. & Swain S. *Rough sleepers: A five year prospective study in Boston, 1999-2003*. Presentation, Tenth Annual Ending Homelessness Conference, Massachusetts Housing and Shelter Alliance, Waltham, MA 2005

O'Connell, J. J. Vulnerability Index. Retrieved on 8/2/17 from jedc.org web site http://www.jedc.org/forms/Vulnerability%20Index.pdf

Seikkula, J. (2011) Becoming Dialogical: Psychotherapy or a way of Life? *The Australian and New Zealand Journal of Family Therapy*. 32(3): 179-193

Stefancic, A. & Tsemberis, S. (2007) Housing first for long-term shelter dwellers with psychiatric disabilities in a suburban county: A four-year study of housing access and retention. *The Journal of Primary Prevention*, 28(3-4): 265-279.

Townsend, P. (1971) *Won't Get Fooled Again*. Who's Next. Performed by the Who. Decca Records, LP.

Tsemberis, S. (2010) Housing First: Ending homelessness, promoting recovery and reducing cost. In I. Ellen & B. O'Flaherty (eds) *How to House the Homeless*. New York: Russell Sage Foundation

10 They do things differently there: PIEs, Housing First and the New Social Psychiatry
Robin Johnson

O wad some power the gift tae gi'e us, to see ourselves as others see us. (Robbie Burns)

Opportunity

This is the story of a journey: in more ways than one.

In the spring of 2016 I was able to spend a few short weeks in the United States. I was originally going out to visit my daughter, who was in university there; but I also hoped to take the opportunity to see for myself how homelessness services actually operate in the US. So let me begin with explaining my reasons for this.

For some years past I have been concerned professionally with understanding the complex interfaces of homelessness and mental health, at all levels, from policy to practice and back again. In the past five years or so we in the UK had been hearing a lot about Housing First, and what appeared to be some spectacularly successful results, a sound and consistent evidence base for the effectiveness of what was described as a very different way of working with people with major mental health problems who have become entrenched in homelessness.

Yet I was frankly sceptical. With people with complex needs, in my experience—before getting interested in homelessness issues I was for many years a psychiatric social worker—it is very rare to find any one solution that is absolutely right for absolutely everybody. Nor was the evidence base in itself quite so convincing. Having read many of the papers on the subject, the evidence, I thought, had been perhaps overstated, and the complex reality of what worked, and why, was perhaps being oversimplified.

By then I had spent five years as editor of an academic journal concerned with research, policy and practice in housing care and support; and what had struck me then—as I had observed in a string of editorials— was how rare it was that the researchers and their confident findings really attempted to identify the social and political context in which their findings were embedded, and which gave them their full meaning. The researchers' descriptions were like the tip of the iceberg; what kept the innovation afloat was barely mentioned, and rarely if ever analysed.

In particular, I suspected that whatever it was that was—quite evidently—working in the US was likely to be deeply steeped in the partic- ular context of the US, its history, its geography, its culture and its economies and institutions. So I wasn't at all convinced that this Housing First approach could simply be exported to another country, with a quite different political system and services—or not, at least without a good deal of translation.

I have been myself once, if only briefly, an adviser with the UK govern- ment. As a result, I was also wary of any programme that is seized upon by government and promoted as best practice, if that means it is taken out of context in which it was first developed. It then must operate to the rules, without the enthusiasm and creativity, the inventiveness of the pioneer and the early adopter. In my experience, it's that sense of "ownership", that creativity at the frontline, that really makes things work.

Contrast

But there was another reason to want to see for myself how services in the US actually worked. Beginning while an adviser to the UK government, I had spent quite a large part of the past ten years trying to describe and analyse the nature and the quality of the best of work that was being done in those accommodation services that we in the UK call "hostels" (or "refuges", for women, and "foyers" for young people), but in the US are all called "shelters".

We had developed, in the UK, a way of working in short term resettle- ment and recovery accommodation that had seemed to me to be very progressive and enlightened. In fact, a lot of what I saw seemed strikingly similar to some of the progressive mental health services I had worked in during my youth. There were some very interesting echoes here—but we'll come back to that later.

The development of these services had made sense in the particular context of UK policy, especially in the funding of social security costs in the 1990s; and a considerable investment of central government funding to improve the design and physical condition of the buildings. Although there was still a lot of work to be done to improve services, that's the work I had been deeply engaged in, these last ten years or more. I was even the one who had actually first coined the term to describe such work – we now talk of "psychologically informed environments".

It's a term that could apply, potentially, to a wide range of human service environments—hospital wards, schools, care homes, even some prisons. But it had been taken up with particular enthusiasm in homelessness services, where for the first time, it seems, we were beginning to describe what the real work of those services is—dealing with the complex psychological and emotional issues that typically underlie entrenched homelessness in the UK. And helping people with such very entrenched problems to find a path to recovery (a word, incidentally, that we here use not just for substance abuse, but for all long-term mental health issues) – that's what we really do.

It had therefore come as a shock to discover that many, perhaps most such homelessness services in the UK would be described and dismissed, in US terms, as "transitional housing", and so by definition therefore wrong, in the eyes of the proponents of HF. Instead we were being told that scrapping such "shelters" was the way forward. They were part of the problem, "research showed". There was something awry here; and I needed to understand it better.

Language

The first clue had come in a conversation with my new found friend, Jay Levy. We had planned a phone call, to try to explore more some of the ideas we seemed to share.

"*But tell me, Robin*" Jay had then asked, "*when you talk of working with people in hostels, is this some kind of social inclusion thing? You place homeless people in youth hostels?*"

I had been amazed to realise, from talking[10] with Jay, that everything that we had written up to that point in the UK about the transformation we had wrought was quite unknown to US readers. The reason for this was that the principal word that we use to describe these developments in the UK – hostel - has a completely different meaning in the US.

---

[10] I later discovered that the spoken word can be even more deceptive than the written. Talking with "shelter" staff in Boston, I described our recent work "in hostel environments". The look of puzzlement alerted me. The pronunciation, the sound of our word "hostel" would be taken to mean, in the US, "hostile". We all breathed a sigh of relief after that.

I later had the opportunity to visit and talk with a woman who was head of support for one of the best known, highly regarded, often cited services in the US. She had told me that some time back she had been searching the net for anything useful written on innovations and improved practice in homelessness. It had simply never occurred to her to use a word like "hostel" in her search terms; and she would, she said, actually have immediately excluded any paper that came up, that talked of hostels.

All that we had done, all the massive investment, of funds and of time, in improvement in our hostels, was quite literally invisible. We were not speaking the same language.

But what, then, was actually happening in the US, that had given rise to HF? Why did we seem to be so different, in the paths we had taken? Just how irredeemably dire was what they, over there in the US (as I had learnt from Jay), called "shelter" accommodation? Was this perhaps the reason that so many in the US seemed to regard them as part of the problem, to have abandoned any attempts to improve them, such as we had undertaken? Should we really be taking the same path as the US, just because it is evidence based?

Variety

As it happened, only a few months earlier I had been sent, in my capacity as the then editor of the "Housing, Care and Support" journal, a paper submitted for publication which described a housing project in Seattle dedicated to accommodating people with substance abuse problems. Entitled "Single-site housing first for chronically homeless people", it discussed the development of 1811 Eastlake as a condominium-style complex of individual units, each with a tenancy; but a place with shared facilities, group activities – all voluntary – and opportunities for shared efforts and participation. On-site staff provided a full range of suitable services from social activities to therapy; there is even a front-desk reception area.

I was intrigued. Here was what seemed to be just the kind of service we were seeing in the UK – a recovery ethos, an integrated development, with opportunities for constructive active engagement, a strong sense of community, formal and informal peer support. This seemed very different to the dispersed, rather isolated housing that I had been given to understand was the preferred model for Permanent Supported Housing (PSH) in the Housing First model. But yet it was described here as being part of the HF program. This was something new to me. Curious, I emailed the authors, to ask how this worked; after a brief interchange, when the authors seemed surprised that I was even surprised, the correspondence eventually fizzled out.

But so it was that I first came across the term "single site" (also known as "congregated" or "clustering") accommodation, as part of the Housing First programme, in contrast to the "scattered site" approach that had seemed to be promoted in all the versions of HF—and of its evidenced base for effectiveness—that we were hearing about in the UK.

Were there, in that case, actually other examples of similarly positive work being done in some places—the United States is after all a very big country—that we simply weren't hearing about over here? Was there other work that was being overlooked, ignored, perhaps even dismissed or side-lined by the enthusiastic adoption of HF, and the rooted hostility towards what is often its apparent target, the "staircase" model of "shelters" and any forms of short term accommodation with tenancy conditions? Was there something else going on? And what could I really hope to see, in three short weeks?

"Systemic" Approaches

Bags all packed, just before setting off to fly to Boston, at the last minute I came across a newly released e-book from Canada, on "systemic" approaches to homelessness. The book was a link in an attachment to someone's tweet that had somehow caught my eye. I don't really follow Twitter a lot, and in the endless blizzard that is the Twittersphere, I could so easily have missed this. But the e-book came with a lengthy foreword, and many chapters; and it promised case studies, examples. It certainly sounded like my kind of thing. One quick click and I had a copy on the iPad to browse on the journey; and (fittingly) in mid-Atlantic, on the plane from Heathrow to Boston, I began to flick through it. (You'll find this book amongst the references in my other chapter in this book, which is more formal and academic in style; in this account I am keeping the style light, and narrative....)

Here I found huge enthusiasm for the game-changing impact of HF there; and many chapters with very useful examples given – and with a fair amount of detail – of what were clearly congregated or single site developments, all in the name of HF. Just as the authors of that earlier paper had said, it wasn't just Seattle; this was happening all over. Or at least, in Canada.

That e-book also used a new term, one I had not come across before, in all my readings on HF in the UK: Housing First as a "strategy". HF was seen here not just as a particular practice, to be adhered to with all due fidelity, but an approach that might then allow within it a variety of pathways, approaches, means to an end. If so, could there then be a constructive role for short term accommodation, even for accommodation with residency conditions, as part of a wider, comprehensive local strategy? If so, what would the guiding principles of such accommodation be?

Arriving overnight in Boston, I was delighted to get to meet Jay Levy himself; and he introduced me to Joe Finn of MHSA (who is also contributing to this book). We spent a whole afternoon together, trying to get to grips with the differences between the social policy context of the US and the UK, the more technical language, the names of different programmes and funding streams, the complex tiers of administration of funds and policy in each locality; and the inevitable tensions in promoting change.

Later I also got to visit and meet some of Joe's colleagues in social work and public health, and began to explore the history of shelter services and philosophies as they had evolved over 30 years or so in the US, the context in which Housing First first appeared - but again, this is something we must come back to. I also heard of concerns that there were some individuals, housed via HF, who had felt cut off from the collusive camaraderie of the street; and the tenancy had failed, through the pain of isolation; all of which needed addressing.

Community

From Boston I went mid-West, to Ann Arbor, in Michigan, and I had – since you ask – a lovely week with my daughter. But since she also had work to do, I also had some free time to fill, and so I took the opportunity to go out with staff of the homeless health outreach team. I got to see for myself the kind of tent cities that homeless people had created; and I heard a remarkable story that speaks volumes about the potential strengths to be found in such communities.

This was something I had simply never seen in the UK, at least in homelessness. I am, as you may have gathered, a firm believer in the potential and the need for community, even for the most marginalised and chaotic; indeed, especially for the most marginalised and chaotic. But I had never envisaged this kind of self-organising community. It was an eye-opener. I had seen many kinds of innovative services, in a community setting; but the idea of community work – as I was later to explore with Jay and his colleagues – was really, as they say in the US, "something else".

This was more like an anarchist collective, or the democratic therapeutic communities I had known and worked in as a much younger man. This was a theme to explore more; and I was to see yet more of this new kind of community support thinking, back in Massachusetts, with Jay; and again later, back in England, now surfing the net to look out for other such stories of a rich community life, in homelessness recovery. In the references, to my other chapter you will find some examples; I am sure there are many more.

In Ann Arbor I also got to see the homelessness community from a different angle entirely. I went to meet the folks who ran the local community newsletter for street homeless people. Not being themselves a housing service—but with their eyes and ears very much open to the views and the feeling in their community—they had a very different perspective on what really worked. What I heard there was far more reservations about the practice of HF, and the isolation that some felt.

Later, at a breakfast club for homeless and otherwise precarious people in a local church hall, another new angle emerged. I fell into conversation with a young man who told me, eagerly, of his experience of being required to live in an abstinence based household for two years, by a Court order, as a condition of his early release, Eagerly he told me how this had been, he said, the making of him. But this was precisely the kind of temporary, abstinence-based housing that HF was so implacably opposed to; and he was telling me how grateful he was to have been made to go there. Short-stay accommodation was taboo in HF; as was "conditionality" – an enforceable participation in a change programme. But court-mandated sobriety accommodation, I later found, was exempted from HF policies.

Furthermore, a study by the same team that had developed the Eastlake project in Seattle had found that 67% of HF participants interviewed were interested in abstinence-based housing, although only 54% believed that they could realistically maintain that kind of supported housing. This raises another awkward question; should services be focusing on meeting the immediate needs for housing, or helping such individuals achieve their real preference? The picture was getting more and more complex; and then we went to Detroit.

Different strokes

It was in Detroit that I really got to see the full extent and character of urban street homelessness in the US. In Detroit, far more than in Boston— where after all, I had deliberately sought "the poorer quarters where the ragged people go"—at every intersection, every stop light on the road as we entered the city, there were people panhandling (as they call it), or sometimes offering to work, standing or slumped behind badly written cardboard placards. Here were evidently homeless people in a state of distress, dereliction and neglect that would have provoked a scandal back home.

I was seeing many more people with outright, obvious major mental illness than we would see in the UK. I began to see more closely the different character of homelessness in the US. In each case, it is the gaps in services that account for a large part of homelessness, but the gaps in mainstream mental health services seem far more pronounced in the US. In the UK, the people who slip through the safety nets of care services into homelessness tend to be those with substance abuse, and long-standing personality problems, which render effective engagement with service harder.

Did this help to understand why homelessness services might have gone in such a different direction? Later, I would need to look into this aspect, therefore, in much more legal and historical detail. After Ann Arbor and Detroit I was in Chicago for a couple of days. Another city, another new piece in the puzzle.

Chicago sees itself, just as Boston does, as an exemplar of HF, and I was escorted proudly to see a number of "single site" permanent supported housing schemes that had been developed there in the name of HF. (It would be difficult, of course, to arrange for me to visit individuals' homes in scattered site projects—and besides, such visits are always intrusive, often rather tokenistic—and I could much more easily visit those accommodated in congregated housing.)

But the thing that was most striking was to discover just how often in the US housing meant in practice not isolated individual tenancies, but congregated or single site housing units where you might find two or three, or five or six, or even ten to twenty individuals.

Sometimes individuals had small flats; sometimes just a single room, and shared facilities. But most if not all such complexes had some kind of communal area, be it a kitchen or a living room. They were living cheek by jowl alongside others, in a social group with companionship for those on a shared journey that seemed to me to have more in common with the smaller hostels or the shared flats in "move on accommodation", that we in the UK had been developing over the past 20-30 years.

The journey progresses. Heading back east, I was able to spend a couple of days with Jay Levy, in Western Massachusetts, and see for myself the way "shelter" actually worked in a much smaller township. A much smaller unit, and something of the flavour of a shared student house – transitional housing for people in transition. It seemed to me that good shelter care was not so very different from hostels in the UK. They just didn't, it seemed to me, have the language to describe what they were doing, and doing well, that we had developed in the UK. But the differences between us were dissolving still further.

Returning eventually to Boston, I had the chance to actually visit some more of the accommodation services that Joe Finn had described – both temporary shelter, and permanent housing. The shelter was indeed a warehouse facility; vast dormitories, with bunk beds and bed spaces that needed to be cleared out by day. No leaving your property here, or it would be stolen, or removed. No way was this offering even the most temporary of homes.

Yet I had some more really useful, insightful conversations with social work and housing staff who were also trying now to understand, looking back on what had happened, and what had changed, in the US and in the homelessness world over the past 30 years. These were the years when HF had suddenly burst upon the world. This was where it all came from. This was where it made sense.

I also found—just as I had done in Chicago—that the services of which they were most proud were doing the things we would have been just as proud of, if they were in the UK. The difference was that here, they were being provided as far as possible in what was, at least technically, permanent supported housing (PSH); and it was at this point that I finally began to see a very different side to HF to the one that I had been presented with in the UK, and then in the US.

It was then I began to understand what may be perhaps the real achievement of Housing First—and how this had been obscured by the rhetoric and the research programmes that point, more contentiously, to other successes. In particular, I began to see the real value, and the real lessons that we might take away.

And so I began to see the UK too, and the services we have, in a new light. For that wider, more historical understanding, I must ask the reader nevertheless to wait a little longer. Because first we need to dispel two or three unhelpful and misleading (i.e. frankly wrong) ideas.

Red Herrings

One thing that seemed to distinguish these PSH services from those we had in the UK, was that there was no fixed time limit to length of stay, whereas many services in the UK still DO have an expectation of move on, even if that is usually these days more flexibly applied. (Indeed, this is part of the reason those individuals still qualify as homeless, and as having some priority in re-housing.)

But the difference between a licence and a tenancy is not a "natural fact", like temperature or altitude. It is a product of law, and laws can vary. In the UK, a full legal tenancy can be for as short a time as 6 months – and at the time of writing, the main opposition party in England is promising to change tenancy law, to extend these minimal times. But when a full tenancy can be as short as 6 months, a tenancy is then in itself no guarantee of permanency.

But where the accommodation service is provided by a socially responsible and accountable agency, such as a charity or housing association, their activities and policies are subject to regulation and best practice standards. Then the guarantee of security for the individual lies not in the tenancy agreement, but instead, in the way that the housing services are regulated, over and above the occupancy terms. If the funding is there to provide decent quality support, personalised to the needs of the individual, permanently supported housing is not essentially a tenancy issue. Rather, it's the supply of support that is the limiting factor.

A second misleading belief is that "conditionality" is never suitable, or never compatible with Housing First. It is therefore welcome that Housing First can now be thought of not just as a specific programme, but as a broader strategy, an overall vision within which a wider range of services can operate, each customised to particular needs and circumstances. This more pluralist approach seems now closer to the route that services and policy in the UK, and the rest of Europe, may find more useful.

Some recent US policy statements on "recovery housing" now do seem to accept a limited role for housing and community support services with conditionality, in the form of sobriety, attached to a tenancy, even if the attention they get seems cursory, and almost a grudging acceptance. Yet we need to remember that the demand for "dry" and "clean" houses came originally not from housing services' tenancy terms and conditions, but from within the substance abuse community, positively wanting that kind of conditionality in their living arrangements. If services are to be needs-led, this has to be an option.

Current US policy seems to accept a very limited scope for conditional housing, and only where there is a clearly demonstrable demand. But to expect chaotic and marginalised individuals to somehow articulate and mobilise to get their needs met seems a recipe for systemic failure.

In reality, socially responsible housing and support providers must be pro-active in anticipating the likely demand, in order to have the services to meet it, based on their own knowledge of the territory and the needs of clients.

A third misleading belief is that phrases such a "personalised" or "holistic" are enough to describe the complexity and sophistication of the "single site" communities that a more strategic HF seems now to be rapidly developing. One thing that most struck me was that almost everything that I heard, up till my all-too brief trip, was concerned with removing barriers to access to housing with support. Knowing better what to look out for, almost all of what I have read since, from the US government, has the same single-minded focus on tenancy rights. I had read almost nothing about what else people might expect or need, once they got there; and, as we say in the UK, "what good looks like". There seemed to be nothing comparable to the programme of improvement in accommodation-based provision that we had developed – and which I had played some role in developing, through the PIE idea.

I have had a number of discussions, before and since my trip, about Trauma-informed Care – the programme in the States that seems in so many ways very close to our term a PIE. In my other chapter in this book, I explore the similarities and differences, trying especially to take my own advice, and properly recognise the social policy context in which they arrived. The impression I have is that we have gone further in describing the practical outcome of trauma awareness, in creating a culture and a whole environment. But as TIC thinking has developed, it seems to be coming to something quite close, with the key features that we had articulated in the idea of a PIE being as relevant and evident in the best of services there as it is here.

I had asked my various hosts in Boston, in Ann Arbor and in Chicago, if they felt there was any way to tell who would thrive in more communal, congregated accommodation and who in dispersed. Could we tell for whom isolated living was preferable, for whom it was intolerably lonely, and maybe needed supplementing with a more community work focus – such as the Clubhouse model. For whom it was a wasted opportunity to get real benefits from shared living?

The simple answer was: no. There was no real pattern they could see; and there was no research being done, so far as they knew. Trial and error seemed the only way to go – though one provider organisation did suggest an implication in this: that it was helpful if a housing provider had a range of styles of accommodation, so that if need be, an individual could be offered a move from one to another with the minimum of disruption. But this valuable learning stays so far within the organisation; it is not part of the programme, and it is not being researched and shared. The emphasis, in the PIEs approach, on action learning and shared learning would be particularly helpful here.

So, following in part from that question of who does well in shared accommodation, we have a fourth misleading assumption – and key to my new understanding of the very real strengths of HF. This is that overall, the population who fall into entrenched homelessness is essentially the same, and that the same solutions should work equally for everybody. Yet although there may be some common features between homeless young people and veterans, women in refuges, and those with major untreated mental illness – most obviously, the lack of a stable home – they also have different needs, and more importantly, different strengths.

But in particular, it might be assumed that the homelessness population is essentially the same in both the US and the UK. Yet major mental illness is evidently now a much larger element in homelessness in the US than it is in the UK. The original versions of HF had been developed creatively to meet the needs of this client group, for whom the existing abstinence-based long-term or transitional housing was going to be ineffective and irrelevant.

One feature of the UK chapters in this book is that in the UK we seem less squeamish about recognition of personality disorder, complex trauma or "traumatised personality"; and this may be because it is THESE problems that are more likely to slip through the healthcare safety nets in the UK; and this is the group that homelessness services in the UK are seeing, and learning to work with.

And this takes us, finally, to what I suspect may prove to be the real achievement of Housing First, in the US.

Moral Treatment Revisited

The past, they say, is another country; and they do things differently there. But if so, might the converse be equally true? Through seeing what happens in another country, can we glimpse some insights into how things could have developed otherwise than they did, in our own? It has become quite common, in recent years, to try to reconstruct imaginatively what alternative courses history might have taken, with just small changes in the start conditions, and think through what might then have happened.

Historians and other theorists call such thought experiments "counterfactuals", and in the messy world of social history and policy, where true experiment is hard to do, it is often the only way to really understand what the options were, what might have been, what could therefore perhaps still happen. But in another country, where things really DID unfold in a different way, we can see such counterfactuals in real life, and in far finer and more confident detail.

After three short weeks in the US, and in only three states I certainly can't claim to be any kind of expert. So I take it on trust the claim that is always made that Housing First, in prioritising the most vulnerable, is accommodating people with major mental illnesses. Certainly the arrival of a new cohort of people in homelessness services in the US in the 1980s after the closure of the mental hospitals and the libertarian reforms to mental health law, combined with the failure to develop community mental health centres, is probably the principal reason for the recognition of a new population with different needs, needing a different solution.

I had assumed, from what I had read, that in the US, psychologists, and particularly clinical psychologists would be involved in running supported accommodation services. Instead what I found was that psychologists were providing much of the thinking and the writing, especially in terms of understanding the significance of trauma, attachment and loss etc. Likewise, with a very strong research tradition in the profession, they were publishing much of the research.

But the services I saw were being developed and managed, and the exciting adaptations, customisations and new learning being supplied, by housing management and social work staff. The values base of Housing First reflects social work's values as much as those of clinical psychology; and the creative pragmatism in inventing variants of the "pure" model of HF - very much a thing for those running services at the frontline – is on the whole more typical of social work than it is of the evidence-focussed worldview of psychology or medicine.

If so, then the truly remarkable fact is that those who, a generation or two earlier, would have been in psychiatric hospitals, run by doctors and nurses, and backed up with medication and compulsory powers, are instead living in small, relatively non-institutional households; and on a voluntary care basis, with no requirement to accept treatment.

For this, we will need a brief aside, into the history of psychiatry and hospital care. Post War social psychiatry, which argued that the hospital itself, as an institution, needed to change, to become more constructive, was the mainspring of progressive mental health care in the mid-20th Century, before the advent of the drug treatments in the 1950s and 60s seemed to offer, for a short while, a quick fix medical solution.

The article that first proposed the term "psychologically informed environments" to describe the progressive work being done in homelessness hostels in the UK usually with little or no intervention or support from mental health services, was part one of a trilogy, entitled "Social psychiatry and social policy for the 21st Century: new concepts for new needs". That article attempted to trace the way some of the ideas of social psychiatry had been re-emerging in social practice, having largely died out in healthcare. What was happening in homelessness services was, we argued, just one example.

I think we can now make a fairly good case for saying that Housing First is also an example of social psychiatry in practice. What we are seeing, I would suggest, may be a return of this way of thinking in the US too - and even a revival of the spirit of "moral treatment" as developed at the famous Quaker home, the Retreat, in York, around the time of Napoleon. (The language is deceptive here, though - a better translation of the original French[11] would in fact be "morale treatment" which better conveys the central stress on compassion, promoting self-respect, and the foundation of trust.)

It may be, then, that the real success of HF has been obscured by the universalism in the "one size fits all" accounts; obscured by the "black box" containment of complexity under the rubric of "personalisation"; and obscured by the emphasis on legal rights in tenancy, rather than human rights and ethical treatment.

So what we are seeing, particularly in Housing First's single site projects, is what mental health care might, and could have been like, if the principles of the York Retreat had been followed, and if the principles of social work and psychology had created the mental health services, with medicine in the ancillary role. But the past was a different country; and sadly, in both our countries, they did do things differently then. But this is now.

---

[11] "Traitement morale". In the Napoleonic era, the terms "moral" and "morale" had not yet separated out into different meanings.

Further Reading

For this account, to keep the tone informal and conversational, I have deliberately not used formal referencing for any of the papers, podcasts or videos that I have mentioned here.

All those cited here, however, are referenced in a more academic styling in the parallel paper that appears in this book: *Principles and Practice in Psychology and Homelessness: Core Skills in Pretreatment, Trauma Informed Care & Psychologically Informed Environments.*

All this material—and much more besides—can also be found on the community of practice website that I run, known as the PIElink—www.pielink.net.

11 The Dialogue Continues...
Robin Johnson & Jay S. Levy

NB: *The initial dialogue between Robin and Jay had begun with a single LinkedIn post, to which Jay had posted a comment that stirred Robin's interest.*

June 2014

Hi Jay,

I am rather interested in your comment on (a recent) LinkedIn post about Housing First: that it "works really well for about 20% or less."

I know a little research that suggests that HF may be more effective with some groups than others, and I am keen to find out more. It seems to me that it's really important to identify what works for whom: and then we can try to see why.

Robin Johnson
Editor, Housing Care and Support

- -

Hi Robin,

Housing First means many things to different people. This makes discussion in forums and conclusions via the media hard to follow and often overly generalized in regard to success rates.

All of the research that I've seen on Housing First is in reference to serving either a chronically homeless population of single adults, or a highly vulnerable unsheltered population based on a vulnerability index rating — which may or may not be in line with chronic homelessness, though the great majority of folks who are unsheltered and vulnerable are also chronically homeless.

The 20% number is a rough estimate based on some of the research on chronic homelessness in Philadelphia and New York City by Dennis Culhane and others... 10% were long-term homeless and 10% have multiple episodes. Current Point In Time (PIT) count numbers indicate a higher percentage of chronic homelessness among individuals, but over an entire year it is less, due to the higher rates of short-term homeless persons.

Much of the research on the success of Housing First has been done on the Pathways to Housing Model by Dr. Sam Tsemberis and others. The results seem to favor this approach for chronically homeless folks who struggle with MI (mental illness) or with co-occurring disorders when MI is primary and addiction is secondary.

That being said, there are some interesting Housing First-led Harm Reduction approaches being tried in Canada, serving folks with active addictions and monitoring how much they drink, while providing access to alcohol and counselling right on the premises. For this approach, they attempt to "screen in" folks who have already had several attempts at trying to sustain sobriety through conventional approaches, but have not been successful.

The point of all of this research is to reduce healthcare costs, save lives, and improve the quality of life for the community and for program participants. I write about how to construct effective support and outreach services, as well as review different types of Housing First approaches and their effectiveness, in my new book *Pretreatment Guide for Homeless Outreach & Housing First: Helping Couples, Youth, and Unaccompanied Adults.*

So, I completely agree with your comment "It seems to me that it's really important to identify what works for whom: and then why."

Take care, Jay

Hi Jay

Thanks for the very prompt reply! I'd rather like to pursue the question a little further with you; there are a couple of papers from the UK that I think are useful; it would be good to have your opinion, from a US angle.

But I am also wondering if your publishers would be keen to get your book reviewed? We don't carry a lot of book reviews (in the journal I edit), and perhaps we should do more.

Robin
Editor, Housing Care and Support

July 2014

Hi, Robin

Sure... just send a request via e-mail in your interest to review a book and I'll forward it to my publisher. LH Press has been very open to these types of requests in the past.

I'd love to review whatever UK literature you can send me, but I can't promise a prompt response. I am in the field, working with staff and folks without homes on a daily basis, so my plate is pretty full at the moment. But I'll be taking some time off in August, so I could definitely get to it then.

Thanks for your interest and understanding,

Jay

NB: *Some time passes at this point; there is some further email correspondence on reviewing Jay's book; plus a little more LinkedIn discussion.*

October 2014

Hi, Jay,

Here attached is a finalised copy of the journal's review of your paper, by my colleague, Lynn. The only real change is that we have added, at the end, some "connective tissue" with some of the issues that we have been pursuing here in the UK, about developing more "psychologically informed environments" (PIEs) in homelessness.

And it's this that I'd really like to talk to you about sometime. There is a lot written on it already — a lot I've written myself, in addition to papers in the journal. But it's an idea that I suspect will resonate too "over the pond," and that's why I am interested to hear more about Safe Havens. (Also "Trauma-Informed Care," which I guess you will know?)

But mainly, this primarily hostel-based work needs to extend into outreach; and this is where your own writing really scores; so I am interested to know how far you can see the same ideas being incorporated into positive environments in US hostels etc? Then I think we might really be on the same page.

One more thing to add, though. I am standing down after this year as editor of the journal, in order to have time to concentrate more on homelessness, and more specifically on PIEs. One thing we are doing is starting to video interview people with something valuable to say (as part of showcasing creative work), and I would be keen to have an interview with you — to complement the review — if we can get the technology to manage the distance problem. I am working with some people at Exeter University at the moment on finding a technology that we can develop.

As it stands, Skype is just not good enough quality for either picture or sound for on-line publishing, but it might be a good place for us to start off with, at least?

Robin

Hey Robin,

Thanks again for the wonderful book review! When do you expect it to be published?

I like the term PIEs better than trauma-informed environments. PIEs comes across as broader, so it can encompass psychologically relevant issues beyond and including trauma. If you could send me something you or others have written on PIEs for the homeless, I would be interested and I am sure it would be highly informative.

A Pretreatment approach is certainly "trauma informed," but it is more based on being sensitive to a broad range of presentations and rooted in meeting folks where they are at, which is why I am biased toward stage-based theories. Whether it is the stage of engagement, common language development, or change, the provider is faced with assessing where the client is at and responding with a stage-appropriate intervention. This also includes understanding the constant and natural flow of transition and adaptation to people, ideas, environments, treatment, and housing.

If we open our eyes and remain alert to all of the natural transitions our residents/clients/shelter guests are facing, then we can join them and support the process. When folks move into hostels, shelters, safe havens, or a residence of their own, the transition process is evident to both the person and the worker, so engagement and setting basic objectives can easily flow from there.

My main point here is that a Pretreatment assessment, which is also a way of thinking, integrates really well with outreach to unsheltered or in-reach to shelters/hostels/safe havens, etc.

Another major Pretreatment principle is promoting safety, and arguably harm-reduction strategies. Crisis intervention is also relevant from the very beginning and can be presented as supporting new transitions by focusing on safety concerns when folks are first moving in to new environments. We can offer basic safety plans that hopefully resonate well when framed via a common language that incorporates building a support network, contact numbers for crises/emergencies, and reviewing specific coping strategies based on a solution-focused approach that explores past and present ways the person has coped and/or what supports have been helpful for managing difficult situations.

There is a basic flow to the work that I am referring to, which is based on supporting transitions to a new environment, which begins with a welcoming and celebration of the person's arrival coupled with orientation to the new environment, neighborhood, people, laundry room, etc... Introduction of basic need items can also be used to promote both transition and engagement to the worker in environment... from there to setting basic objectives in regard to being successful in the environment (getting along with neighbors, taking care of space/property, paying rent or doing required activities (hostel 'chores') in exchange for lower rent)... to establishing a basic safety plan in case anything goes wrong or the person feels really stuck.

This defines the basic overview of a Pretreatment approach to the first 48 hours of a new move in... whether it be Housing First, or other new environments that a person may enter from an unsheltered setting. Currently, I overlook a PATH team of master level clinicians who are directly connected to shelters and attempt to engage folks with MI, co-occurring disorders, or tri-morbidity. We also work closely with Health Care for the Homeless (HCH) nurses and doctors who are situated in the same shelter environments.

The REACH model that I espouse includes the outreach worker having direct access to housing, and then being part of a team of helpers who continue to work with the (now housed) client to successfully transition to their new environment and to hopefully connect to some meaningful day structure.

I am a big fan of incorporating the outreach worker with the basic transition plan, so as to include the person who has already developed trust and common language with bridging this knowledge to the new environment through direct intervention, modelling, and sharing helpful information including specific stage of change information (Re: MI, SA, Medical and housing issues) with staff/helpers connected to the new environment.

The work in unsheltered environments goes much slower, but we have found that the transition to in-shelter settings can really spark more productive goal oriented work, if we "catch the transition bus."

Perhaps you can tell me a bit more of how Hostels are used to serve folks without homes?

Jay

Hi Jay,

Simplest question first: *Emerald* journals are published online before they come out in the printed issue copy many weeks later, and they are usually available in a pre-proof-reading copy as soon as they are accepted. I'll check with the production team, but I think the review should be already available. But I'll have to check if it's behind the journal's paywall.

Still, I am sure we can get you a copy, and if I talk nicely to Lynn (which is easy to do — she IS nice) she will give her consent to put a copy on the website that we have set up, for sharing ideas and practice on PIEs developments.

And that's another whole story. The simplest thing to do, if you are interested in reading up on this PIEs stuff, which is really a whole new development from the UK in the last decade, is to go to that website, have a bit of a browse around, and if you want to read some more, you can register (its free) and that will give you access to Lynn's review (when I've put it there, at least) and all the rest of the library area.

One reason I am standing down as editor of HC&S is to be able to devote much more time to developing this programme, our new social enterprise, and the whole web-based on-line community angle.

If you would be interested, I would be inclined to create a page there on pre-treatment principles. But if so, it would make a lot more sense for you to write it than for me to! And then we can get a video interview with you, to go with the page. And thus we spread the word...

Robin

Robin,

Great! I'll definitely check out the link and review some of the writings on PIEs.

Also interested on how Hostels serve the homeless. Is it currently set up as a main number that people in need call and then they are referred to openings via the Hostel Network? In this way folks without homes are mainstreamed with other travellers? Are they provided with any outreach or other specialized services via the Hostel or do they check in somewhere else for case management and other services?

Let's definitely talk come January about setting up a Pretreatment page and potential interview.

Thanks again for your interest, Jay

NB: It is around this time that Jay and Robin manage to schedule a phone call; and it was in the course of this phone call that they realise that the word "hostel" in the UK means something quite different to its US meaning. (For an explanation of this difference, see the Glossary; and Chapter 10, Robin's "They do things differently there.") In the light of this confusion over the meaning of the word, some of Jay's questions and Robin's replies suddenly make sense...

Jay,

Good stuff.

PIEs is an idea, as much as a practice; and a general overview of many practices; the PIElink is about sharing ideas, as well as sharing practice. (So, we host and post relevant research and policy analysis as well as frontline service issues.)

But it's not a client referral service. I suppose we really ought to have links to them; but outside London (we are mainly UK based for the moment, though we mean to grow), all One Stop Shop services go through the local authority — even if many voluntary sector services also advertise their local provisions on the web. So, mainly we'd just be linking to them.

As for the work in the hostels themselves, yes, some services do have counsellors or clinic sessions in situ; many more have some training and support consultancy etc. to help them deal more constructively and imaginatively with psychological and emotional needs. But as you'll see if you watch that 15 minute "handy guide," the real work in becoming a PIE happens when people convert training and support and big ideas into real differences in the way the service itself is set up and runs.

We don't actively discourage, but we don't promote access to off-site case managers or healthcare input, because in our experience, marginalised and serially excluded people just won't attend; or attend so erratically that they get struck off as "hard to engage." No, the mountain must go to Mohammed. We want to see psychological input embedded — and that doesn't mean just psychologists, but awareness and empathy.

But now I am in danger of getting onto my soapbox. For now, let's just say that your work shows all the imaginativeness, awareness and empathy that we want to promote, whether in outreach or in hostel, refuge, foyer and shelter work, and onwards, into second stage housing and beyond.

Robin

TNB: The review of Jay's book is published in the Housing Care and Support journal, and the discussion by email continues, as they try to get to grips with the differing vocabularies for services in the US and the UK. Here they are trying to explain the term "Safe Haven," to see if this matches the work on UK's "hostels" better than "shelter" does. They are also discussing the means of identifying vulnerability and eligibility for such additional support services, and also integrating outreach approaches with "Experts from Experience."

December 2014

Hi Robin,

In addition to Safe Havens, our local REACH housing program for rough sleepers, we have also used working farms for housing placement and vocational training, as well as college dorm type training programs with work focus for homeless young adults via job corps and Boston University's Psychosocial Rehabilitation approach to vocational training and housing.

All the best,

Jay

January 2015

Hi Robin,

In the spirit of sharing, I've attached both a Vulnerability Index and the VI-SPDAT. You already know my reservations about the VI-SPDAT, but I still believe it is a useful tool for informing assessment. I do like the ease in which a Vulnerability Index can be used by outreach workers to get a quick handle on risk of death for a sleeping rough population. Dr. James O'Connell and Dr. Hwang developed the VI and I am a big fan of their work and research via Health Care for the Homeless (HCH).

Great talking to you too!!!

Jay S. Levy, LICSW

Jay,

I'll have a look at these. In the meantime, you might be interested in the suite of tools that are for the moment most commonly used in the UK — the Outcome Stars.

The main point of the Star approach, though, is not to confirm their eligibility, but rather to plan, and to identify the progress users make — and thus what the services have achieved. This first article (attached) is more "philosophical." There is a second, more pragmatic, about more technical concerns over rater reliability, which I will fish out if you are interested.

After our conversation, though, I have in mind to start drafting a paper for publication on the extent to which there is as yet any real transnational vocabulary that allows us to translate and transfer development, learning and research from one country to another. (My target here being as much the European adoption of HF; but also wanting to see more real interest in research on the part of practitioners...)

But I am thinking that a good way and place to start some discussion might be to launch a discussion topic via LinkedIn. It seems to be starting to be useful.

Robin

February, 2015

Jay,

Re: *Pretreatment Guide for Homeless Outreach & Housing First*

I quote:

"A really important book... in years to come, people are going to look back and say, this changed everything."

That's from Victoria Aseervatham, who is the rough sleepers' commissioner for the City of Westminster (the heart of London), who is promoting your book any chance she gets. This is still a small niche world — the whole PIEs network is. But where Westminster starts, the rest of London often follows. "First we take Manhattan; then we take Berlin...", as Leonard Cohen says...

We should perhaps talk about how (if at all?) all this might play in the States. I'm home now for a good fortnight or so; so maybe we can find a time to phone? My afternoon is your morning, by about 4 hrs, I think?

Robin

Hi Robin,

That's great news!!! Please pass on my appreciation to Victoria. My books and journal articles have gotten some play in the States, but not as much as I thought considering some of the people that have endorsed and gave wonderful reviews. This included the Community Liaison for the National Coalition for the Homeless, the Director of Boston's Healthcare for the Homeless, and the head of Massachusetts's Housing and Shelter Alliance, among several others.

Book or two sells each day somewhere across the USA, so you never know what might come of it.

By the way... I like the Leonard Cohen quote!

Thanks, Jay

Hi Jay,

Glad you liked Victoria's piece. She's great — and her role in Westminster has been pivotal for us in establishing SO much creative practice. I have more examples on the way; a huge backlog of material to process.

Here's the video link for the Street Buddies. I think you'll like it. It's not particularly a pre-treatment approach — a lot of their work is pre-verbal! — but it IS all about the extraordinary delicacy involved in meeting people where they are at.

R

Hey Robin,

Thanks for sharing... this is the note I left in response to Street Buddies...

"Quite interesting! One of the areas I write about in Homeless Narratives & Pretreatment Pathways (HNPP) is Pre-engagement strategies. Years ago, I used to do work in NYC, and our outreach team was composed of a combination of professionals and folks who have experienced homelessness. Sometimes the person with "lived experience" would take the lead and we would stand back... even at a distance.

We actually engaged well over time with long-term homeless folks and would leave need items from a distance, as described here. Also, we would eventually pair a need item with notes and other offerings... a kind of de-sensitization. Also we would try to engage with others who were homeless, yet more easily engaged within the same vicinity to model the helping process in a non-threatening way.

Much more to say on this, though basically, thinking in terms of stages of engagement is helpful. Thanks to Louise and Robin for sharing this video!"

Through my years of outreach I have found that the most important thing is to completely separate outreach from enforcement! So, I am glad Louise strongly highlighted that point. People with long-term homeless histories can be reached by professionals and/or peers, as long as they actively work toward meeting folks where they are at.

Breaking down the engagement process into various stages is helpful, and staying aligned with the proper stage (the stage the relationship is truly at). With some folks, the stage of pre-engagement can last a long time or re-occur when the worker mistakenly believes that the person is ready to engage more fully to begin making goals. My first book (HNPP) gives many examples of this process with long-term homeless individuals.

All the best, Jay

Thanks, Jay.
We are really on the same page here, aren't we?
Robin

Robin
The short answer is that I too believe that we are on the same page, but there is also a great deal of "unsaid" that could go off into many interesting directions.

No doubt that trauma history impacts the engagement process with people with long homeless histories, and depending on the nature of the trauma and the severity of it, could lead to an array of outcomes around whom folks are apt to initially trust, if anyone. The relevant Pretreatment question is then "What do we do?"... hence Pretreatment Strategies.

How the Peer movement[12] intersects with this is not necessarily straightforward, though it can be, and often is very helpful toward engaging with some real hard-to-reach folks. Thanks for sharing the Street Buddies work with me, and I hope to hear more about it. I am commenting more than usual because I am on holiday and have a little more time to reflect on things.

In regard to Pielink: I am thrilled about what you are doing and I am also happy to contribute material to the site in line with its mission...

---

[12] Jay shares his views on the Peer Movement and their critical advocacy for inclusion in chapter 7.

podcasts, videos, and book excerpts all sound good to me. Just let me know about pacing...

Thanks, Jay

Hi Jay

It occurs to me, before we talk tomorrow, to send you as promised this presentation done by John Conolly, which makes good use — I hope you agree? — of your work.

Attached is the original guidance paper from 2010 — often known as "the complex trauma paper" — which launched this whole development in the UK.

And I thought you might also be interested to read this other paper (as it happens published in the same year, which is why it doesn't mention ours), which explores the relative contribution of HF with different client groups and in different contexts; and also expresses some concerns, even back then, that much effective practice may be overlooked and marginalized by an excessively simplistic interpretation of the evidence for HF.

Delighted, too, to find you and Suzanne Quinney already in contact, via LinkedIn!

Robin

Robin,

Wow!!! I love John's presentation and the PIE practice guide for homeless services. Suzanne Quinney's application of Appreciative Inquiry to transform hostels into PIE is phenomenal.

Jay

To: Jay Levy
Subject: RE: Greetings

Great to talk with you.

I've already had an email exchange with John, and he is very happy to draw out both the narrative and the harm reduction elements. (I should have mentioned that he is now embarked on a doctorate, looking specifically at the use of narrative in telling the stories of homelessness in a healing relationship, so he is not at all averse to having that teased out!)

Robin

September 2015

Hi Robin,

I took the liberty of setting up a Powerpoint presentation on Pretreatment. It still doesn't capture the narrative and harm reduction elements, but the examples of its application through case illustration would definitely explore those issues more fully.

I basically reworked John's slides, but excluded the complex trauma slides. I thought you might want to look at how I framed things and then John could re-integrate the complex trauma and personality disorder slides. I also think that it was very good via John's original version, so there is no need to make changes.

I am just sharing a little bit more of my thinking... I am planning to integrate in John's thoughts on complex trauma and homelessness in future presentations, though I am not there yet.

Jay

January 2016

Hi. Jay

HAPPY NEW YEAR!

You may have spotted — or maybe you get notifications? — that I've responded to your last LinkedIn post. I was thinking to try to continue the discussion there — whilst also starting to syphon off some longer discussion threads to the PIElink, and also to advertise a Blab discussion for later in January. Ray Middleton from Fulfilling Lives is keen on hosting a transatlantic discussion on homelessness.

Meanwhile, I've been working on a draft of a paper of psychology in homelessness that attempts to situate PIEs, TIC, HF and Pretreatment alongside each other (I'm using the independent emergence of agriculture as the comparison or metaphor).

That's now on the umpteenth draft, but it's not far off ready to send to you, as I imagine you'll be able to suggest other observations especially on PT, and maybe on other links. (Perhaps mention Safe Havens, Transitional Housing etc., where you are far more knowledgeable than I?)

Robin

Hi Robin,

Welcome to 2016!

I look forward to reviewing your writing... I am sure that it will also help me with my current long-term project. In the end it is all related; and I do like your metaphor on the emergence of agriculture, though our work is not quite as pivotal to the development of Western civilization.

: -)

Also, I would love to participate in a video dialogue with you and Ray. All in good fun, Jay

----

Morning, Jay

(Well, you may remember Ghandi's reply, when he first came to England, and he was asked what he thought of Western Civilisation? He said he thought it would be a very good idea...)

At some point I'd be interested to hear your "take" on Trauma Informed Care. There has been some growing interest in TIC over here in the last year or so, especially after a colleague of ours went on one of the exchange trips run by Homeless-Link and the National Alliance to End Homelessness.

The impression I get is that TIC and PIE are pretty much the same thing, with different names — or at least, that there is so much overlap, it's probably better to see them as twins.[13]

But I'm interested to explore how they both relate and interface with Housing First. I know you have located PreTreatment firmly within the HF programme. But it's quite unclear to me how we reconcile the wish to radically improve "hostel" ("shelter") and services with some of the HF rhetoric of dispensing entirely with them, in the belief that they are ALL just "staircases"?

Regards, Robin.

Hi Robin,

My last book took what I developed for outreach and rooted it in HF because that was needed to better serve folks who were being quickly housed without adequate transition and/or informed support services. In a very real sense, for HF to be successful, we need to provide quality outreach to folks in housing, and the Pretreatment model is a nice guide.

Pretreatment is really an outreach philosophy of providing human services to hard-to-reach individuals, couples or families in a variety of environments. I also believe that you are right to classify it as a psychological model that fits in well with a PIE approach.

---

[13] For further reading on the comparison between PIE and TIC, see Robin's contribution- chapter 2

My views on Trauma Informed Care (TIC) is a much longer dis-cussion[14], but for now it is suffice to say that both PIE and Pretreatment are already trauma-informed models that have much broader implications. As you like to say, Psychologically informed! Trauma informed is a subset of this. Much like how widespread addiction issues appear to be, so it is also true with trauma.

Therefore, all our services would benefit from being both trauma and addiction informed, which begs the question... How do we do this well? What types of training do staff from various human services need?

I believe that both PIE and, whether as part of it or separate from it, Pretreatment provide a good set of principles and a scaffolding that can welcome various specific research based trainings, as well as upholding person centered relationships and demonstrating how to do that well.

The beat goes on, Jay

Robin,

Our transatlantic dialogue/interview and other videos that Ray produced are really good! : -)

I'll definitely share with my publisher and also promote Ray's training films via Twitter and Facebook. By the way, I have a Facebook group page entitled Homeless Narratives & Pretreatment Pathways and will soon be adding his PIE films one by one for review by interested group members. If you are on Facebook, feel free to join the group.

Thanks, Jay

February 2016

Hi, Jay

Everything is now in place for the new website for the PIElink — we only now have the kind of glitches you only hear about from feedback. So perhaps "released into the wild" is another way of putting it.

One of the trickiest tasks is to create a vocabulary that works on both sides of the Atlantic! In fact, it seems to me that that task is a subject in its own right, so I am thinking to post something on LinkedIn, inviting a discussion.

One immediate question, for example, is whether I was right to lump "safe havens" in with "hostel/foyer/refuge," using the UK terminology here? And "Safe Haven" — is that exclusively for former homeless people? Or do

---

[14] See appendix i for further discussion of TIC and Pretreatment

you also get SHs for folk who were, for example, in mental hospital, but are then discharged, and had nowhere to go to? And one of the key features is: no tenancy agreement?

In other news, I have abandoned the struggle to get an article on HF, PT, PIEs at TIC written in under 2,500 words. Instead, I've sent SITRA this (attached), hoping they can use it. It might work for LinkedIn, too. What do you think? But now I have thrown off the corsets of 2k word count, I'm finding the original paper idea starts to flow again. So with luck and a following wind I'll have something for you before long.

What I am writing might even be a chapter in your book! Though I'd want to share it around a bit first.

Cheers!

Robin

Hi Robin,

Just as a heads up to try and clarify things around transitional housing. The Department of Housing and Urban Development (HUD) is indeed moving away from "transitional housing" as a matter of policy and evidence-based practice in an effort to house permanently very vulnerable, at-risk, chronically homeless folks. As you've written about... it questions the effectiveness of the staircase model for this at risk population of homeless individuals.

But I was using the term in a more generic sense as in some shelters in the UK turning into smaller hostels — in your UK sense of transitional programs with staff supports. Safe Haven is literally for unsheltered or rough sleepers with major mental illness. So, if a person is inpatient directly from the streets then they may qualify, but certainly not if they can make it in shelter temporarily or if they came from housing to the shelter, but can't return to housing.

HUD has also moved away from Safe Havens models, but we continue to open new safe havens as a safe residential setting for unsheltered homeless persons with severe mental illness, and these places are without sobriety requirements (type of HF, though not really permanent housing) so the discussion can get complicated as to whether we consider Safe Havens a small, specialized shelter or transitional housing. So, I think it does fit well in the same category as hostel/foyer/refuge[15].

-----

[15] For more information on the definitions of '"hostel", "foyer", "refuge", and "safe havens" see the glossary of terms located in appendix ii

Further, some of the Youth housing programs are still considered transitional housing in line with the developmental challenges and constant transitions that young adults bring or even desire. So the picture is complicated on what a transitional housing program means, depending on who funds the programs and expectations connected to this, as well as the research connected with specific populations served or targeted.

Even the HUD-funded transitional programs were more targeted to people in transition around addiction and work issues, as opposed to highly vulnerable chronically homeless persons, which is now the norm for HUD-funded programs.

Our residential care is for people with major mental illness, not normally for Personality Disorders, though a primary diagnosis of Borderline Personality Disorder (BPD) is a notable exception. But normally the residents served in MH group homes and congregate settings are diagnosed with major thought disorders or Bipolar or Major Depressive disorders paired with low functioning/compromised ADLs (Activities of Daily Living).

In fact, the Massachusetts Department of Mental Health recognizes BPD as a qualifying diagnosis and I've worked directly with several people with BPD staying in residential programs in NYC and Boston. These options are few and people are wait listed, so homeless persons rarely get access to group homes for MI, though it is more available as an option for addiction, which is separate from Mental Health services. This is one of the reasons HF and Safe Haven programs were embraced, as so many folks who were homeless with major MI had no place to go.

I hope this clarifies my usage to set the table for further conversation.

Jay

March 2016

Hi Jay,

Pretty much the same over here. The health service has recently started to recognise BPD — because people with BPD tend to demand help — but it's not anything like so good, generally, in spotting any of the other (12 other!) sub-types, apart from the anti-social; and so the other PDs end up in prison or homeless, or in A&E (that's our equivalent of your "ER"). It's one of the reasons why it has been our "hostels" that have developed the skills in working with this group...

But thanks for these clarifications — it all goes to show how hard it is to specify tight definitions in a world where context and complexity must rule!

To my mind, it really brings home the point that we need a much richer dialogue between us all, and I am really looking forward to the chance to take that further.

Meanwhile, I am packing a bag to head for London for the annual conference of the Faculty of Homelessness and Health Exclusion. I am giving a talk myself on the second day — Transatlantic Dialogues, on (you've guessed it!) the relationship between HF, PIEs, TIC, PTx and System Change Brokerage.

Things are certainly warming up.

Robin

Hi Robin,

Great to hear about your upcoming presentation! I look forward to seeing some of the video from the London conference. I am sure that folks will be intrigued by the Transatlantic Dialogue on HF, PIEs, TIC and Pretreatment.

When you meet with Joe Finn,[16] you *may* notice that he is quite an advocate and more entrenched than me in Housing First approaches, while perhaps seeing less need for transitional programs.

Nevertheless, I think he will present a well thought out viewpoint for you to consider and his advocacy has resulted in many types of housing with support services along the spectrum of HF throughout Massachusetts.

Jay

Thanks Jay — including for the slight word of warning!

But I'm probably best off getting the full "HF fan club" treatment in the first instance, and then we can talk about what questions I have.

(Good discussion with a housing association chief exec last week, on her concerns that HF in the UK is becoming a policy steamroller. It covers all the issues, and the recording is decent quality; that'll probably make a good podcast.)

Robin

Robin then sets off for the US. Chapter 10, entitled "They do things differently there" describes in some greater detail Robin's tour, beginning in April.

---

[16] Robin and Joe Finn, who wrote the US foreword for this book, had already planned a meeting in Boston to further compare and contrast transatlantic approaches to housing and homelessness.

April 2016

Jay,

It's been an absolutely brilliant first few days; the visits to BHCH (Boston's Health Care for the Homeless) and then Beth and David at the shelter were really illuminating. I already feel I have the pieces of the jigsaw puzzle coming together in my mind. My head is stuffed full of experiences, and I have two days more to cram in more, here; I am beginning to feel like the policy equivalent of *pate de foie gras*; but it's all good — really good.

But I am trying hard to suspend judgement and keep an open mind, until at least the next couple of days here in Chicago, where they are so confident they have got it right.

And I am really looking forward to scrambling it up some more with new experiences.

Still, I am forming already a pretty workable hypothesis of whom HF really works for, and if so, why. (Which is the converse of why it works, and if so, for whom. Which is, come to think of it, how this whole correspondence began!)

Robin

Robin,

That's interesting news... we can discuss your theory, as I have an array of thoughts on that from my own research via Pathways Model and first-hand experiences with HF. I experienced two different types of HF programs connected with my outreach team based on the REACH model that I featured in my books.

Thanks, Jay

Jay,

That's good — I need my temporary interim conclusions to be constantly shaken up by new accounts!

R

At this point, Robin arrived in Western Massachusetts, to visit Jay and some of his services there. On the PIElink website, there are several videos made of interviews at Jay's home, in which Robin quizzes Jay for the camera, on his thoughts on finding new ways to understand and forge relationships with homeless people, on his experiences in setting up the REACH programme, and his views on Housing First.

After his return to England, Robin and Jay continued to correspond, partly in the crafting of this book — and this chapter — and also over new issues that continued to arise for further discussion and exploration.

The Dialogue continues...

The PIElink:

www.pielink.net

Housing Care and Support Journal's review of the book:

http://pielink.net/download/vickery-l-2014-book-review-pretreatment-guide-for-homeless-outreach-housing-first/

Homeless Narratives Facebook page:

https://www.facebook.com/groups/136548916369874/

Street Buddies interview:

https://youtu.be/tGb_LXWjR5M

Robin's interview with Jay on the work of REACH:

http://pielink.net/videos/a-pie-of-pathways-the-work-of-reach-in-western-massachussetts/

"Back on your feet: Building Resilience with Hostel Residents":

More viewing on Suzanne Quinney's application of Appreciative Inquiry in transforming a Central London hostel:

https://vimeo.com/37232992

LinkedIn Topic: 'Transatlantic Dialogues on Homelessness' located in the LinkedIn group: Homelessness and Housing Professionals

https://www.linkedin.com/groups/1289557

(You must ask to Join the group to navigate to this topic)

12 Cross-Cultural Connections: Homelessness, Costs and Interventions
Jay S. Levy

This chapter is an exploration into the uncertain terrain of data. Here we present, compare, and contrast data from many different places. Our hope is to provide a lens into homelessness trends, effective interventions, and cross-cultural considerations. However, both the collection and interpretation of data always bears watching.

"Rough sleeping" in England

Unfortunately, many people in both the US and England do not or cannot access shelters, transitional housing, or hostels. Instead, they end up among the unsheltered homeless who live primarily outdoors. People in the UK refer to this as "sleeping rough."

The Department for Communities and Local Government (2017) reports that during the autumn of 2016 (see Fig. 12-1, p. 198), England's rough sleeping single night count estimates revealed that there were 4,134 persons (16% increase since 2015) sleeping on the streets, or in abandoned buildings, vehicles, or other places not meant for human habitation. This count included 964 rough sleepers (3% increase from 2015) residing in London, which accounted for 23% of the National figure. The rate of rough sleeping per 10,000 households stands at 2.7 for London vs. 1.8 for all of England.

Outreach and resettlement teams, in conjunction with workers from day centers and hostels have also compiled data (Combined Homelessness and Information Network- CHAIN database) of an unduplicated count for the entire fiscal year 2015/16, as opposed to a point in time count, and found a total of 8,096 rough sleepers throughout London, which is an increase of

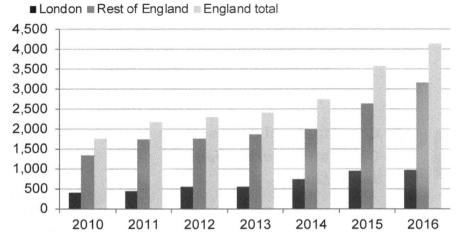

Fig. 12-1: England/London Rough Sleeper Totals 2010-2016
(DCLG, 2017, p.1)

7% from 2014/15 report. Past CHAIN numbers indicate that over 500 rough sleepers throughout London have a history of serving in the Armed Forces, as well as a steady increase over the past five years in Youth Homelessness (18-24 years old).

The most recent CHAIN numbers (2015/2016) indicated more than 800 youth sleeping rough on the streets of London. In addition, of the rough sleepers throughout London who agreed to complete a needs assessment, 43% reported alcohol support needs, 31% drug support needs, and 46% mental health support needs, 13% reported having all three needs, and 26% reported having none of these needs.

In summary, *Homelessness Monitor* (2017) data reports that rough sleeping levels in England have increased by 132% since 2010 and by 16% since 2015. The levels of increase have been higher in the South of England at 166% and London at 132% since 2010. In the past year, there was a higher increase in rough sleeping levels outside of London at 21%, compared to only 3% in the capital.

Overall, homeless numbers for the entire year in England are much larger than this, due to unaccompanied adults accessing homelessness hostels, where over 38,000 beds (*Homeless Link*, 2015) are available and often filled to capacity. According to the *Homelessness Monitor* report (Fitzpatrick, et al., 2016) recent research *estimates* that single night rough sleeper counts throughout England could be as high as 8,000 persons.

UK Homeless Households: Labels and Numbers

In England, the "homeless households" category consists of families with children and other vulnerable persons experiencing homelessness. Applications are only granted to those who can demonstrate eligibility, which single people don't, unless deemed "vulnerable," and for that, they need evidence of "illness." Local government — statutorily responsible for housing those vulnerable like this, will try to deter people from making an application, so these stats are distorted downward to reduce the demand and the costs for both temporary and permanent (not supportive) housing assistance.

Nevertheless, over 112,000 people actually submitted homelessness applications in 2014/15 (26% rise since 2009/10), and thousands of families are provided with temporary accommodation via Bed and Breakfast motels, or other short-term arrangements (e.g., limited local authority room rentals) until the facilitation of a housing placement. 58,000 households were accepted as homeless in 2015/16, a 34% increase since 2009/10 (assessed as unintentionally homeless and in priority need), with a 6% rise in the past year. The British Broadcasting Corporation[17] with confirmed numbers from the UK's Department of Communities and Local Government (DCLG) reported that as of June, 2015 there were 66,980 households (mostly families) registered as homeless in England, with close to 100,000 (99,080) children reported as living in temporary accommodation.

Currently, there is no reliable count of homelessness across the entire UK (England, Scotland, Wales, and Northern Ireland). Nevertheless, other UK countries also report significant homeless numbers. Scottish local authorities (Scottish Government, 2015) in 2014-15 reported that 29,565 people were assessed as homeless, with homeless individuals making up two-thirds of all homeless applications. The startling fact is that in Scotland, ALL citizens have a right to housing. Not just the vulnerable and families with children — ALL!

So in Scotland, housing the most vulnerable first really is about housing THEM first, not about getting them housed before treatment.

An alarming fact is that in Scotland, over 44% of homeless individuals were under 21 years of age. This appears to be a new and disturbing trend with the accompanied risks of long-term negative consequences for the younger generation. And this uptick in youth homelessness is not just in Scotland, but also a trend in both the US and England. We need immediate and successful interventions to house youth, while providing educational and vocational training to support their transition to adulthood. Otherwise, we may lose a significant proportion of young adults to a lifetime of perpetual poverty and illness, as well as suffering the inevitable social costs.

Scotland's local authority statistics report that 1,737 people slept rough during 2013/14. Wales (Crisis, 2016) also shares some limited government figures on homelessness, which includes 14,160 households (individuals/ families) applying for assistance during 2014/15, and 36% were deemed as being homeless, and in "Priority Need." The most recent rough sleeper count available recorded 141 people on a single night in November 2016, and 313 people over a two week period in October, 2016. Data from the 2016 count cannot be compared to previous years due to differences in timing, methodology and coverage.

As of this writing, there is no recent authoritative data from the province of Northern Ireland, though some reports indicate significant homelessness numbers on the increase (Fitzpatrick, et al., 2014) due to unemployment, low wages, and high costs of living, as well as family and relationship breakdown. *Northern Ireland Homelessness Monitor* (Fitzpatrick, et al., 2014) states that in 2012/13, some 19,400 households presented as homeless in Northern Ireland. Of these, just over half (9,900) were assessed as "Full Duty Applicants" (FDA), which is equivalent to acceptance as unintentionally homeless and in priority need. This was a significant increase from 2005/6, and this trend has apparently continued.

US Data

Numbers in the US are considerably higher than in the UK. The HUD Point In Time count (HUD-AHAR Part 1, 2017) aggregate data reports that on a single night in 2017, there were 553,742 homeless people in the United States, including 369,081 who were homeless as individuals (67%) and 184,661 (33%) people who were homeless in families. This is approximately a 1% increase in homelessness numbers from the prior year, bucking a trend of 6 consecutive declining years. The higher number is almost entirely due to higher numbers of unsheltered individuals living in major urban settings. These numbers include a staggering total of 192,875 people (35% of homeless population) sleeping in unsheltered environments not meant for human habitation.

A state by state analysis based on the same report reveals that half of all people experiencing homelessness did so in one of five states: California

---

[17] http://www.bbc.com/news/uk-34346908

(25% or 134,278 people); New York (16% or 89,503 people); Florida (6% or 32,190 people); Texas (4% or 23,548 people); and Washington (4% or 21,112 people). California and New York accounted for more than 40% of all homeless people throughout the US. In fact, NYC alone reported 76,501 homeless people (HUD-AHAR, 2017) on a single night living in shelters and in places not meant for human habitation (unsheltered-rough sleepers). The same HUD PIT count (2017) found more than 3,900 New Yorkers sleeping rough or unsheltered within NYC's five Burroughs.

Meanwhile, California (HUD-AHAR Part 1, 2017) accounted for nearly half of all unsheltered people (91,642) in the country in 2017 (49%). Unduplicated count estimates throughout an entire year (Burt & Aron, 2000; Burt et al., 1999), as opposed to Point in Time methods, state that there are more than 2 million people homeless across the USA. This includes almost 1.5 million (1,484,576) people who accessed shelter beds throughout 2015 (HUD-AHAR Part 2, 2016).

US numbers indicate some notable improvement since 2007 (see Fig. 12-2, p. 202) as evidenced by more than 100,000 fewer people in homeless shelters. The good news (NAEH Report, 2016) is that since 2007, there has been a 31% decline among chronically homeless individuals, as well as a 32% decrease in people residing in unsheltered settings. Much of this success is attributable to providing Housing First type options that prioritize long-term homeless individuals with disabilities for permanent affordable housing with support services.

Further good news is that the national numbers on Veterans without homes have shown a significant reduction of 45% since 2009 (even when accounting for a larger number of unsheltered veterans in 2017), due to major government initiatives by the Department of Housing and Urban Development in conjunction with Veterans Affairs. This has led to an influx of funds for the Veterans Affairs Supportive Housing (VASH) program, which consists of a subsidized housing voucher matched with case-management services for veterans without homes, as well as Supportive Services for Veteran Families (SSVF) dollars to pay for moving costs and other related items to transition veterans to housing.

On the flipside, we are bracing ourselves for the continued ramifications of two wars (Iraq & Afghanistan), and the inevitable fallout that wars bring: broken families, Post-Traumatic Stress Disorder, Traumatic Brain Injury, and Homelessness.

Data Comparison

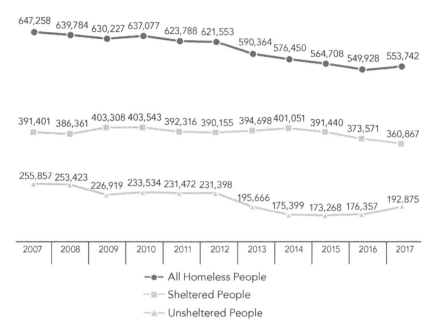

Fig. 12-2: US - PIT Estimates of People's Homeless Status 2007-17
(HUD AHAR, 2017, p. 8)

On the surface, there appear to be major transatlantic differences, and one reasonable conclusion is that the US has a flimsier safety net as evidenced by much higher overall homeless numbers. However, one must consider the cultural differences around the imperative to make it on one's own versus accepting help from others, which may ultimately impact the availability of natural supports via family or the community, as opposed to a safety net that is largely in place due to government initiatives.

US culture values liberty and personal responsibility, while England's universal tax-funded medical care for all citizens may be indicative of a society that endorses greater community responsibility. This is further reflected by involuntary psychiatric commitment law, which in the US errs on the side of respecting personal liberty with the exception of imminent danger to self/others, while in England it is more concerned with getting people with severe mental illness desperately needed treatment, even if it ends up being involuntary, and thereby a bit more protective of both the person and the community.

Another reason for the large disparity is that the UK's population of approximately 70.4 million (Office of Records, 2011; National Record of Scotland, 2016; NISRA, 2015;) is nearly five times smaller than that of the USA — 321.3 million (US Census Bureau, 2015). The US national rate of homelessness (HUD-AHAR, 2017) is 17 homeless persons per 10,000 *people* in the general population. Unfortunately, as of this writing, the national rate for England and/or the UK is unknown and in some circles it is considered to be an enigma.

Perhaps the most accurate comparison between the US and England is in reference to the sleeping rough population (see Fig. 12-3). The unsheltered-sleeping rough population in the US is at a rate of about 14 per 10,000 *households* compared to 2.7 for London and 1.8 for all of England. While in the Autumn of 2016 about 964 people slept rough on a single night in London, in NYC, with a similar size general population, the 2016 street count (HUD-CoC Dashboard Report-NYC) revealed approximately 2,835 individuals. On the face of it, NYC's unsheltered homeless population appears to be about 3 times larger than that of London. Further, as of this writing preliminary numbers for 2017 indicate that NYC's unsheltered homeless population has grown to more than 3,900 people, or to 4 times that of London. Interestingly enough, the Annual Assessment report to the US congress (HUD-AHAR, 2017) analysis highlights that NYC's unsheltered population is only a small proportion of NYC's larger homeless

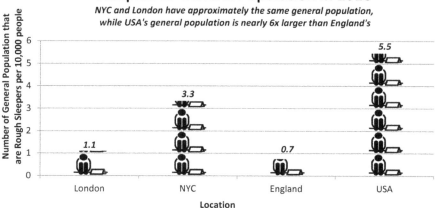

Fig. 12-3: US/England 2016 Rough Sleeper Comparison

population of 76,501. This is in part due to NY state policy of granting all homeless persons a right to shelter. A right that is not provided by most other states and municipalities throughout the US. This makes the disparity between NYC's and London's sleeping rough population all the more remarkable.

Despite these dramatic differences, it is clear that homeless numbers throughout the UK and in particular in England appear to be on the rise (Homeless Monitor, 2015; Crisis, 2016), as evidenced by rough sleeper counts increasing by 37% in London and 14% in England from 2013 to 2014 and then the numbers increased again by 27% in London and 30% throughout England from 2014 to 2015, and once again by 3% in London and 16% in England from 2015 to 2016.

UK government austerity measures since 2010 have resulted in economic hardship, a fraying of the social safety net, and the closure of 4,000 hostel beds over 4 years, as well as a greater than 50% cut in funding for homelessness services. According to the national homeless charity Crisis (2016), all forms of homelessness has risen, after many years of declining trends prior to 2010. Many fear that we may be witnessing an unraveling of essential resources paired with rising economic costs resulting in an enduring negative impact of poverty and homelessness throughout the UK.

A Flawed Comparison?

One may fairly question whether this is a flawed comparison. While the US and England have made some progress in tracking homelessness numbers, we should remain cautious about the validity and reliability of our data, as well as be hesitant to make quick conclusions. This is in part due to different methodologies, tracking systems, and definitions of homelessness, as well as difficulties in measuring and comparing hidden homeless sub-populations who choose not to report to authorities.

If we are to be candid, we must admit that there are some real and direct conflicts of interest that most of these numbers embody. Many government officials are looking for ways to show success and thereby reduce expenditures. This has spurred government agencies to change the definitions of who qualifies as officially homeless in order to show a (superficial) reduction in homeless numbers. For example, in the US, the term "chronically homeless" has been redefined in a more narrow manner that limits eligibility for housing and services to a smaller subgroup than in the past, as well as demanding more formal evidence for meeting the chronically homeless label's criterion.

Further, the people and agencies who report data to government officials are pressured to demonstrate that their program-based interventions are successful and warrant continued funds. Other annual variables that impact the accuracy of Point in Time Count results include the unpredictability of the weather, as well as variance in staff training and how many people assist with the counting process. The end result is at times confusing, and certainly can and should be questioned.

This limits our ability to compare statistics from one region to another let alone between countries with different climates, cultures, economies, and varying definitions of homelessness. However, this does not take away from the fact, based on overwhelming statistical evidence, that the US has significantly reduced the homelessness of certain subgroups (i.e., Veterans, Chronically homeless, and unsheltered persons) since 2007, while still exhibiting much larger numbers, with many more people sleeping rough on a daily basis, than what is seen in the UK. This has led to a homeless crisis being declared by the mayors of several US cities including Seattle-Washington, Los Angeles-California, Honolulu-Hawaii, and NYC, among others. Further, there is ample evidence to show that homelessness is on the rise throughout the UK, while access to services and resources has become more restricted.

The Costs of Homelessness

Reducing homelessness remains a challenging issue when you consider the lack of affordable housing, unemployment rates among minorities and youth, as well as high rates of under-employment, coupled with being disconnected from a support network of family, friends, faith based groups, or other available community resources and services. In addition, many folks with jobs are just not making livable wages. These economic issues need to be more fully addressed, if we want to see long-term progress in stemming the tide of homelessness.

In summary, homelessness issues and the trauma inherent in this experience persists on both sides of the Atlantic. In the end, we are all in the same boat as we try to grapple with the negative ramifications of homelessness and its heavy toll on individuals and societies.

Urban homelessness in the US and UK is well documented and even more magnified by the realities of rich and poor living closely together in places such as London and NYC. An often underappreciated aspect of homelessness in poor rural areas is the lack of a reliable and economical transportation system, so people cannot easily travel to work and healthcare appointments, while also having a harder time maintaining important social ties, or connecting with needed assistance. Other direct causes of homelessness consist of institutional discharges from hospitals, prisons, or youth aging out of foster care, among other things. Many of the people who end up homeless in these ways have experienced a great deal of trauma and are compromised by mental health, addiction and medical issues.

In particular, people without homes who have complex needs due to trauma, addiction, as well as mental and physical disabilities have historically been denied access to affordable housing, support services, and needed treatment due to not meeting a "readiness standard" and/or specific eligibility criteria. In some cases, eligible individuals have rejected offers of programs that come across as overly regimented, authoritative, and unconcerned about individual preferences. This segment of homeless individuals and couples often value their autonomy above most things and will do what they can to meet their immediate needs for food, warmth, and safety, while often not prioritizing longer-term concerns of housing and healthcare. In addition, affordable housing alternatives with support services that are geared for meeting people "where they are at," as opposed to demands of treatment readiness are too few in number to meet the ever-present demand.

This has resulted in the continuation of long-term homelessness, high rates of emergency care use, inpatient hospitalizations, incarcerations, and premature deaths. In fact, there have been a number of studies (Hwang, 2000; O'Connell, 2005; Babidge, Buhrich, & Butler, 2001) in the US and abroad that have demonstrated the complex link between homelessness and early death. James O'Connell's (2005) meta-study review on homeless mortality rates concluded that despite a diversity of methodologies utilized across multiple continents, there is remarkable consistency that transcends borders, cultures and oceans: homeless persons are three to four times more likely to die prematurely than the general population, and the average age of death is between 42 and 57 years old.

Unfortunately, the findings are even more alarming when one considers the death rates and life spans of people sleeping rough. Dr. Hwang, Dr. O'Connell and colleagues (1998) studied the vulnerability of particular homeless subgroups, and found that people who were unsheltered or living outside for at least six months were at high risk of death if they fell into any of the following categories:

- Triple diagnosis of mental illness, substance abuse, medical condition
- 60 years of age or older
- History of frostbite, hypothermia, or trench foot

- At least three emergency room visits over the prior three months

- More than three emergency room visits or hospitalizations in a year

- Diagnosis of HIV/AIDS, liver or renal disease

Over a five year period, 40% of the people who were among these categories died, and the average age of death was 47 (O'Connell, 2005). Further, the latest ten-year longitudinal study (Roncarati, 2016) on 445 unsheltered/sleeping rough persons (mostly white men) in Massachusetts confirms a much higher death rate than the general population at a significantly younger age. Its findings showed that the average age of death was 53 years old and the risk of mortality in comparison to the general Massachusetts population was nearly ten times higher, as well as three times greater among unsheltered/sleeping rough persons, as compared to the general homeless population, which includes people in shelter. Over a ten-year time period, 134 deaths out of 445 individuals (30%) occurred even though there was nearly universal access to health insurance and care in Massachusetts. This further demonstrates the need for housing and/or housing with support services as an essential part of a successful healthcare for the homeless policy.

The evidence gathered in both the US and England demonstrates that there is a high financial cost to homelessness. England's Department of Health study (2010) found that people sleeping rough and in homeless hostels in London were 3.2 times more likely than the general population to require inpatient care, and once admitted to the hospital, the cost was 1.5 times higher for required treatment. Bretherton & Pleace (2015), who researched the effectiveness of nine Housing First programs in England, concluded that the high costs of emergency service usage, inpatient stays and involvement with the criminal justice system can be potentially reduced or removed by a Housing First service. In fact, many studies in the US have shown this to be true. This is especially the case when considering the impact of unsheltered homelessness or people sleeping rough.

This is evidenced by a five-year study of chronically homeless persons (O'Connell, et al., 2005), which found that 119 street dwellers accounted for 18,384 emergency room visits and 871 medical hospitalizations. The average annual health care cost for individuals living on the street was $28,436 compared to $6,056 for individuals who were formerly homeless. We know that Housing First options (Levy, 2013) comprised of affordable housing with support staff, costs considerably less than the status quo. The expenditure for subsidized housing and support services (Levy, 2013) ranges from $12,000 – $20,000 per year, as compared to the significantly higher price of inaction.

While Housing First programs are not a cure, nor guarantee improvement of difficult issues such as social isolation, relapse, or ongoing mental health concerns, there is an impressive track record of significantly reducing life-time medical costs and successfully maintaining people in permanent housing whose primary diagnosis falls into the broad category of major mental illness, as opposed to a primary diagnosis of addiction or substance use disorders (Bretherton & Pleace, 2015, pp. 12-13; Padgett, Henwood, & Tsemberis, 2016; Tsemberis, 2010; Stefancic and Tsemberis, 2007).

One interesting finding in England is the high prevalence of Personality Disorders among the homeless population. There is some evidence to suggest that up to 70% of single homeless people have a personality disorder (PD), (Maguire et al., 2009, cited by the DOH, 2010). This compared to 4% of Great Britain's general population (Coid et al., 2006). Thus far, we have little information on how well suited Housing First programs are for serving this subgroup, who often present with complex needs.

This is in part because the US has not done comparable studies to track the incidence of PD among the homeless, let alone in regard to tracking the success of HF with serving PD. However, the success of transforming homelessness hostels into Psychologically Informed Environments (PIE) throughout England has helped people with PD. So, perhaps a similar approach of instituting PIE with HF programs could lead to effective housing with support services alternatives for this underserved group who present with significant trauma issues.

Advocacy for Effective Outreach and Housing Alternatives

This is a call to action! It is clear that the burden of homelessness includes unacceptable mortality rates and financial costs. In addition, our quality of life suffers from the societal ill of homelessness. Quality of life issues are evident when homelessness comes into our purview, while visiting a local park, playground, or commuter transit station such as a subway or bus depot. We are often confronted with the quandary of helping or turning away from people who are in need.

People in urban environments see this day after day, and many have become hardened to other people's suffering. Perhaps this is done to protect ourselves from other people's pain and our own sense of helplessness. We are tempted to think in terms of us vs. them and therefore turn away, as opposed to reaching out a helping hand. The societal ill of homelessness impacts all of us and certainly challenges us to do better.

Our focus on chronic homelessness and rough sleepers is crucial, because people who remain homeless over long periods of time under the harshest of conditions incur high healthcare costs due to frequent emergency room usage and inpatient stays, and the great majority of them are at high risk of death. This is why my past writings have focused on Pretreatment outreach methods and successful Housing First models that don't require treatment, yet still provide support services. A Housing First approach matched with effective outreach methods that follow a Pretreatment philosophy of care reduces costs and, most importantly, provides us with the opportunity to save lives.

Fortunately, there have been noteworthy responses to the crisis of homelessness on both sides of the Atlantic. Evidence of systemic change can be found within the peer advocacy movement (experts by experience) and their integration into outreach teams and residential support staff; or system-wide staff training resulting in the implementation of Pretreatment strategies, Trauma Informed Care and the formation of Psychologically Informed Environments (PIE). People working within traditional networks have begun to realize the gravity of the situation, and we have made progress with silo-busting strategies to promote access to comprehensive services for people with complex needs. Regional networks of providers have been organized to collaborate on galvanizing resources and services in a targeted manner toward reducing chronic or long-term homelessness. Outreach teams and shelter/hostel staff have direct and improved access to needed healthcare options and housing resources that may include Housing First Programs or other supportive housing alternatives.

Nevertheless, serious challenges remain, and every day the health and safety of many people experiencing homelessness is at considerable risk.

References

All Roads Lead Home, (2008) The Pioneer Valley's Plan to End Homelessness. Supported by the Cities of Holyoke, Northampton, Springfield, MA. Funded by One Family, Inc.

Babidge, N. C., Buhrich, N. & Butler, T. (2001) Mortality among homeless people with schizophrenia in Sydney, Australia: 10-year follow-up. *Acta Psychiatrica Scandinavica*, 103(2): 105-110.

Bender, K., Thompson, S. J., McManus, H., Lantry, J., & Flynn, P. M. (2007) Capacity for survival: Exploring strengths of homeless street youth. In *Child and Youth Care Forum* 36(1): 25-42 Bretherton, J. & Pleace, N. (2015) *Housing first in England: An evaluation of nine services*. Center for Housing Policy: University of York

British Broadcasting Corporation (2015) *Homelessness figures: Nearly 100,000 children in England 'homeless'*. Retrieved from: http://www.bbc.com/news/uk-34346908

Burt, M .R. & Aron, L. Y. (2000) *America's homeless II: Populations and services*. Washington, DC: The Urban Institute

Burt, M. R., Aron, L. Y., Douglas, T., Valente, J., Lee, E. & Iwen, B. (1999) *Homelessness: Programs and the people they serve. Findings of a national survey of homeless assistance: 1996 summary report*. Washington, DC: The Urban Institute

Coid, J., Yang, M., Tyrer, P., Roberts, A. & Ullrich, S. (2006) Prevalence and correlates of personality disorder in Great Britain, *British Journal of Psychiatry*, 188(5): 423-431.

Common Ground Website (2012) Housing First Research: www.commonground.org/mission-model/our-results/ & www.commonground.org/mission-model/why-common-ground-works/

Crisis: The National Charity for Homeless People (2016) About Homelessness – Definition And Numbers. UK. http://www.crisis.org.uk/pages/homeless-def-numbers.html

Culhane, D. P. and Metraux, S. (2008) Rearranging the deck chairs or reallocating the life boats? *Journal of the American Planning Association*, 74(1): 111-121

Department for Communities and Local Government (2017) *Rough Sleeping Statistics — Autumn 2016, England*. Comp. Mike Young. London: Communities.gov.uk

Department of Health (2010) *Healthcare for Single Homeless People*. DH Office of the Chief Analyst. Retrieved from: http://www.qni.org.uk/docs/healthcare%20for%20single%20homeless%20people%20NHS.pdf

Farrow, J. A., Deisher, R. W., Brown, R., Kulig, J. W. & Kipke, M. (1992) Health and health needs of homeless and runaway youth. *Journal of Adolescent Health*, 13(8): 717-726

Frankl, V. E., (1985) *Man's search for meaning*. New York: Washington Square Press

Fitzpatrick, S., Pawson, H., Bramley, G., Wilcox, S. & Watts, B. (2016) *Homelessness Monitor: England*. Heriot Watt University and University of York, Crisis, and JRF.

Fitzpatrick, S., Pawson, H., Bramley, G., Wilcox, S. & Watts, B. (2014) *The Homelessness Monitor: Northern Ireland 2013*. Heriot Watt University and University of York, Crisis, and JRF.

Gulcur, L., Stefanie, D., Shinn, M., Tsemberis, S. & Fischer, S. (2003) Housing, hospitalization, and cost outcomes for homeless individuals with psychiatric disabilities participating in continuum of care and Housing First programs. *Journal of Community and Applied Social Psychology*, 12(2): 171–186

Home and Healthy for Good Report (2010) Compiled by Massachusetts Housing & Shelter Alliance Staff. Retrieved from website: http://www.mhsa.net/matriarch/MultiPiecePageText.asp?PageID=60&PageN ame=HomeHealthyforGoodArchive.

Homeless Link (2015) *Support for single homeless people in England*. Annual Review. London: Homeless Link.

HUD AHAR (2016) *2015 Annual Homeless Assessment Report to Congress – Part 2*. Retrieved from website: https://www.hudexchange.info/onecpd/assets/File/2015-AHAR-Part-2.pdf

HUD AHAR, (2016). *2016 Annual Homeless Assessment Report to Congress*. Retrieved from website: https://www.hudexchange.info/resources/documents/2016-AHAR-Part-1.pdf

HUD AHAR, (2017). *2017 Annual Homeless Assessment Report to Congress*. Retrieved from website: https://www.hudexchange.info/resources/documents/2017-AHAR-Part-1.pdf

HUD CoC Dashboard Report–NYC (2016). Retrieved from: https://www.hudexchange.info/resource/reportmanagement/published/CoC_Dash_CoC_NY-600-2016_NY_2016.pdf

Hwang, S. W., Lebow, J. J., Bierer, M. F., O'Connell, J., Orav, E. J. & Brennan, T. A. (1998) Risk factors for deaths in homeless adults in Boston. *Archives of Internal Medicine*, 158(13): 1454-1460

Hwang, S. W. (2000) Mortality among men using homeless shelters in Toronto, Ontario. *Journal of the American Medical Association*, 283(16): 2152-2157

Kuhn, R. & Culhane, D. P. (1998) Applying cluster analysis to test of a typology of homelessness: Results from the analysis of administrative data. *American* Journal of Community Psychology 17(1): 23-43

Levy, J. S. (2013) *Pretreatment guide for homeless outreach & housing first: Helping couples, youth, and unaccompanied adults.* Ann Arbor, MI: Loving Healing Press

Maguire, N. J., Johnson, R., Vostanis, P., Keats, H. & Remington, R. E. (2009) *Homelessness and complex trauma: a review of the literature.* Southampton, UK, University of Southampton retrieved from http://eprints.soton.ac.uk/69749/ cited in Healthcare for Single Homeless People, p. 12, Department of Health, March 2010, Office of the Chief Analyst

McMillan, T. M., Laurie, M., Oddy, M., Menzies, M., Stewart, E. & Wainman-Lefley, J. (2015) Head injury and mortality in the homeless. *Journal of Neurotrauma.* 32(2): 116-119

National Alliance to End Homelessness (2016) *The State of Homelessness in America: An examination of trends of homelessness, homeless assistance, and at risk populations at the national and state levels.* Washington, DC: Homeless Research Institute

National Record of Scotland (2016) *Population projections for Scottish areas.* Retrieved from: https://www.nrscotland.gov.uk/news/2016/population-projections-for-scottish-areas

NISRA (2015) *Northern Ireland's mid 2015 population estimate.* Retrieved from: http://www.nisra.gov.uk/

O'Connell, J. J. (2005) *Premature Mortality in Homeless Populations: A Review of the Literature.* Nashville: National Health Care for the Homeless Council, Inc.

O'Connell, J. J., Swain, S. (2005) Rough sleepers: A five year prospective study in Boston, 1999-2003. Presentation, *Tenth Annual Ending Homelessness Conference*, Massachusetts Housing and Shelter Alliance, Waltham, MA 2005

Office of National Statistics (2011) *2011 Census of United Kingdom (England & Wales).* Retrieved from: http://www.ons.gov.uk/census/2011census/2011ukcensuses

Padgett, D., Henwood, B. & Tsemberis, S. (2016) *Housing First: Ending Homelessness, Transforming Systems, and Changing Lives.* New York, New York: Oxford University Press

Pearson, C., Montgomery, A. & Locke, G. (2009) Housing stability among individuals with serious mental illness participating in Housing First programs. *Journal of Community Psychology, 37(3)*: 404–417

PIElink (2015) http://pielink.net/

Rogers, C. R. (1957) The necessary and sufficient conditions for therapeutic personality change. *Journal of Consulting Psychology*, 21(2): 95-103.

Roncarati, J. S. (2016) *Examining the Mortality of an Unsheltered Homeless Cohort From Boston, MA, 2000 Through 2009.* Doctoral dissertation, Harvard T. H. Chan School of Public Health. http://nrs.harvard.edu/urn-3: HUL.InstRepos: 32644540

SAMHSA & National Homeless Resource Center (1997) *In from the cold: A tool kit* for creating safe havens for people on the streets. Washington, DC: HHS: HUD

Scottish Government (2015) *Operation of homeless persons legislation in Scotland.* Scotland Government Publications.

Stefancic, A. & Tsemberis, S. (2007) Housing first for long-term shelter dwellers with psychiatric disabilities in a suburban county: A four-year study of housing access and retention. *The Journal of Primary Prevention* 28(3-4): 265-279

Tsai, J., Mares, A. & Rosenheck, R. (2010) A Multisite Comparison of Supported Housing for Chronically Homeless Adults: "Housing First" Versus "Residential Treatment First." *Psychological Services, 7(4)*: 219–232.

Tsemberis, S. (2010) Housing First: Ending homelessness, promoting recovery and reducing cost. In I. Ellen & B. O'Flaherty, (eds) *How to House the Homeless.* New York: Russell Sage Foundation

Tsemberis, S. & Eisenberg, R. (2000) Pathways to housing: supported housing for street-dwelling homeless individuals with psychiatric disabilities. *Psychiatric Services, 51(4)*: 487–493.

Tsemberis, S., Gulcur, L. & Nakae, M. (2004) Housing first, consumer choice, and harm reduction for homeless individuals with a dual diagnosis. *American Journal of Public Health, 94(4)*: 651–656

US Census Bureau (2015). *2015 National Population Estimates.* Retrieved from: https://www.census.gov/popest/data/national/asrh/2015/

Wasserman, J. A. & Clair, J. M. (2010) *At home on the street: People, poverty and a hidden culture of homelessness.* Boulder, Colorado: Lynne Rienner Publishers

13 The Calculus of Inclusion
Jay S. Levy

> The restoration of positive spiritual and cultural values is
> important since these contribute toward restoration of
> individual self-confidence, empowerment and identity."
> — Wangari Maathai (2006)

Our central theme is to share and encourage transatlantic dialogues on homelessness that include our narratives, challenges and successes. The essential task of facilitating dialogues remains the same whether it is across oceans, between workers and clients, staff members, or throughout systems of care.

The spirit of our dialogue is reflected through the sharing of multiple perspectives with our readers. It is one of fostering connection and positive change. The gift to our US readership is all things PIE and its informed development of policy, programs, and services for people without homes with complex trauma histories. The UK readership can hopefully benefit from the additional perspective that Pretreatment provides to one's direct care practice, as well as our nuanced discussions of Housing First, which may help inform its fit within the UK context. Just as Robin and I have found, I know that we all benefit from a dialogue that helps us to reflect beyond the familiar terrain of our experiences and ideas, as this provides the seeds from which new effective approaches to homelessness can grow.

Each chapter of this book presents lessons learned from the field in our attempts at helping, as well as a variety of perspectives and approaches that both US and UK practitioners have to offer. The universal principles of Pretreatment and the major elements of PIE were utilized together and separately, to help us assess and better understand the multifaceted and complex reality of homelessness, trauma, and loss from direct care services to the creation of programs and governing policy throughout a variety of ecological and cultural contexts. Our shared experience indicates that we are in it together and there is undoubtedly much that we can learn from one another.

In the end, it is about access to the narratives that guide our work, while promoting inclusion of the people we serve throughout our communities. This encompasses access to affordable housing, and establishing meaningful connections with one's neighbors and the greater community, as well as fuller participation in the economy and having quality healthcare options (medical and behavioral health services) to promote healing on a physical, mental, and spiritual level. To do this effectively requires everyone's efforts working in tandem with one another across locales, rather than developing and relying upon sub-regional fiefdoms of policies, resources and services.

Stronger Together

Wangari Maathai, 2004 Nobel Peace Prize recipient for her contribution to sustainable development, democracy, and peace, shares the Myth of the Hummingbird (2010, https://tinyurl.com/HBIRD00):

> Once there was a great forest fire. All the animals fled to safer terrain and felt powerless as the giant blaze engulfed their home. In their midst, a small hummingbird said, "I must do something," and frantically flew to the nearby stream picking up a few drops of water at a time to sprinkle upon the raging fire. Up and back the hummingbird flew, carrying as much water as he could muster in his tiny beak to splash upon the ferocious flames.
>
> The larger animals that watched became indignant and began to mutter to themselves and to one another "what good can a little hummingbird do in this time of crisis... why does he waste his time and efforts on such an impossible task?" But still the hummingbird persisted; flying to and fro from the stream to deliver drops of water at the all-consuming fire. Just then the elephant, while swinging its long, voluminous trunk, yelled out to the hummingbird, "There is nothing you can do... the fire is too big and you are too little." For a moment, the hummingbird turned its gaze upon the large, docile animal and quickly responded, "I am doing the best I can!"

Let's all heed the advice of the hummingbird by doing what we can to dramatically reduce the societal ill of homelessness. For far too long, too many people without homes have been excluded from needed healthcare, housing, and even from their own communities. This is especially true for those who are among the long-term homeless and/or people sleeping rough who invariably present with complex needs. We can no longer afford to look away, while the dire consequences of homelessness are felt throughout our communities, emergency rooms, hospitals, and prisons.

Old models that have left us with ever-increasing medical, correctional, and emergency costs matched with high mortality rates among our most vulnerable, homeless neighbors are simply unacceptable. We must join together throughout our cities and towns to make a critical difference.

The first chapter of this book opens with the words of Martin Luther King, Jr. (1963), who states, "Injustice anywhere is a threat to justice everywhere. We are caught in an inescapable network of mutuality, tied in a single garment of destiny." Our sense of community, moral and spiritual health is under threat by our own inaction. Let's make no mistake about it; homelessness is a social justice issue that demands our attention. It's up to each of us to act and do what we can... much like the hummingbird.

It's All About Relationships

Whether we follow Pretreatment, PIE, and/or Trauma Informed Care principles, creating dialogues remain at the center of our practice. Regardless of geography, philosophy, or the lessons derived from "hands on" practice and successful programs, we keep coming back to the transformative power of relationships.

This project is full of examples that provide a roadmap for successful engagement with vulnerable persons who are homeless with longstanding, unmet, complex needs. People's stories from both sides of the Atlantic demonstrate over and over again that the formation of person-centered relationships is the very foundation for our work. This book demonstrates inclusion at every turn, such as helping Miguel to reconnect with the Latino Community, or John Conolly's use of Pre-treatment Therapy to build pathways with Ted to access treatment, or when Suzanne Quinney shows us how Appreciative Inquiry can foster greater participation in communities by transforming hostels to PIEs. Pretreatment strategies, Open Dialogue, and Appreciative Inquiry can guide us through the terrain of individual, cultural, and systemic differences in an effort to establish positive communications, lasting connections, and pathways out of homelessness.

These are effective tools for reaching out to excluded populations, and to directly include them in the conversation of their own health and well-being, thereby promoting a safe and trusting relationship with a sense of empowerment. Judith Herman (1992, p.134), the renowned author of *Trauma and Recovery*, states, "The core experiences of psychological trauma are disempowerment and disconnection from others. Recovery is therefore based upon the empowerment of the survivor and the creation of new connections."

The Peer movement, self-help groups, and our efforts to reintegrate people without homes with their families, faith groups, or other cultural gatherings are all part of the road to recovery. It is through meaningful connections with others that we are truly revitalized. Beyond outreach to individuals is the quest for belonging to something larger than ourselves; membership and acceptance within a community that shares our values and beliefs. As Wangari Maathai (2006, p.48) states, "The restoration of positive spiritual and cultural values is important, since these contribute toward restoration of individual self-confidence, empowerment and identity."

This means finding ways to welcome those who have been most isolated and marginalized back into our communities and thereby reducing stigma, as opposed to creating institutional settings that remain separate from the rest of us. The success of the Housing First movement very much depends on its willingness to uphold the value of community integration. Otherwise, we are simply moving the trauma of the streets and shelters into a housing environment without addressing the issues of exclusion, oppression, and isolation. It is critical that support services for Housing initiatives are adequately in place to facilitate transition of our clients to naturally occurring community supports. Our hope is to foster a greater sense of community membership; a sense of belonging, acceptance and connectedness to a culture that may provide a greater sense of purpose and/or spiritual meaning.

The Multiple Benefits of Cross-Cultural Dialogues

One of the pleasant surprises of our cross-cultural exchange was our shared value of fostering relationships by carefully attending to the nuances of language. This was reflected throughout the text by examining "Open Dialogue" (Bakhtin, 1981), "Appreciative Inquiry" (Watkins, et al., 2011), and the stages of "Common Language Construction" (Levy, 2004). All three approaches can aid us in better understanding the universe of the client, while establishing a person-centered relationship. Once trust and respect for client autonomy are established, our communications can become goal focused, and together we can journey down pathways to housing and/or recovery.

Outreach depends on our efforts to begin a dialogue with those in need, crossing the border from one world to another in search of a common language. It is in our willingness to cross the cultural divide, and faith that an open dialogue can result in mutual understanding and goal focused work that opens the door to new possibilities. This sets the stage for healthy change. It is an opportunity for the worker and the client, as well as our systems of care to get "unstuck" by shifting their perspectives.

The counselor is challenged to work with, not against, people's strengths, values, and meaning. This means listening carefully, and "tuning in" to the person's universe of language, while letting go of our "program speak" in favor of individualization. Likewise, the client is challenged to take the risk of trusting someone and once again believing in the possibility of positive change. Finally, our systems of care need to be equipped to support both staff and clients by providing cross-cultural trainings that promote Pretreatment strategies and Psychologically Informed Environments, as well as maintaining and developing needed resources and services to help to end homelessness.

Similarly, we have crossed the cultural divide in our work with colleagues at various conferences (e.g., International Street Medicine Symposium), sharing insights from around the globe. Of course, this is not limited just to conferences, as cross-cultural perspectives on homelessness flow via journal articles, university coursework, staff trainings, and easily accessible podcasts on YouTube, as well as through a variety of websites such as the www.pielink.net that offers interviews and library materials on transatlantic homelessness issues. In fact, I recently taught the first graduate studies course on PIE and Pretreatment, utilizing multi-media resources from PIE-Link, with college students in the US. These forums, as well as the exchange programs between the US and UK, share insights of PIE and Trauma Informed Care approaches to homelessness, and this book is among the transition buses bringing information to and fro, which in turn continues the evolution to new hybrid models.

New Hybrids

New hybrids have arisen since the inception of PIE and Pretreatment, as reviewed throughout these pages. These include: Pre-Treatment Therapy as now practiced in Central London; Homeless services workers are being trained to utilize elements of PIE & Pretreatment principles to help inform direct care practice; the development and implementation of the REACH Housing model that combines Pretreatment and Housing First principles of care. Other approaches that have emerged include Dialogical PIE, which is the convergence of Open Dialogue with a psychological model developed by Ray Middleton called Ladder4Life (Middleton, 2016), as described in Chapter 6, as well as the coming together of PIE and Appreciative Inquiry practice as highlighted by Suzanne Quinney in chapter 8.

Of course, this is just a sampling of what has occurred, with many more possibilities to come. As our communications flourish, new and exciting ideas can and will arise. I dare say that our attempts to greatly reduce homelessness will not be answered by a single model or a one size fits all approach. I am confident that innovative hybrids will become part of the solution. Our hope is to develop policies, programs, and strategies that can be piloted, tested, and ultimately applied as viable approaches to the vexing issue of homelessness.

Coming Home

Generating ideas, learning from one another, and instituting innovative practices such as Housing First, Coordinated Entry, Pretreatment, PIE, and Trauma Informed Care are all steps on the road home. A helpful acronym that represents many of the challenges that lie before us is RAPP.

- **R**- Resource sustainment and development inclusive of an array of targeted housing options such as Housing First, Transitional Housing, and half-way house options

- **A**- Access and Availability of Resources for those who are most in need based on inclusionary "best fit" criteria of eligibility, not exclusionary exact match measures

- **P**- Prevention Strategies and Programs inclusive of healthcare and affordable housing for all as well as job development, training and education to help provide a livable wage

- **P**- Pretreatment Approach informs direct care work and instituting PIE to further develop homelessness policy, systems of care, and targeted programs

The RAPP acronym reflects the policy, funding, and training needed to support our efforts toward inclusion. We need to build an adequate safety net of resources and services that is accepting of people with complex needs who are homeless. This means not only having enough affordable housing resources and support services, but also providing access to those in need. Prevention strategies inclusive of adequate healthcare coverage and access to recovery based addiction, mental health, and medical services, as well as education and employment training opportunities are all part of the solution. Training for homeless service providers, policy makers and advocates in PIE, Trauma Informed Care, and Pretreatment approaches is an essential ingredient that promotes high quality care, policies, and programs.

Perhaps this is only the beginning. Joining with others, developing a language to help create systemic change, and taking part in an open dialogue beyond geographical limits are all part of the process. The PIE movement in England has made significant progress in transforming shelters/hostels into Psychologically Informed Environments that support people with complex needs in their transition from homelessness to housing in the community. Housing First has been a proven transatlantic practice that has been successfully piloted in many countries including the US, Canada, UK, and France. There is widespread agreement regardless of locale on the importance of relationship-centered work, and the necessity for trauma-informed care, as well as the need to better address economic realities, such as unemployment, under-employment, and the lack of affordable housing that produce homelessness. We could also benefit from an interconnected system of seamless care that is inclusive, rather than exclusive. Our hope is to have a positive and significant impact on policy, systems of care, and on the frontline work being done to help end or at least greatly reduce the societal ill of homelessness.

In closing, I give much of the credit to all those who shared our transatlantic journey. The community of authors who contributed to this book, the readers, and many others have added to the philosophical base as well as expanded and humanized our outreach, pathways to recovery, and housing opportunities for people who are homeless with complex needs.

I am grateful to Robin Johnson for being the touchstone that brought people together and made this project a reality. Exciting opportunities with real applications to help guide policy and "hands on" practice lie ahead as we work together to construct a better future for those without homes, the people who serve them, and ultimately for us all. Our goal is to reach out to those who are most in need in order to provide a greater sense of safety, dignity, and a place they can call home.

References

Bakhtin, M. M. (1981) *The Dialogical Imagination*. Austin, TX: University of Texas Press

Herman, J. L. (1992) *Trauma and Recovery*. New York, NY: Basic Books

King, M. L. Jr. BrainyQuote.com. excerpt from April 16, 1963 letter from Birmingham jail. Retrieved March 19, 2017, from BrainyQuote.com Web site:
https://www.brainyquote.com/quotes/quotes/m/martinluth122559.html

Levy, J. S. (2004) Pathway to a common language: A homeless outreach perspective. *Families in Society: The Journal of Contemporary Human Services*, 85(3): 371-378

Maathai, W. (2006) *The Greenbelt Movement*. New York, NY: Lantern Books

Maathai, W. (2010) Animated clip from Dirt! The movie: I will be a hummingbird https://www.youtube.com/watch?v=IGMW6YWjMxw

Middleton, R. (2016) *Ladder4Life: Narrative social-psychological framework*. Newcastle, England: JUMP

Myth of the Hummingbird (2010). [video]
https://www.youtube.com/watch?v=IGMW6YWjMxw

PIE-Link (2015). http://pielink.net/

Watkins, J. M., Mohr, B. & Kelly, R. (2011) 2nd edition. *Appreciative Inquiry: Change at the speed of imagination*. San Francisco, CA: John Wiley & Sons, Inc

Appendix i – Pretreatment Approach

What is Pretreatment?

I first introduced the term "Pretreatment" as an approach to help people without homes who experience mental health and/or addiction issues in an article published in the *Families in Society Journal*, entitled "Homeless Outreach: On the Road to Pretreatment Alternatives" (Levy, 2000). This was the outgrowth of my witnessing too many people being ignored by a treatment-biased culture that continually refused to serve those who were most in need. As mentioned earlier, these folks were often considered "not ready," "non-compliant," or "beyond service capabilities." In response to this dilemma, a Pretreatment philosophy was developed from an outreach perspective, which is naturally person-centered because the work begins literally and figuratively where the client is at.

The term "Pretreatment" initially appeared as "Pretreatment Variables" through research that predicted successful outcomes for addiction and recovery treatment approaches (Joe, et al., 1998,; Miller & Rollnick, 1991,; Salloum, et al., 1998). A psychologist named Bruce Wampold (2001) took this a step further by conducting a meta-analysis of pretreatment variables on the success of different counseling methods for addressing mental illness. He concluded that particular therapeutic models mattered less as a predictor for success than an array of general factors such as the client's hope and expectation for change, belief in the effectiveness of the therapy, and a positive working alliance between the client and therapist.

The main conclusions from research on both mental illness and addictions support the value of client-centered approaches (Rogers, 1957; Levy, 1998; Wampold, 2001), the importance of motivation and problem recognition, as well as belief in the therapeutic model or approach by both counselor and client. Other studies on assisting people with severe mental illness uphold the effectiveness of Psychosocial Rehabilitation principles (Anthony, et al., 1990), which instills hope and motivation by being goal-focused. An integral part of the work is for counselor and client to jointly identify barriers to achieving their objectives and thereby develop strategies to overcome these obstacles. This is a goal-centered approach that helps people to recognize certain concerns over time based on their aspirations, rather than being dependent upon persons presenting with initial problems and/or declaring themselves in need of help.

I have found that many people without homes, who have experienced significant mental health issues including trauma, often minimize their problems and/or define them differently: not in a treatment language. However, when engaged and supported by an outreach counselor/worker, many are often open to working on goals that speak to their circumstances, which includes addressing their daily needs, sense of safety, and future aspirations.

Most people who experience the detrimental effects of homelessness and trauma are struggling just to survive and meet their immediate needs of health and safety. The research literature (Babidge, Buhrich, & Butler, 2001; Burt et al., 1999; Hwang, 2000; Johnson & Haigh 2012; McMillan et al., 2015; O'Connell, 2005) confirms the high risk of premature death and increased rates of chronic health issues such as arthritis, diabetes, and cancer, as well as significant rates of psychological trauma and traumatic brain injury (TBI) experienced by homeless individuals.

The conclusions from these types of research, coupled with the persistence of a treatment-biased culture that doesn't adequately provide access to homeless persons, indicate the need for a Pretreatment approach. It is relationship-driven work based on five guiding principles of care (Levy, 2000):

> **Relationship Formation:** Promote trust, and respect client autonomy via Stages of Engagement, resulting in a client-centered relationship that is goal driven
>
> **Common Language Construction:** Listen, understand and utilize a person's words, ideas and values in an effort to develop effective communication
>
> **Ecological Considerations:** Support the process of Transition and Adaptation to new ideas, people, environments, housing, and recovery, etc.
>
> **Facilitate Change:** Utilize Stages of Change Model and Motivational Interviewing techniques to facilitate positive change

> **Promote Safety:** Apply Crisis Intervention and Harm Reduction Strategies to reduce risk, increase safety, promote stability, and embrace the opportunity for positive change

Pretreatment (Levy, 2010, p.15) is defined as "an approach that enhances safety while promoting transition to housing (e.g., housing first options), and/or treatment alternatives through client centered supportive interventions that develop goals and motivation to create positive change."

An outreach counseling model based on a pretreatment philosophy affords us the opportunity to become both interpreters and bridge builders (Levy, 2013). Potential resources and services are therefore reinterpreted and reframed, so the client can more fully consider these options and their potential impacts. This is the first major step toward building a bridge to needed resources and services that include housing and treatment options. It is a bridge consisting of a safe and trusting relationship between worker and client, as well as a common language that fosters communication. This is in line with our striving to understand people's values and stories in a manner that dignifies the meaning and purpose of their narratives.

Developing client centered relationships, understanding their worlds, and providing or accessing essential community resources and services are the mutual goals of homeless service workers, residential support staff and their clients. In many respects, the definition of Pretreatment and its five principles of care are universal and timeless. They are cross-cultural concepts that can be applied on both sides of the Atlantic to help those who are most in need. Similar to the elements of PIE, a Pretreatment approach is trauma informed.

Interconnections of PIE and Pretreatment

Psychologically Informed Environments (PIE) and Pretreatment approaches can be instituted on a systemic level of coordinated entry design, and on a programmatic level of residential or shelter care, as well as on a personal level of outreach or direct services to people without homes. These approaches keep us in line with the person, so we can listen and respond in a humanistic manner. Our aim is to uphold the client's dignity as an essential part of the helping process.

As noted earlier in chapter 9, in our necessary rush to become housing focused, use standardized assessment tools, and input data, we risk losing person-centered insights such as sensitivity to the stage of engagement to enhance trust, or working with, not against, a person's sense of meaning and purpose, as well as providing adequate levels of follow up care after a person is housed to combat isolation and instability due to the impact of complex trauma.

When one looks at the human service world through the lens of a Pretreatment model, the emphasis is on direct care and building person-centered relationships with the people we serve. PIE is a much broader concept that provides guidance for large systems of care, as well as the development of particular programs. What PIE helps to assure is the quality of care needed throughout multiple systems of care including shelters, hostels, and residential settings, drop-in centers, various treatment facilities, etc. It encompasses a Trauma Informed Care philosophy and goes beyond it to consider the broader challenge of being psychologically informed in the development of all systems of care and their programs, resources and services.

The propagation of Psychologically Informed Environments and its precepts would help assure that persons with complex and multiple needs who have experienced the detrimental effects of homelessness are better served in a variety of human service settings. Greater professionalism in the workforce and better outcomes for people without homes have been attained through training programs, supervision, and reflective practice based on the nuances of PIE and Pretreatment principles of care, as discussed and demonstrated throughout these chapters.

In many respects, a Pretreatment approach fits nicely into PIE as a Psychological Model, as well as under the PIE element of Relationships, by upholding the central importance of engagement, as well as supporting the process of adaptation to new environments, and enhancing staff training activities. A focus on helping processes consists of stages or phases of engagement, common language construction, and change, to guide homeless service and/or residential staff interactions with people who are often excluded from services due to complex trauma, multiple needs, and other behavioral health issues.

Further, sensitivity to person-in-environment issues follows Ecological Social Work principles that support the process of transition and adaptation. Similar to PIE, the term "environment" is defined broadly and encompasses not only the physical environment, but also interpersonal aspects, exposure to ideas, values, and rules that govern social structure, other participants, and even the different phases of a client-worker relationship.

For example, the concerns associated with the early stage of engagement may be quite different from the last stage of termination. Whether it is the safety concerns and trust issues associated with meeting a homeless service worker, or the fears of terminating a professional relationship, the process of transition and adaptation is supported by different types of interventions in accordance with the particular stage of relationship formation, common language development, and change. In this manner, a Pretreatment approach can be the psychological model to help guide counselors, support key relationships with clients and others, as well as support transitions to new environments.

The question for both the homeless and human service sectors is how to best serve people without homes who present with complex and multiple needs, as opposed to writing them off as unwilling or treatment resistant. The implementation of PIE in England and its expansion throughout the UK provides a needed perspective to meet the remarkable challenge of reaching, supporting and housing the very people who have been unfairly stigmatized and in many cases have suffered the most from our past inaction.

In response, the PIE movement has had a positive impact on the transformation of homeless services, which includes a focus on creating a hostel network of Psychologically Informed Environments. Further, the integration of peers or "experts from experience" onto outreach teams, hostel and residential staff have brought about greater sensitivity to the plight of people without homes. In fact, Ray Middleton, who wrote the foreword and chapter 6 of this book, is an "expert from experience" who provides systems brokerage consultation in the North of England.

The PIE perspective provides a needed emphasis on developing program education on trauma (such as reframing a person's diagnosis of Personality Disorder as someone with complex needs) and its impact on people's lives, implementing an appropriate psychological model to better address these issues, as well as helping staff to be more sensitive and connected with the people they serve.

Both the development of PIE and Pretreatment have much in common with Trauma Informed care (TIC), due to the central concerns of providing care to excluded populations with high rates of trauma. Hopper and colleagues (2010) reviewed research in the US on Trauma Informed Care, and found that the following four basic tenets are essential to positive outcomes for programs and the people that they serve.

1. **Trauma Education** for all staff
2. **Promote physical and emotional safety** for trauma survivors through needed environmental modifications, clarifying worker-client boundaries/roles, and developing supports and

skills to address triggers, implement safety plans, as well as crisis intervention, etc.

3. **Rebuild Control** by providing choice and promoting a greater internal locus of control (respect client autonomy); empower clients to actively promote self-care and recovery. Provide an environment with supports that are safe, consistent, and predictable

4. **Strengths-based work:** Identify, reinforce, enhance and develop client strengths, coping skills/strategies

Final Thoughts on a Pretreatment Model

A fuller conception of the outreach counseling process that is derived from a Pretreatment approach includes ten guidelines for outreach counseling (Fig. i-1, p. 231) and the stages of pre-engagement through termination as represented here (Fig. i-2, p. 232), based upon my (Levy, 1998) integration of Eric Erikson's (1968) Psychosocial Developmental stages and Germain & Gitterman's (1980) Ecological phases. This includes developmental stage sensitive interventions to help guide the worker throughout the counseling process, while always remaining within the context of the person's narrative.

In closing, a Pretreatment approach embraces a dynamic set of processes that are simultaneously considered by the worker, which is based upon five universal principles of care. A Pretreatment approach helps us to truly meet people where they are at, and thereby develop critical person-centered relationships. The worker is always assessing for safety concerns and is ready to respond through the use of crisis intervention or harm reduction strategies. Our task is to become goal focused, while taking part in an ongoing dialogue with some of the most excluded members of our society. This, along with our undying optimism, provides the fertile ground that supports the unfolding of a person's story toward new possibilities of healing and recovery.

Fig. i-1: Ten Pretreatment Guidelines for Outreach Counseling

1. Meet clients (both literally and figuratively) where they are at!
2. The relationship is most important — Promote trust and respect autonomy
3. Develop a common language of shared words, ideas and values
4. Be goal centered — Join the person in setting goals that resonate well in his or her world
5. Mutually define or characterize particular difficulties to achieving goals and jointly develop strategies or plans
6. Carefully support transitions to new ideas, relationships (stages of engagement), environments, resources, and treatment (bridge client language to treatment language)
7. Promote Safety via Harm Reduction strategies and Crisis Intervention techniques
8. Utilize crisis as an opportunity to promote positive change
9. Respect the process of change — understand its stages and relevant interventions
10. Understand the person's narrative and integrate a person's sense of meaning or purpose with movement toward positive change

Originally published: Levy, (2011).

Fig. i-2: Outreach-Counseling Developmental Model

Ecological Phase	Psychosocial Challenge	Intervention
Pre-Engagement Initial Phase	Trust vs. Mistrust Issues of Safety	Observation, Identify Potential Client, Respect Personal Space, Safety Assessment, Attempt Verbal & Non-Verbal Communication, Offer Essential Need Item, Listen for Client's Language, Establish Initial Communication, etc.
Engagement Initial Phase	Trust vs. Mistrust Issues of Dependency Boundary Issues	Communicate with Empathy and Authenticity, Learn Client's Language, Actively Listen by Reflecting Client's Words, Ideas, and Values, Identify and Reinforce Client Strengths, Provide Unconditional Regard, Avoid Power Struggles, Emphasize Joining the Resistance, Introduce Roles, Begin and Continue Development of Healthy Boundaries, Establish Ongoing Communication, Identify Current Life Stressors, etc.
Contracting Initial Phase	Autonomy vs. Shame Issues of Control Initiative vs. Guilt	Further Define Roles & Boundaries, Address Shame by Universalizing Human Frailty and Reviewing Client Strengths, Point Out Discrepancy and Explore Ambivalence, Negotiate Reachable Goals to Alleviate Life Stressors, Explore Client History in Relation to Goals, Determine Eligibility for Potential Resources & Services Regarding Client Interests, Further Define Shared Objectives by Utilizing Client Language, Jointly Consider Housing Options, etc.
Contract Implementation Ongoing Work Phase	Initiative vs. Guilt Issues of Stability Industry vs. Inferiority	Jointly Assess Goals, Strengths, and Obstacles, Identify and Address Fear, shame, Guilt, and Anger Issues Through Listening, Joining, Validating and Redirect Focus to Achievable Tasks, Review & Reinforce Current Coping Strategies, Promote Self Care, Educate re: Symptom Management, Further Develop Skills and Supports, Refer to Indicated Services, Enhance Coping Strategies, Mobilize Client Strengths, Support Transition and Adaptation to New Programs, Services and Housing, Reinforce Positive Change
Termination Ending Phase	Relationship Identity vs. Confusion of Roles Boundary Issues Issues of Loss	Review the Work Completed Together, Emphasize Gains, Share Feelings of Loss, Connect to Past losses, Differentiate, and Explore as Needed, Reinforce and Consolidate Change, Review and Reinforce Support Systems, Review and Redefine Provider Roles, as well as Client-Worker Relationship, Redirect to Established Support Systems

    * Many of the interventions listed are applicable to different phases (stages) of the outreach-counseling process, yet have particular relevance to the indicated stage.

References

Anthony, W., Cohen, M., & Farkas, M. (1990) *Psychiatric rehabilitation.* Boston University: Center For Psychiatric Rehabilitation

Berger, P. & Luckman, T. (1966) *The social construction of reality.* New York: Doubleday

Babidge, N. C., Buhrich, N. & Butler, T. (2001) Mortality among homeless people with schizophrenia in Sydney, Australia: 10-year follow-up. *Acta Psychiatrica Scandinavica,* 103(2): 105-110

Burt, M. R. & Aron, L. Y. (2000) *America's homeless II: Populations and services.* Washington, DC: The Urban Institute

Burt, M. R., Aron, L. Y., Douglas, T., Valente, J., Lee, E. & Iwen, B. (1999) Homelessness: Programs and the people they serve. *Findings of a national survey of homeless assistance: 1996 summary report.* Washington, DC: The Urban Institute

Epston, D. & White, M. (1992) *Experience, contradiction, narrative, and imagination: Selected papers of David Epston and Michael White, 1989-1991.* Adelaide, Australia: Dulwich Centre Publications

Erikson, E. H. (1968) *Identity: youth and crisis.* New York: Norton

Germain, C. B. & Gitterman, A. (1980) *The life model of social work process.* New York: Columbia University Press

Hopper, E., Bassuk, E. & Olivet, J. (2010) Shelter from the Storm: Trauma-Informed Care in Homelessness Services Settings. *The Open Health Services & Policy Journal.* 3: 80-100

Hwang, S. W., Lebow, J. J., Bierer, M. F., O'Connell, J., Orav, E. J. & Brennan, T. A. (1998) Risk factors for deaths in homeless adults in Boston. *Archives of Internal Medicine,* 158(13): 1454-1460.

Hwang, S. W. (2000) Mortality among men using homeless shelters in Toronto, Ontario. *Journal of the American Medical Association,* 283(16): 2152-2157

Joe, G. W., Simpson, D. D. & Broome, K. M. (1998) Effects of readiness for drug abuse treatment on client retention and assessment of process. *Addiction,* 93(8): 1177-1190

Johnson, R. & Haigh R., Editors. (2012) *Complex trauma and its effects; Perspectives on creating an environment for recovery.* Brighton: Pavilion

Levy, J. S. (1998) Homeless outreach: A developmental model. *Psychiatric Rehabilitation Journal,* 22(2): 123-131

Levy, J. S. (2000) Homeless outreach: On the road to pretreatment alternatives. *Families in Society: The Journal of Contemporary Human Services,* 81(4): 360-368

Levy, J. S. (2010) *Homeless narratives & pretreatment pathways: From words to housing*. Ann Arbor, MI: Loving Healing Press

Levy, J. S. (2013) *Pretreatment guide for homeless outreach & housing first: Helping couples, youth, and unaccompanied adults*. Ann Arbor, MI: Loving Healing Press

McMillan, T. M., Laurie, M., Oddy, M., Menzies, M., Stewart, E. & Wainman-Lefley, J. (2015) Head injury and mortality in the homeless. *Journal of Neurotrauma*. 32(2): 116-119

Miller, W. R. & Rollnick, S. (1991) *Motivational interviewing: Preparing people to change addictive behavior*. New York: Guilford

O'Connell, J. J. (2005) *Premature Mortality in Homeless Populations: A Review of the Literature*. Nashville: National Health Care for the Homeless Council, Inc.

O'Connell, J. J. & Swain S. (2005) *Rough sleepers: A five year prospective study in Boston, 1999-2003*. Presentation, Tenth Annual Ending Homelessness Conference, Massachusetts Housing and Shelter Alliance, Waltham, MA [same query as before regarding this paper.]

Prochaska, J. O. & DiClemente, C. C. (1982) Trans theoretical therapy: Toward a more integrative model of change. *Psychotherapy: Theory, Research, and Practice*. 19(7): 276-288

Rogers, C.R. (1957) The necessary and sufficient conditions for therapeutic personality change. *Journal of Consulting Psychology*, 21(2): 95-103

Salloum, I. M., Moss, H. B., Daley, D. C. & Cornelius, J. R. (1998) Drug use problem awareness and treatment readiness in dual diagnosis patients. *American Journal on Addictions*, 7(1): 35-42

Wampold, B. E. (2001) *The great psychotherapy debate: Models, methods, findings*. Mahwah, New Jersey: Lawrence Erlbaum Associates

Appendix ii - A US/UK Glossary of Homelessness terms

In this glossary, more technical terms used in this book are spelled out in alphabetical order. Where in these descriptions a term is used that is defined elsewhere in the Glossary, this is indicated with "qv."

Other, more pervasive or more subtle connections, and any contrast or overlap between terms, are conveyed more schematically in Fig. ii-1 (p. 236). In this way, we hope, the connections between needs and services can be made; and the wider connections issues can be accommodated without too much irksome repetition.

NB: In this list we also distinguish US and UK terminology, both where similar and where they differ — typically in the more technical language of government-funded funded programs — with the simple initials (US) and (UK).

~ ~ ~

Chain data (UK) is quite a broad-ranging set of data collected on rough sleepers *(qv),* and others with a "street lifestyle," such as street drinking or begging — but in the London are only. Outreach workers, day services and hostels and other more specialist services record basic demographic data, support needs, pre-homelessness circumstances, contacts with outreach and other services, and any outcomes or events.

Chronic Homelessness (US) A person is considered to be experiencing chronic homelessness when he or she has a disability and has been continuously homeless for one year or more or has experienced at least four episodes of homelessness in the last three years where the combined length of time homeless in those occasions is at least twelve months.

Clubhouse (UK & US) is a social support network with a strong peer- and community participation ethos, built around a recovery model, whether from mental health or substance abuse issues; some are specifically for

A Homelessness Glossary

US and UK service terminology compared

Chronic Homeless (US)

Unsheltered homeless (US)

Rough sleeping (UK)

Sofa surfing (UK)
Doubled up (US)
Couch surfing (US)

Veterans (US & UK)
Unaccompanied Youth (US)

Vulnerably housed (UK)

Sheltered homeless (US)

Emergency shelter (US)

Point in Time count (US)

Rough Sleeper count (UK)
Chain data (UK)

Homelessness (US & UK)

Rapid Rehousing (US)

DV Shelter (Us)

Refuge (UK)

Night shelter (UK)

Hospitalisation (US & UK)

Continuum of Care (US)

Strategic Housing First (US)

Housing First (US)

Housing First (UK)

'Staircases' (US & UK)

'Elevators' (UK)

Recovery Housing, 2015+ (US)

Permanent Supported Housing (US)

Transitional Housing (US)

Recovery Housing, pre-2015 (US)

Foyer (UK)

Safe Haven (US)

PIE of Pathways (UK)

Clubhouse (US & UK)

Hostel (UK)

Core and cluster (UK)

Residential Care (US & UK)

Supported Housing (UK)

Fig. ii-1: A Homelessness Glossary

young people. Clubhouses usually have programmes of activity for members. Users of the service are seen as 'members' of a 'club', with rules of membership suited to the nature of the issues that brings them together for mutual support.

As with a core-and-cluster services (qv) a clubhouse will usually have a building as its base—the clubhouse itself- and will sometimes have 'satellite' accommodation units there and/or in the vicinity. But where a core-and-cluster service typically has a dedicated staff team, many clubhouses aim to minimise reliance on professional staff, and seek to promote mutual support instead.

Continuums of Care (US) CoCs are local planning bodies responsible for coordinating the full range of homelessness services in a geographic area, which may cover a city, county, metropolitan area, or an entire state.

"Core and cluster" (UK) describes a network of accommodation units where one (the "core") is staffed, and the other units (the "cluster") accommodate others with less need for intensive support on-site, but all residents are seen equally as members of the support community. Cluster flats are often used for individuals moving on from the Core unit.

(NB: This is a term originally used in Canada to describe independent living arrangements for those with learning difficulties, as part of the hospital closure programme there. It was adopted in mental health services in the UK, and has lately spread to the homelessness sector, to describe flexible support services mixing short-stay and ongoing support, as needed.)

Doubled Up or Couch Surfing (US) staying with friends, family or acquaintances temporarily. "Couch Surfing" denotes multiple short stays (doubled up) moving from one place to the next in order to avoid homeless shelters or living outdoors.

DV Shelter (US) Domestic Violence (or DV) Shelter: A women's shelter, also known as a women's refuge and battered women's shelter, is a place of temporary protection and support for women escaping domestic violence and intimate partner violence of all forms. DV Shelters help women to be safe, while gaining tangible resources to help them and their families create a new life. In the UK, the term used is **refuge** (qv).

"Elevators" (UK) was the term suggested by Crisis, a major UK national charity in 2010, in a review of the effectiveness of Housing First *(qv)* programmes, to describe the different approach to change management that they saw in short-stay homelessness accommodation services in the UK, in contrast to the "Staircase" models *(qv)* criticized by Housing Firsts' proponents.

(NB: the term "psychologically informed environment" was only first proposed a little later that same year.)

Emergency Shelter (US) is a facility with the primary purpose of providing temporary shelter for homeless people.

Foyer (UK) is an approach to meeting the needs of homeless young people, which entails providing a range of other supports, often on-site, including emotional and peer support, assistance with resuming education and social security benefits.

(NB: The age range for eligibility of foyers may vary, but tends in practice to mean 16+. This primarily reflects the view that it is unhelpful for such young people to be in homelessness services for adults, but in practice the element of age-appropriate peer support seems genuinely valuable in its own right.)

Homeless (US-Health and Human Services Definition) A homeless individual is defined in section 330(h)(5)(A) as "an individual who lacks housing (without regard to whether the individual is a member of a family), including an individual whose primary residence during the night is a supervised public or private facility (e.g., shelter) that provides temporary living accommodations, and an individual who is a resident in transitional housing."

A homeless person is an individual without permanent housing who may live on the streets; stay in a shelter, mission, single room occupancy facilities, abandoned building or vehicle; or in any other unstable or non-permanent situation. [Section 330 of the Public Health Service Act (42 U.S.C., 254b)]

Homeless (literal homelessness definition) describes a person who lacks a fixed, regular, and adequate nighttime residence living in shelter, outside or a place not meant for human habitation such as a vehicle or abandoned building.

(NB: the HUD definition utilized for Point In Time counts does not include people who are doubled up or couch surfing, or persons residing in institutions, e.g., jails, juvenile correction facilities, foster care, hospital beds, detox centers).

Hospitalisation (US & UK) short or long-stay inpatient status in a designated hospital. Care and treatment programmes in the US and the UK are largely comparable, but major differences in the funding of medical care, and in the scope of the law on powers for compulsory detention, mean that the continuity between hospital and community facilities can vary widely, especially for client groups with complex needs.

Hostel (UK) is the term generally used in the UK for any form of short-stay staffed, supported accommodation, though the term is typically used for those formerly homeless. Hostels are typically medium-sized (10-30 bed spaces) and usually provide individual rooms, rarely en-suite; and provide a range of support and recovery-oriented services.

(NB: The term "psychologically informed environment" was coined to describe some of the features of the more successful or innovative of homelessness hostel approaches.)

Housing First (US) A homeless assistance approach that provides people experiencing homelessness with permanent housing as quickly as possible, while prioritizing people who are most vulnerable — and then providing voluntary supportive services as needed. Typically, it does not exclude people from housing because of ongoing substance use or mental illness, nor does it demand that people participate in treatment.

Housing First (UK) In the UK, Housing First (HF) has been promoted within and by the homelessness sector itself, and government has been more cautious in giving it support. As a result, there has not been the same centrally imposed definition of eligibility or fidelity to the model, nor the same attempt to use government funding to force services in the sector to adopt this approach.

(At the time of writing, it seems plausible that in the UK, as in other parts of Europe, HF will be seen as an important and valuable approach, but one that co-exists with recent improvements in short stay or "transitional" accommodation.)

HUD VASH (US) A collaborative program between HUD and VA combining HUD housing vouchers with VA supportive services to help Veterans who are homeless and their families find and sustain permanent housing. (From HUD Website)

Permanent Supportive Housing/PSH (US) is a program designed to provide housing (project and tenant-based) and supportive services on a long-term basis to formerly homeless people. HUD McKinney-Vento-funded programs require that the client have a disability for program eligibility, so the majority of people in PSH have disabilities. As of this writing, most people served are chronically homeless (qv).

Night shelter (UK) also called "direct access," refers to short-stay "hostel" *(qv)* services for meeting the immediate accommodation needs of homeless people. But other health and welfare services are often available, and night shelters in the UK have a triage role in identifying what further support an individual may need to escape the homelessness situation.

PIE of pathways (UK) is a term that has been suggested for the coordination and commissioning of multiple services in a locality to ensure that the "pathways" into and between services reflect and take into account an understanding of the psychological and emotional issues that confront homeless or vulnerably housed individuals.
(Creating a local PIE of pathways may be the primary responsibility of commissioners and policy makers in a locality, but a large organisation, or a consortium of organizations each providing a range services in any locality may also work towards a PIE of pathways; and individual workers, in work with clients, will need to be aware of the coherence or lack of coherence of services outside their own.)

Point-in-Time Counts (US) are unduplicated one-night estimates of both sheltered and unsheltered homeless populations. The one-night counts are conducted by Continuums of Care *(qv)* nationwide, and occur during the last week in January of each year.

Rapid Rehousing (US) is a housing model designed to provide temporary housing assistance to people experiencing homelessness, moving them quickly out of homelessness and into permanent housing.

Recovery Housing (US) Pre-2016, this was the term in widespread use in the US to describe specialist accommodation, whether short-term or long-term or mixed with an expectation of compliance with a treatment or peer support program, typically involving abstinence from drug or alcohol use. There usually are a range of group activities and/or common projects, in addition to simple residence.
(NB: Individuals must choose to move to such housing, in order to get the additional support of the program. They have been described as "intentional" communities, both because individuals must choose to move there, and because they work primarily on strengthening the individual's choice, or resolve, to remain abstinent.)

Recovery Housing (US) Toward the end of 2015, the US department of Housing and Urban Development, (HUD) issued a statement on how it saw Recovery Housing — where continued residence is dependent on partici-pation in the program — as being nevertheless compatible with a Strategic

Housing First approach *(qv)*, which is otherwise broadly opposed to such "conditionality," provided that (1) a degree of "elastic tolerance" is used, and (2) there are other options available that do not make such demands of compliance.

(NB: HUD states that in the future it will only favor, for funding, Recovery Housing that meets the tighter criteria that they have proposed, and CoCs that adopt this strategy.)

Refuge (UK), often called specifically "women's refuge," refers to a safe house for those escaping domestic violence. Refuges will usually be staffed, for extra security. Length of stay may vary, but is usually a matter of months. Some refuges have dedicated "move on" accommodation nearby.

Residential Care (US & UK) refers usually to long-stay accommodation for people with chronic disabilities. In the UK, residential care is seen as a form of social (or social plus nursing) care, and is regulated and inspected by the health and social care regulators, as distinct from hostels, which are outside this inspection and regulation regime.

Rough Sleeping (UK) People sleeping in the open air (such as on the streets, in tents, doorways, parks, bus shelters or encampments or other places not designed for habitation (such as stairwells, barns, sheds, car parks, cars, derelict boats, stations, or "bashes"). The definition doesn't include people in hostels or night shelters, sofa surfers, people on campsites or other sites used for recreational purposes or organised protest, squatters or gypsies/Travellers.

Rough sleeping count (UK) Rough sleeping counts and estimates are single-night snapshots of the number of people sleeping rough in local authority areas. Local authorities decide on the best method to use in their area: a street count or an estimate.

Safe Havens (US) are projects that provide private or semi-private long-term housing for unsheltered (qv) people with severe mental illness and are limited to serving no more than 25 people within a facility. People in safe havens are included in the one-night PIT count but, at this time, are not included from the one-year shelter count.

Sheltered Homelessness (US) refers to people who are staying in emergency shelters *(qv)*, transitional housing programs *(qv)*, or safe havens *(qv)*.

Sofa surfing (UK) staying with friends or acquaintances, with no home to go to.

Staircases (US & UK) is the term used, primarily by critics of this approach, for a design of specialist support and rehabilitation accommodation services such that the individuals in need must move from one service to another, tackling each of their problems in turn, in stages of recovery.
(Pressure on resources means that all but the final stages of this "progress" involve transitional accommodation, with no security of tenure; and failure to comply with treatment, or to improve, may result in loss of residence.)

Strategic Housing First (US) describes an approach to Housing First *(qv)* as an overall strategy for local services development, in which other and different kinds of supported accommodation programs may also fit, provided they comply with the overall aim of offering choice.

Supported Housing (UK) is a term that covers a very wide range of housing services covering a wide range of support needs, from sheltered accommodation for seniors to supported living for people with disabilities or learning difficulties, "alternatives to admission" or "step down" (early discharge) short stay accommodation for people with mental health problems, etc., etc.

Transitional Housing Programs (US) provide people experiencing homelessness a place to stay combined with supportive services for up to 24 months.

Unaccompanied Youth (under 18) are people who are not part of a family with children or accompanied by their parent or guardian during their episode of homelessness, and who are under the age of 18.

Unaccompanied Youth (18 to 24) are people who are not part of a family with children or accompanied by their parent or guardian during their episode of homelessness, and who are between the ages of 18 and 24.

Unsheltered Homelessness (US) refers to people whose primary nighttime residence is a public or private place not designated for, or ordinarily used as, a regular sleeping accommodation for people (for example, the streets, vehicles, or parks).

Veteran (US) refers to any person who served on active duty in the armed forces of the United States. This includes Reserves and National Guard members who were called up to active duty.
(This term is increasingly being used also in the UK, where otherwise the term is "ex-services personnel.")

Vulnerably housed (UK) is the term used in the UK to indicate a broad range of situations in which individuals might find themselves, including hostel *(qv)* residence, on which the (originally centralized and "ring-fenced") Supporting People grant monies could be spent.

(NB: This meant that the same locally funded organisations would in principle be able to provide the same ongoing support as an individual moves through the service. To what extent this actually happened was determined by local decisions on commissioning of services with greater or less "joined-up thinking," and more or less narrow "outcome measures.")

* Most of the above US definitions were derived from the Department of Housing and Urban Development (HUD)

About the Authors

Jay S. Levy, MSW, Clinical Social Work

Jay S. Levy has spent more than 30 years working with individuals who experience homelessness. He is the author of the highly acclaimed books *Pretreatment Guide for Homeless Outreach & Housing First* and *Homeless Narratives & Pretreatment Pathways*. He has also published a monograph and several journal articles on Homelessness issues. Jay developed Pretreatment as an approach for helping people without homes. He has helped to create new Housing First programs such as the Regional Engagement and Assessment for Chronically Homeless program (REACH).

Jay is currently employed by Eliot CHS-Homeless Services as a Regional Manager for the statewide SAMHSA-PATH Homeless Outreach Team. He is also an adjunct teacher at Anna Maria College and recently taught a unique graduate psychology course on Outreach Counseling, which integrated Pretreatment and PIE perspectives with the clinical challenges of homeless services work.

He has achieved formal recognition from the Commonwealth of Massachusetts Department of Mental Health for his ongoing efforts to help under-served homeless individuals through his direct service, clinical supervision of staff, and program development. Jay received his MSW degree in clinical social work from Columbia University in 1988.

Jay lives in Western MA with his wife, Louise. His two children, Talia and Sara, are off to college and beyond. He is an avid stargazer. More information on Jay and his work can be found at www.jayslevy.com.

Robin Johnson

Robin first became interested in understanding mental health and mental illness when studying social science and philosophy in the radical years of the late '60s. He then came across the therapeutic community ("TC") approach — a movement for a more communitarian, "social" psychiatry —

and worked and lived in a number of such communities through the 1970s, including the Henderson, probably the best known of all "TCs," which specialised in work with those we would now describe as having a personality disorder.

Robin went on to train as a psychiatric social worker, and became interested in—and impressed with—the role of housing and homelessness services in working with some of their more vulnerable and chaotic clients, some of those most "hard to reach."

In 2001, he left social services, to pursue an interest in research and development on mental health and housing, and soon found himself an adviser to various government departments on innovative practice. He was one of the leading authors of two government guidance papers on mental health needs that argued for better recognition of the work of homelessness services.

He was for five years editor of the Journal of Housing, Care and Support, a visiting fellow at several universities, and worked on the Royal College of Psychiatrist's "Enabling Environments" working group, which was tasked with adapting the TC approach for the era of community psychiatry — work which indirectly gave rise to the concept of a "psychologically informed environment" in homelessness resettlement services.

He has one remarkable daughter, of whom he is enormously proud; now lives in West Cornwall; and plays the baritone saxophone with more enthusiasm than competence. He claims to be trying to retire; but no one seems to believe it.

John Conolly, UKCP reg Psychoanalytic Psychotherapist, Lacanian Analyst, MA, MA

Exclusion has always been a major theme of John's professional life. As an Organisational Psychologist, he conducted research on the service usage patterns of homeless people in East London, and as a trainee Psychotherapist, his clinical placement was in a counselling charity for homeless people. He remained seven years, until he became manager of clinical assessments, upon his registration with the United Kingdom Council for Psychotherapy (UKCP) in 1998.

John joined a NHS trauma stress clinic for Refugees and Asylum Seekers in 2002, and has led the Westminster Homeless Health Counselling Service, at the Central London Community Healthcare NHS Trust since 2009, where he developed a special interest in Personality Disorder. He is an accredited trainer for the National *Knowledge and Understanding Framework* (KUF), on Personality Disorder.

He is a member of the Homeless and Inclusion Health Faculty, and sits on its education and training committee. He wrote the counselling section of the Faculty's *Health Service Standards for Commissioners and Service Providers* (2013).

John taught counselling skills at Middlesex University Mental Health Department, and has authored several articles and book chapters. He recently accepted to teach on the Irish Health Research Board's "Psycho-traumatology of homelessness" PhD programmes, at Trinity College, Dublin. He is a UKCP registered Psychoanalytic Psychotherapist and Lacanian Analyst.

He lives in North London with his wife, two daughters and a cat.

Ray Middleton, B.Sc., Doctoral Researcher in Social Psychology

Ray Middleton has developed a "Training the PIE facilitator" programme and PIE resources, such as YouTube films. As Work Force Development lead at Fulfilling Lives in England, he has written a psychological framework, in plain English, called Ladder4Life, which makes up one of the key elements in PIE. His research positively evaluating Ladder4Life PIE has been published.

Ray has previously managed Personality Disorder services and been a senior Care Coordinator in Early Intervention in Psychosis (EIP) service. He has spoken at National events about Ladder4Life PIE, such as at The Kings Fund, and the first PIE conference in 2017. He is a Systemic Practitioner within Systemic Family Therapy and studied at Leeds. He is also completing a PhD in Narrative/Dialogical and alternative approaches to "Personality Disorder."

Ray has drawn from his personal experience of complex needs and using services in the 1990s to create the Ladder4Life framework, implement PIE training for staff, and directly help people with complex needs. His journey of getting better from these difficulties has motivated his work in improving services for this client group.

Ray lives in a coastal village the North East of England with his wife, Elizabeth, and two Basset Hounds, Kippy and Poppy. More information on Ray and his work can be found at www.ladder4life.com

Suzanne Quinney, MA, Rural Social Development and Agricultural Extension

Suzanne has worked with a wide range of organisations — the NHS, Housing Associations, Richmond Fellowship, Barnardos, British Red Cross, Oxfam, and in community development. Following the work with a large number of Westminster hostels and engaging with the concept of PIEs, she co-authored two articles for the Journal of Housing Care and Support in 2014. She is currently supporting a Liverpool Homeless service to develop as a PIE using Appreciative Inquiry, and to be PIE-oneers, exploring the 4th dimension of appreciation.

Suzanne and her husband Tim Slack are co-founders of *Appreciating People* www.appreciatingpeople.co.uk/ and of *How to Be More Awesome*, and uses Appreciative Inquiry and Positive Psychology to support organisational and individual learning. She loves sharing this approach with interested people, and is part of the amazing team that won a Patient Safety Award in 2017, for the Learning from Excellence training work done with the Patient Safety Collaborative of the West Midlands Academic Health Science Network. She was a conference organiser and workshop leader for the Findhorn Foundation — the internationally renowned educational centre and eco-village.

Suzanne is a trained facilitator of The Work of Byron Katie, inviting people to investigate their stories, and also loves Sci-Fi and Quantum Physics for the way they challenge beliefs. She expands her construction of the inner and the outer world (and she loves being an aunt because it does something similar!).

Joe Finn, MA, Sociology, MA, Theology, JD

Joe Finn was named Executive Director of the Massachusetts Housing Shelter Alliance on October 14, 2003. He has dedicated the last twenty-five years to working in the area of homelessness and is committed to the challenge of ending homelessness.

MHSA's initiative under Joe's leadership, *"Home & Healthy for Good"* has led to the housing of 981 chronic homeless persons across Massachusetts for one of the state's first cost-benefit analysis of housing as opposed to emergency resources. This was recognized with a 2010 innovation award by Root Cause's Social Innovations Forum. MHSA also led the effort during this period to create CSPECH, a nationally recognized homeless community support service reimbursement by Medicaid. He was awarded the 2010 Pioneer Institute's national *Better Government Award* for his work "Containing the Cost of Medicaid by Providing Housing for Chronic Homelessness."

In July of 2012, under Joe's leadership, MHSA was awarded the Massachusetts "Pay for Success" social innovation financing contract to house chronic homeless persons. One of the first PFS to deal with homelessness in the world, to date it has housed 584 people.

Throughout his career, Joe has concentrated on the expansion of permanent supportive housing opportunities for individuals, including chronic homeless individuals. He is married to Dolores McIlmail, and is the father of six boys and one girl.

Index

stigma, 25
  negative-identity, 52
Strategic Housing First, 242
street medicine, 5–6, 8, 219
supported housing
  defined, 242
Supporting People, 21, 30, 242

T

Tapert, S., 43
TBI, 78, 155, 201, 226
therapeutic nihilism, 17
therapist
  stigma, 41
Thomas, B., 130
TIC, xi, 14, 16, 23, 27, 190, 191, 209, 217, 219–21, 228, 229
  defined, 23
  overlap with PIE, 26
toxic help, 57, 61
  defined, 55
transitional housing, 13, 20, 24, 26, 45–46, 155, 163, 168, 172, 192, 193, 197, 238, 241
  defined, 242
trauma, xiv, 8–9, 13–27, 39–42, 50–54, 72–78, 88–89, 180, *See also* complex trauma
Trauma-Informed Care. *See* TIC

traumatic brain injury. *See* TBI
traumatised personality, 50–54
trench foot, 206
Tsemberis, S., 8, 13, 150, 178, 208

U

unaccompanied youth
  defined, 242
unsheltered homelessness
  defined, 242

V

veteran, 201, 205
  defined, 242
  disparities, 44
  HUD and VA, 239
  needs, 172
  peer counseling, 110
  priority housing, 36

W

Walter, J., 80
Wampold, B., 225
Westminster Council, xiii
White, M., 7, 43, 47, 96, 109, 129
Winnicott, D., 60
Withers, J., 8

Pretreatment Guide for Homeless Outreach & Housing First

This book provides social workers, outreach clinicians, case managers, and concerned community members with a pretreatment guide for assisting homeless couples, youth, and single adults. The inter-relationship between Homeless Outreach and Housing First is examined in detail to inform program development and hands on practice. *Pretreatment Guide for Homeless Outreach & Housing First* shares five detailed case studies from the field to elucidate effective ways of helping and to demonstrate how the most vulnerable among us can overcome trauma and homelessness. Readers will:

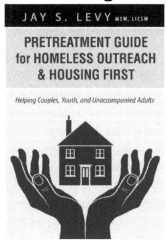

- Expand their assessment skills and discover new interventions for helping people who have experienced long-term or chronic homelessness.
- Understand and be able to integrate the stages of common language construction with their own practice.
- Learn about the positive measurable impact of a Housing First approach and its moral, fiscal, and quality of life implications.
- Understand how to better integrate program policy and supervision with Homeless Outreach & Housing First initiatives.
- Learn how to utilize a Pretreatment Approach with couples, youth, and unaccompanied adults experiencing untreated major mental illness and addiction.

"Jay S. Levy's book is essential reading to both people new to the movement to end homelessness and folks who have been in the trenches for many years. Learn how to do effective outreach with the chronic homeless population, and the ins and outs of the Housing First model. The personal stories and the success cases will give inspiration to work even harder to help both individuals and for ending homelessness in your community."

Michael Stoops, Director of Community Organizing
National Coalition for the Homeless, Washington, DC

ISBN 978-1-61599-201-0
From Loving Healing Press

On any given night, there are over 643,000 homeless people residing in shelters and on the streets across America.

Homeless Narratives & Pretreatment Pathways

From Words to Housing

Jay S. Levy, MSW, LICSW

"Levy crafts stories of characters who sear the memory: Old Man Ray, the World War II veteran who resents the VA system and regards himself as the de facto night watchman at Port Authority; Ben who claims to be a prophet disowned in his own country, crucified by the government and enslaved by poverty finds a bridge to the mainstream services and a path to housing through the common language of religious metaphors, including redemption and forgiveness; and Andrew who has been 'mentally murdered' is helped to understand his own situation and gain disability benefits through the language of trauma; among others.

"These stories are deftly interwoven with theory and practice as Levy constructs his developmental model of the engagement and pretreatment process. The outreach worker strives to understand the language and the culture of each homeless individual, builds a bridge to the mainstream services, and helps those providers to understand the special circumstances of these vulnerable people. Levy bears witness to the courage of these pilgrims who wander the streets of our cities, and his poignant book is a testament to the healing power of trusting and enduring relationships."

Jim O'Connell, MD - President and Street Physician for
Boston Health Care for the Homeless Program

- Understand and be able to utilize the stages of common language construction in your own practice.
- Learn about pretreatment principles and their applications with persons experiencing untreated major mental illness, addiction, and medical issues.
- Discover new interventions via outreach counseling, advocacy and case management with people experiencing long-term or chronic homelessness.
- Understand how to better integrate policy, programs (e.g. Housing First), and supervision with homeless outreach initiatives.

ISBN 978-1-61599-026-9
From Loving Healing Press